The Alabama,

BRITISH NEUTRALITY,
AND THE
AMERICAN CIVIL WAR

The Alabama,
BRITISH NEUTRALITY, AND THE AMERICAN CIVIL WAR

Frank J. Merli

Edited by David M. Fahey

INDIANA UNIVERSITY PRESS

BLOOMINGTON • INDIANAPOLIS

This book is a publication of

Indiana University Press
601 North Morton Street
Bloomington, IN 47404-3797 USA

http://iupress.indiana.edu

Telephone orders   800-842-6796
Fax orders   812-855-7931
Orders by e-mail   iuporder@indiana.edu

The paper used in this publication meets the minimum requirements of
American National Standard for Information Sciences — Permanence of
Paper for Printed Library Materials, ANSI Z39.48-1984.

Manufactured in the United States of America

Library of Congress Cataloging-in-Publication Data

Merli, Frank J., 1929–2000.
The Alabama, British neutrality, and the American Civil War /
Frank J. Merli ; edited by David M. Fahey.
p. cm.
Includes bibliographical references (p.) and index.
ISBN 0-253-34473-5 (cloth : alk. paper)
1. United States — Foreign relations — 1861–1865. 2. United States — Foreign
relations — Great Britain. 3. Great Britain — Foreign relations — United States.
4. Alabama (Screw sloop) 5. Semmes, Raphael, 1809–1877. 6. United
States — History — Civil War, 1861–1865 — Naval operations.
I. Fahey, David M. II. Title.
E469.M47 2004
973.7′2 — dc22
2004006412

1   2   3   4   5   09   08   07   06   05   04

Contents

Seven

THE CONFEDERACY'S CHINESE FLEET, 1861–1867   158

Illustrations

Frank J. Merli (1929–2000)

Frank J. Merli spent his professional life studying British neutrality during the American Civil War. At the time of his death, he was writing a multivolume, expanded version of his monograph, *Great Britain and the Confederate Navy* (1970).[1] His new work offered a provocative reinterpretation of Britain's wartime neutrality and the South's failure to obtain European assistance. Here, in brief, are his major arguments.

An Anglo-American war in 1862 would have meant the breakup of the United States, the independence of the secessionist states, and probably the perpetuation of slavery. A combination of naïve and inept diplomacy and ill-timed military defeats cost the South active European support. The Confederacy's leaders did not understand the importance of European intervention or how to obtain it. To learn why the European powers failed to intervene, diplomatic historians need to break free from the spell of the classic histories of American Civil War diplomacy. Present-mindedness and factual errors disfigure the pioneering work of E. D. Adams (1925) and Frank L. Owsley (1931).

Other than direct foreign intervention, British shipyards offered the Confederacy its best chance of survival. Allowing the South no favors, the British government pursued a policy of neutrality as British law defined it. Those who accuse the foreign secretary or the prime minister of connivance in the *Alabama*'s escape are unfair to them.

They also are unfair to the Confederate naval agent, James D. Bulloch, who deserves most of the credit for providing the *Ala-*

bama with the opportunity to savage northern shipping and, as a
result, helping to drive from the high seas merchant ships flying
the United States flag. Despite inadequate support from Richmond, Bulloch attempted to sail a fleet of commerce raiders
and blockade-breaking ironclad rams through the intricacies of
British neutrality law. He merits comparison with Robert E. Lee
as a Southern officer whose genius might have saved the Confederacy. Although Bulloch's work is now largely forgotten,
the skill with which the sailor from Georgia conducted his
European mission merits his designation as the Confederate
Franklin.[2]

When on 22 December 2000 an aneurysm cut short forty
years of study, much of what Merli had learned died with him,
but a substantial part of his legacy lives on in the present volume. Despite the limitations of posthumous publication, this
book is vintage Merli, a memorial to a lifetime of research and
analysis. It is not a miscellaneous collection. The seven chapters
are united in their focus on British neutrality and the CSS *Alabama,* the commerce raider that became a symbol of the problems besetting British neutrality law and practice. The book
combines two kinds of work. Most of it consists of chapters from
Merli's uncompleted books. Although they lack his trademark
exhaustive documentation, they reveal the state of his thinking at the height of his powers. A single reprinted essay that
appeared in hard-to-find conference proceedings and a completed but unpublished coedited naval memoir show Merli as
he wanted to be read.

The entire volume embodies Merli's historical method. Thor-
oughness in research mattered more than quantity in publication. In a self-study he explained, "I have not only read prac-
tically every British state paper pertaining to the Confederacy,
but I have read each in the various stages of development, from
prime minister to foreign secretary to the government clerks."
Although happiest in the archives, he also analyzed with great
care a variety of printed sources, some of them — such as contemporary pictures — neglected by other historians. New books
that rehashed old research disappointed him. He was even
more frustrated when they perpetuated factual errors that had

been corrected decades earlier (sometimes by Merli himself). He considered sacred that principle which all historians are taught but frequently forget: always check secondary sources against contemporary documents. He regarded an accurate chronology of events as indispensable.

Although Merli spent most of his life writing history with "a heavy underpinning of footnotes," he recognized that as a mature scholar he had begun to change: "The nature of my work has led me more and more in the direction of the essay form, even to some essays of a speculative nature."[3] The volume begins with a speculative essay on the topic that provided the framework for Merli's research, the international dimension of the American Civil War.

For Merli, the formative years occurred at Indiana University where as a graduate student he worked under the direction of Professor Robert H. Ferrell. He often spoke about the painstaking "Ferrell method" as the model for his research, editing, and writing. It also was at Indiana where Merli met his wife, Margaret. He spent most of his career, more than thirty-two years, at Queens College in the City University of New York.

After *Great Britain and the Confederate Navy* had established his reputation, Merli never published another monograph, but he was not silent. He coedited a collection of essays on American diplomatic history and edited a special issue about the CSS *Alabama* for the short-lived *Journal of Confederate History*. He published substantial essays (such as "The Confederate Navy, 1861–1865" and "The American Way with Blockades: Reflections on the Union Blockade of the South"), edited documents, contributed to reference works, and presented conference papers. An omnivorous reader, he mastered the literature of American Civil War diplomatic and naval history, old and new. He was responsible for the Civil War chapter in the standard bibliography for the history of American foreign relations.

During these decades he also worked on his unpublished books. At first, he planned a trilogy on the period 1856–1872, beginning with the Treaty of Paris when the European powers proposed a new definition of neutral rights and responsibilities, and ending at Geneva with the *Alabama* claims. His 1970 book would have served as the middle volume. When this project proved too ambitious, he focused on the war years. Trained as a diplomatic historian, he developed new expertise as a naval historian and as a historian of nineteenth-century British neutrality law.

He unselfishly shared the "Merli archive" with others. It included more than 160 rolls of microfilm and dozens of boxes stuffed with photocopies, handwritten spiral notebooks, and hard-to-find books. Merli's first research trip to England took place in 1961. His last archival research notes, written two months before his death, record what he found in the letters of the British diplomat Sir Frederick Bruce in the Seward papers at the University of Rochester.[4]

Merli was more than a hard worker. He possessed a gift for startling insight. He marveled at the creative process, how ideas came to him or didn't. There were many times when the wonderful moment of insight illuminated his work. He was an original thinker who challenged deeply rooted orthodoxies.

Merli had a network of friends to whom he periodically mailed handwritten drafts and typescripts. In editing this book, I sometimes found myself reading comments that I had scribbled in margins many years ago. As my central critique, I pleaded with him to complete an article or book and submit it for publication. Too much the perfectionist, Merli nearly always found another way of telling his story that postponed possible publication. He refused to be rushed. For a long time, he wouldn't even tell me about his research on the Confederacy's Chinese fleet but only hinted that he had discovered a topic for a book that would write itself. Alas, no book does that.

After Merli's sudden death, his wife, Margaret, and their sons, Robert and David, provided me with a large box packed with typed and handwritten manuscripts from which I assembled this volume. Throughout the editorial project, Margaret repeatedly ransacked the Merli archive to find answers to my queries. Without the Merli family's love and commitment, this book could not have appeared.

Editing Merli's unpublished writings presented problems. He never used a computer. Although he sometimes typed his correspondence, he composed his historical writings in longhand, in later years typically at the East Northport public library near his Long Island home, and went through many handwritten revisions before he paid a secretarial service to type an advanced version. He then revised it with pen or pencil. For many papers there is no easy way to know which version with the same title is the most recent, and manuscripts with different titles overlap. Merli often experimented with how best to present his arguments. In fact, three of his four books-in-progress were, to a considerable extent, alternative ways of writing the same book. In editing these materials, I have sometimes combined chapters, sometimes compressed them, and sometimes excerpted them to supplement other material. To produce a book of manageable length, I have left out a great deal.

Merli could be impatient about sloppiness over details, so I must apologize for any errors of mine that result from ignorance or carelessness. Lacking familiarity with his documents, all that I could do where he did not provide footnotes is to identify the secondary works to which he alluded and sometimes add a list of relevant publications, including a few that appeared after his death.

I remember Frank Merli as more than a scholar. He was a generous and loyal friend. We met in the 1960s when both of us taught at Indiana University's Gary campus. In later years we resumed our friendship in England during summers of research. When I was completing a book in the 1990s, his editorial advice was indispensable. My preface to that volume acknowledges that "perhaps vainly, he urged the merits of clarity and conciseness, transitions and topic sentences, and chapters that do not just stop but conclude."

It is as a Londoner that I remember Merli most vividly. He often worked at the old Public Record Office on Chancery Lane. For somebody with his long-legged stride, it was an easy walk from London House on Mecklenburg Square, where he lived. Although a great walker, he mastered the underground better than the typical transient American. For him it was a source of pride that at every station he knew on which side of the train to disembark and where the lift or the stairway was located. He delighted, too, in his expertise on London's Italian restaurants (his favorite was the now defunct Peter Mario's). As a basis for comparison, he always had to start with the minestrone.

But the emphasis here must be on the work and not on the man. His contribution to our understanding of the American Civil War needs to escape the prison of his filing cabinets.

This volume begins with Merli's controversial overview of the international dimension of the war. He launched a fierce attack on the mind-set and personnel of Confederate diplomacy, in his judgment the fatal weakness of the secessionists in the American Civil War. He argued that European hostility toward slavery did not in itself prevent support for the South, and he underscored the importance of the timing of events in his explanation of the failure of Europe to intervene. Writing provocatively about British policy in the *Trent* affair and the mediation maneuvers, he assessed the danger of an Anglo-American war. He depicted the foreign secretary Russell — half giant, half child — more generously than many diplomatic historians. Merli analyzed Russell's acceptance of the Union's version of blockade and pointed out that the new Confederate secretary of state, Judah P. Benjamin, for all his brilliance, could not see beyond Southern blinders. This chapter also features a vigorous critique of the historians E. D. Adams and Frank L. Owsley.

In 1970 when I read Merli's then brand-new book, *Great Britain and the Confederate Navy*, I protested to him that it omitted what in many conversations he had told me about his disagreements with Adams and Owsley. He responded that if one carefully read the text of the book, the endnotes, and the annotated bibliography and compared what each said, his critique of Adams and Owsley would become apparent. In reply I grumbled that there weren't ten historians in the world who would read carefully enough to discover the secret. Over the next few decades Merli's disagreements with Adams and Owsley became more radical, and he lost his inhibitions about stating them forcefully.

In addition to being the most controversial, chapter 1 was the most difficult to edit. I began by synthesizing two papers with different names and different structures that covered the same topic. Originating as an encyclopedia article, these papers became too lengthy and too speculative to be published in such a format. The longer essay, examining most aspects of the story, was an early draft. Then I excerpted material from several other papers not included in this volume, such as Merli's never completed chapter on Secretary of State Benjamin and his "note on blockade."

. Before Merli died, he wrote an introduction to the book that he planned on the CSS *Alabama.* Always interested in process as well as outcome, he provided a short, intellectual autobiography. He also sketched his objectives in writing about the *Alabama,* particularly its escape from British territorial waters. In the present volume, the introduction for a book never completed serves to introduce the middle chapters on the famous Confederate cruiser.

The third chapter is the longest one in the book. In the draft available to me, Merli's description and analysis of the "law of the *Alabama*" broke off in the midst of his account of the final report issued by the law officers of the Crown, so I have completed it. Merli's missing paragraphs don't affect his argument. In fact, he focused neither on the law nor on the evidence but on the process: how documents and opinions moved from American diplomats to British officials at various levels of government, back and forth. Merli's persuasive conclusion was that the British responded to American complaints with reasonable efficiency and that the Americans deserved most of the blame for the delays that allowed the *Alabama* to escape. Finally, the Confederates were lucky. The principal law officer of the Crown suffered a mental breakdown that slowed the legal process at a crucial moment.

The brilliantly conceived and argued fourth chapter, combining two of Merli's manuscripts, criticized E. D. Adams for his account of the escape of the *Alabama* and offered an imaginative explanation for his errors. Sir Roundell Palmer's speech in the House of Commons in March 1863 led Adams astray. The chapter also chided Frank L. Owsley. The key to Merli's analysis was careful reconstruction of chronology. Omitted in this edited version is Merli's detailed account of later historians that traced their errors to Adams and Owsley.

Merli objected to the conspiracy theory that somebody in the British government, in most accounts a Foreign Office clerk, telegraphed Bulloch or the shipbuilder on 26 July 1862 to warn that the *Alabama* had to leave British jurisdiction as soon as possible. Merli pointed out that for an insider's betrayal of a government secret the date didn't make sense: the government had acquired no crucial new information on the 26th. More important, there is no substantive evidence that establishes the source of the telegram as a government leak. Merli was convinced that the foreign secretary and prime minister had not betrayed their responsibilities. He did not deny the possibility of a lower-level official doing so, without the knowledge of his superiors, but he doubted it in the absence of credible evidence.

The fifth chapter is a document that Merli edited in collaboration with Renata Eley Long. She generously has authorized publication in this book. The document is a memoir, written many years after that event, by the English captain who sailed the *Alabama* out of British territorial waters. I include the document in part for its intrinsic value. It is virtually unknown, although the text was printed, with few annotations and no commentary, in a Liverpool maritime journal in the late 1980s. The other reason why I include the Merli and Long version of the document is to illustrate the massive documentation characteristic of Merli's work but lacking in the uncompleted drafts that make up most of the present volume.

The sixth chapter looks at Raphael Semmes, the *Alabama*'s captain, and the brief battle at Cherbourg where a Union ironclad sank the Confederate commerce raider. The topic — Semmes's motives at Cherbourg in 1864 and his unhelpful 1868 memoir — may not seem as important as the topics for previous chapters, but Merli's treatment of it epitomized his detective-like reconstruction of events, his autobiographical explanation about when and how he learned what he did, and his delight in the process of discovery. For instance, he found out that the novelist and poet George Meredith was the anonymous author of the first and final chapters of a contemporary British account of Cherbourg, an account that — despite its sympathy to the Confederate cause — Semmes attacked with virulent scorn. Merli sees Semmes's reaction as suggestive in explaining a larger story: the South's difficulty in understanding Europe and Europe's importance to a successful outcome of the war and, as a result, the failure of the Confederacy to win European support.

The final chapter, about what Merli characterized as the Confederacy's Chinese fleet, is the only reprinted one. Pictorial Histories Publishing Company of Missoula, Montana, kindly has granted permission to reprint Merli's contribution to a volume of conference proceedings for the International Commission for Maritime History and the North American Society for Oceanic History. According to a standard database, only fifteen libraries claim a copy of the book, with the Library of Congress not being among them. So this paper is hardly well known. After he happened upon this topic during a research trip to London, Merli worked on it for decades. He told a friend, "The CCF file must have crossed the Atlantic almost as many times as I did."[5]

In this essay Merli enlarged the scope of his inquiry into the practice of British maritime neutrality by comparing government policy toward mid-nineteenth-century civil wars in America and China. Discovering an episode that earlier American Civil War historians had overlooked, Merli points to what he calls the Confederacy's Chinese fleet. It had been constructed for the Chinese imperial government to use against pirates, emboldened by the Taiping rebellion, but the deal collapsed after the flotilla reached China. The situations were not identical: Britain never granted the Taipings belligerency status, and it was a government enjoying diplomatic relations with the Queen that wanted to build warships in Britain. Yet both cases raised questions about the responsibilities of a neutral government, questions that Britain answered very differently for the Chinese empire than for the Confederate States of America.

There was another reason why Merli found this episode fascinating. He argued that it offered a last-minute opportunity for the South to purchase a small British-built naval squadron. Apparently, it was to prevent this possibility that the British government reluctantly purchased the ships. Merli meant to expand his essay into a small book. Shortly before his death, he completed a draft of his first chapter, "The Chinese Context." I have added excerpts from it as a postscript to the reprint. In addition, I have changed the endnote format to that of Indiana University Press.

Although I regret excluding from the present volume essays for which Merli left manuscripts, the most painful omission, in my opinion, is that of an essay specifically about Merli's hero, James D. Bulloch. In the materials that I have seen, there are only scattered bits and pieces dealing with the great Confederate naval agent (including Merli's brief entry in the *Encyclopedia of the Confederacy,* published in 1993). For the most part, the paper with the promising title "At the Height of His Powers: James D. Bulloch and the Escape of the CSS *Alabama,*" duplicates what Merli wrote in other manuscripts about the *Alabama*'s escape.

This draft does add something new. In it Merli provided his fullest analysis of Bulloch as historian, Bulloch's two-volume memoir, *The Secret Service of the Confederate States in Europe; or, How The Confederate Cruisers Were Equipped,* published in the mid-1880s. Merli described it as "in many ways a great book, and it is also an underappreciated one." He praised it for being mostly free of "that whiny spite and small-mindedness that make the reminiscences of Jefferson Davis and Raphael Semmes so tedious." In contrast, Bulloch's memoir is "fair-minded and judicious." Yet it also is characterized by a "studied, deliberate ambiguity." "Everything in it is not as straightforward as it may seem on first reading." Bulloch didn't tell the full story: "He gives, he takes away; he reveals, he conceals."

In a manuscript written in the last year of his life, Merli offered this sketch of his favorite Confederate:

It might be said of Bulloch that in 1861 a man and a mission had found each other. Shrewd, affable, discreet, tactful, and wise in

James D. Bullock (right), with his younger half brother Irving,
one of the *Alabama*'s junior officers (who here wears a uniform
inappropriate to his rank, perhaps because he lost his own uniform
in the sinking of the *Alabama*). The picture probably was taken in
1864 or less likely in 1865. Courtesy of Henry Skinner and also
of Roy Rawlinson's website, "When Liverpool was Dixie."

the ways of the world, he possessed in full measure all the traits
and skills that his task required. Moreover, he also had a firm
confidence in his ability to get the job done — and to this day no
one has ever charged him with neglect of duty, defects of character, or personal dishonesty. In my detailed and comprehensive
study of his career — one that stretches over some forty years — it
has been virtually impossible for me to discover any serious imperfections in the conduct of his mission, except for one unwise

choice of a subordinate, that of the turncoat Clarence R. Yonge. And that black sheep may have been foisted on him by higher authority.[6]

In the outline for one of his projected books, Merli listed a chapter about the sea captain from Georgia whom he described as the "naval diplomat *par excellence*" and provided a descriptive paragraph. Apparently Merli never drafted this chapter. In the outline Merli said that "if [Bulloch's] mission to Europe had been properly financed, if it had had the full support of Richmond's State and Naval Departments, if it had been free from divided counsel and bureaucratic infighting, Bulloch *might* have given Jefferson Davis even that which Lee could not deliver — independence and international recognition."

David M. Fahey

The Alabama,

BRITISH NEUTRALITY,
AND THE
AMERICAN CIVIL WAR

ONE | THE INTERNATIONAL DIMENSION OF THE AMERICAN CIVIL WAR

$\mathscr{A}$LTHOUGH the Civil War is the most studied event in United States history, the crucial importance of Europe's response remains largely unrecognized. For instance, that monumental, many-houred TV coverage of the Civil War created for the Public Broadcasting System by Ken Burns barely hinted at its international dimension. Civil War history is dominated by a nationalistic perspective that focuses narrowly on the war as a confrontation of North and South. As in the case of the American Revolution, Americans appear loath to recognize the Civil War's international dimension. In fact, the war's outcome was determined more in Europe than it was at Gettysburg.

Hostility to slavery did not prevent Britain and France from supporting the Confederacy. National interests, rather than sympathy for one side or the other, dictated the ways in which the European powers answered the questions posed by the war. The forces for and against intervention in late 1862 were in such a state of equipoise that almost any alteration in the balance might have tipped the scales in the South's favor. The problem was that Richmond never devised an effective way to sell its cause in Europe.

Few Americans remember that President Abraham Lincoln internationalized the war soon after it began by his decision to blockade the entire 3,500 miles of the Confederate coast. None

1

but the most astute supporters of the Lost Cause know that long before the secessionists had fired on Fort Sumter, President Jefferson Davis had sent agents to Britain and France in search of the sinews of war. Almost nobody knows that one of the greatest of Confederate heroes worked unsung in Liverpool and London to create an arsenal of naval might to forestall Lincoln's Anaconda Plan to cut off European supplies and strangle the South into submission.

Most of the few historians who have studied the international dimension have failed to understand the combination of timing and intangibles that thwarted foreign intervention. At least from their research there has emerged this consensus: foreign participation in the American Civil War would have changed the course of history.

When the fire-eating faction of Southern nationalists launched its attack on Fort Sumter in April 1861, the shots sent screaming over the harbor at Charleston, South Carolina, set in motion a sequence of events that forever altered the nature of the American republic. Accepting that challenge, Northerners too took actions that would profoundly change the nation's future. When Abraham Lincoln decided to suppress the rebellion, rather than let the "erring sisters" go in peace, he invoked a wide range of presidential powers inherent in his conception of the Union. He understood that the Southern bid for separate nationhood would require a foreign "lifeline."[1] Lincoln's order for a blockade, moving the war to the sea, compelled an official response from the neutrals of Europe, especially from Britain, the nation with the largest stake in maritime affairs.

In a war filled with what might have been, the establishment of an independent Confederacy in America with British sanction remains one of history's most terrible "ifs." Jefferson Davis *might* have created a nation capable of outlasting the war, *if* he had been able to orchestrate any sort of active foreign response to his cause. To succeed in their bid for independence, Southern leaders would have needed to emulate their Revolutionary War forefathers by calling on the Old World to redress the balance of power in the New. It is a sad commentary on Southern diplomacy that so few in the upper echelons of Richmond understood the importance of the European response to the war and how to make it favorable to their cause.

The South frittered away the advantages that it enjoyed on the world stage when the war broke out in 1861. Despite the incubus of slavery that, in the unfortunate phrase of Vice President Alexander Stephens, was the "cornerstone of the Confederacy," the South entered its struggle with a surprisingly good press in Europe. Much of this stemmed from foreign misunderstanding about the nature of the war, about Union objectives in it, and about the supposed impossibility of Washington conquering the South. In Britain and France, those who opposed the perpetuation of slavery might favor national self-determination and consequently be sympathetic to secession. They also could see advantage for their own countries in a transformation in the North American balance of power. Other things also generated pro-South sympathy abroad: the underdog status of Confederate cavaliers, Northern tariff policy in an era of free trade, and a long-standing antipathy to the brag and bluster of pushy, money-grubbing Yankees (and aristocratic sympathy toward the plantation owners of the South). Commercial relations with the cotton kingdom were strong in parts of Britain and France. It was said that Liverpool flew more Confederate flags than Richmond.

Unfortunately for the Confederacy, it had no Benjamin Franklin or Thomas Jefferson to represent it in Europe. Such diplomats, rare in any age, were especially needed when the scepter of Europe's statecraft was passing from one generation to another, from Palmerston to Bismarck. The South's bid for independence coincided with a major European challenge to the Vienna compromise of 1815.

＊　　＊　　＊　　＊　　＊

Two classics of American Civil War diplomatic history remain required reading: Ephraim Douglass Adams, *Great Britain and the American Civil War* (1925), and Frank Lawrence Owsley, *King Cotton Diplomacy* (1931). Part of the difficulty in understanding the international dimension of the American Civil War stems from a simple fact: Our two leading historians on that subject have led us astray. They were pathfinders: early proponents of multiarchival research who made important and enduring contributions. Yet their books — which still dominate the way we see the foreign response to the war — are incorrect on many factual and substantive matters. More important than the mistakes on details, both books are defective in their central interpretive framework. As a result, the picture presented is out of focus.

If there is a key to Europe's response to the war, it will not be found in either Adams or Owsley. After several close readings of their more than 1,200 pages, despite their many insights, I cannot find in them a satisfactory explanation of Europe's reluctance to aid the Confederates. Nor do the works of Adams and Owsley come to grips with the South's failure to exploit those advantages it possessed on the world stage when war broke out.

Let me begin with the historian who proclaimed his problematic interpretation in the title of his book. The blatant economic determinism of Owsley's *King Cotton Diplomacy* tells us more about that distinguished scholar's Southern populist mind-set of the 1930s than it does about the diplomacy of the 1860s. His concluding chapter, "Why Europe Did Not Intervene," recaptures that anticapitalist mentality, influential on the eve of the New Deal era, better than it does the *Realpolitik* of the ruling elites in Palmerston's London and Napoleon III's Paris. According to Owsley, King Wheat had outdone King Cotton. When he blamed Europe's "merchants of death" for the Southern failure to obtain foreign support, he effectively absolved Southerners of responsibility in their self-destruction. His accounts of some specific events of the war are so seriously flawed as to be useless (for instance, his account of the escape of the Confederate cruiser *Alabama*). Other critics have identified aspects of his work as defective, especially his treatment of the ways British workers responded to the war. One must give up those simpleminded dichotomies between the working class and aristocracy in describing British reactions to the war.

Owsley's work has led generations of scholars astray. Despite several decades of research in the public and private archives of Great Britain, I have failed to find much evidence to support Owsley's thesis that economic concerns dictated the way foreigners responded to the war. It is not just that British leaders did not often talk in economic terms. The problem is more complex than that. It might be said that those leaders did not think in those terms — or, at least, not in the way Owsley ascribes to them. Queen Victoria's wartime ministers possessed a pre-Marxist worldview.

To be sure, British statesmen were well aware of the economic realities of their era, but it is equally true that they did not assign to economic forces the impact that later historians do, especially those who came of age in the shadow of Charles A. Beard and grew up under the domination of the Southern agrarian fixation with the "money interests." In the politics and diplomacy of the mid-nineteenth century, money did indeed talk. It just did not say what Owsley tells us it said. Economic concerns were merely one — and not the most important one — of a myriad set of problems that confronted European statesmen during the war. Their responses to those problems were far more richly nuanced than Owsley allows.

The work of E. D. Adams poses more complex interpretive problems. In many ways Adams's treatment of wartime diplomacy is superior to Owsley's, though it too is seriously defective in its account of the *Alabama*'s escape. More important, Adams's great work also suffers from a retrospective thesis, from a reading of 1920s sensibilities back into the Civil War. In this case, however, democracy triumphant and the afterglow of early-twentieth-century Anglo-American rapprochement substitutes for Owsley's economic determinism. Unfortunately, Adams's "progressive democracy" has even less validity than Owsley's "economic determinism" in explaining Britain's failure to intervene. Once again, I must note that my long reading in the records of the policy makers and their subordinates has failed to find any substantial support for Adams's charming contentions about the influence of democracy on the deliberations of the upper-class realists who conducted British foreign policy in the 1860s. Nor is Adams's characterization of British neutrality as "cold" the best way to describe the way Queen Victoria's ministers responded to the war. The statesmen who decided policy in London understood that a new Southern republic might alter the North American balance of power in Britain's favor, and they were not mesmerized by any "glittering illusion" of Southern military invincibility that would guarantee Confederate victory without help from overseas.

These masterworks share an unusual feature that helps explain their continuing influence. They have been able to bridge the emotional and ideological differences that usually separate Northern and Southern accounts of the war. Some version, some subtle blending of their views, has found favor both north and south of the Mason–Dixon line. Why? In putting the blame for Davis's defeat on Britain's supposed "democratic and liberal" proclivities, Adams nearly matches Owsley's obtuseness on the great moral issue of the war and its impact on the foreign response. In his emphasis on "nationality" (as the dominant mode of the Union's response to the war), Adams had to downplay slavery as well as the South's tendency to self-destruct in the international arena. A new generation of professional Confederates can read Adams as well as Owsley and find what they want.

The end of the Civil War virtually coincided with the death of Lord Palmerston. His death, in turn, signaled the end of an era in British political history. It has been difficult for Americans who study the war's international dimension to comprehend the peculiar way that politics and diplomacy worked in the last years of that great statesman's career. Roy Jenkins's recent biography of William E. Gladstone has much enhanced my own understanding of the foreign response to the war.[2] That work has many wise things to say about politics in the waning years of Palmerston's leadership and about the relations between the prime minister and his volatile chancellor of the exchequer. To simplify complex problems, one might begin by recognizing that for Lord Palmerston and his foreign secretary, Lord Russell, other considerations ranked higher than the march of democracy. Both of them believed that the concessions of the 1832 Reform Bill toward popular participation in elections had gone far enough and were "final." It is also difficult to find evidence that economic considerations dominated their approach to wartime problems. Both were ardent advocates of free trade and devoted to Britain's mercantile interests, but such concerns did *not* make them champions of the Confederate cause. To accuse British leaders of crass economic motives or of advocating the creation of a Confederate slave state under British auspices distorts history. The record of cabinet debate on the mediation maneuvers of 1862, as I have read it, suggests that humanitarian concerns loomed as large as economic or geopolitical ones in generating the push for involvement at that time.

The time for a new synthesis of Civil War diplomacy is long overdue. There is room for revisionism in the Civil War as well as in the cold war.

*   *   *   *   *

Beyond all doubt the powers of Europe, especially Britain, possessed a vital interest in the course of the American Civil War. At a number of points, transatlantic affairs directly impinged on the national well-being of Britain and France. One of the most important of these was the possibility of war by inadvertence, the chance that an incident at sea might accidentally involve Europe in the war. To forestall that event, Queen Victoria in May 1861 issued a proclamation of neutrality and recognized the belligerent status of the South. That policy can best be described as a "fair neutrality," neither pro-North nor pro-South. Britain also adopted a wait-and-see attitude toward the Northern blockade. France soon followed a similar course.

In the nineteenth century, much ink had been spilt to resolve the rules of proper neutral conduct in wartime. The crux of that problem revolved around a simple question: When did a blockade become "effective," that is, when did it merit international recognition? Bitter experience had taught that there was a danger in "paper" blockades, those that were merely declared, without sufficient naval strength to prevent entry to or exit from particular ports. In the 1856 Declaration of Paris at the end of the Crimean War, the powers of Europe had worked out a code of conduct for such cases, but it soon proved inadequate for history's first modern war. Lincoln's closure of the Confederate coast by fiat struck Europeans as a paper blockade of the most blatant kind. They knew that the Union navy lacked the ships to give its blockade even a semblance of that effectiveness envisioned by the peacemakers of Paris in 1856.

An effective blockade precluded *all* trade with an interdicted port, while one not so closed presented enormous potential for private profit. It immediately became apparent that the blockade threatened Europe's need for cotton. It became equally clear that the South needed many things that only Europe could supply. Running the blockade quickly became big business. An attempt in the early months of the war to resolve these difficulties did not succeed.

The United States had not accepted the 1856 principles of Paris, but when the war broke out, the British foreign secretary, Lord Russell, tried to gain the assent of the North and South to those about blockade and privateering. The commissioning of private ships as vessels of war—a traditional weapon of small naval powers against stronger ones—had been taken up by Jefferson Davis at the outset of the war to counteract the blockade. These early extensions of the Civil War to the sea posed danger to Europe's lawful commerce. Russell attempted to blunt them by inviting both belligerents to accede to the provisions of Paris. Naturally enough, the South could not accept the prohibition of privateers. Without that surrender, the North saw no advantage in a retrospective acceptance of the Paris principles. Because of its preponderance of naval power vis-à-vis the South (and because of the neutrality of Britain, the mistress of the seas), the Union navy saw opportunity for significant innovation in the rules of war.

Problems involving principles of international law, concerns over wartime neutral trade, and fears of a maritime incident that might trigger a war were embedded in a context that had cotton at its center. This idea, usually called King Cotton diplomacy, rested on an illusion that the thin fiber of the cotton plant possessed sufficient power to bind Europe to the will of the South. The folly of this conception did not become apparent at once. In the flush of enthusiasm after the fall of Fort Sumter, many otherwise rational people overestimated cotton's power and not without some justification. Britain and France consumed the bulk of the American cotton crop. Without cotton from the seceding states, the hungry mills of Lancashire and Lyons would starve. Unemployed operatives in these cities and their superiors at the mills and mercantile communities would pressure their governments to get cotton at any cost. Such attempts would of necessity challenge the blockade, antagonize the North, and bring Europe into the war. No one could resist the power of King Cotton — or so went the prognosis in Richmond.

Why did the scenario not go as planned? Many forces and factors came together to blunt the mighty monarch's influence. The last prewar crop reaching Europe had been one of the largest on record. This meant that when the war started Europe confronted a glut of cotton, rather than a shortage that might have prompted a more vigorous pro-South stance. When the so-called cotton "famine" did begin to cause genuine hardship in Europe's cotton textile industry, other concerns blunted any serious consideration of an active response on behalf of the South.

Careful and detailed analysis of those events that might have triggered a European involvement in the war has failed to find any evidence that cotton was a decisive factor in any of them. Southerners never learned that the interests of Lancashire did not always coincide with policy in London. The leaders of the South allowed themselves to be mesmerized by a myth. Alternative sources of cotton were soon found in India, China, and Egypt, and while these never measured up to the quality of the best Southern fiber, they filled a gap. Wartime expansion of shipbuilding, munitions, woolens, and a host of other industries offset the disruptions caused by the demise of the king. Other parts of the story include alterations in the military balance in America (Europe's need for cotton never coincided with a convincing Confederate victory on the battlefield) and the revulsion against the South's attempt at economic coercion. Russell, the man most responsible for coordinating the British response to the war, confessed himself put off by heavy-handed Confederate tactics. Of course, the South blunted its own weapon by its ill-advised, self-imposed cotton embargo.

Ironically, the cotton embargo made a shambles of arguments that the blockade was ineffective. If Union cordons were as porous as Confederates claimed, why did so little cotton reach Europe, and why did they complain so much about Yankee interference with the trade?

The cotton embargo had a more destructive consequence. It blinded Southern leaders until too late to a more imaginative use of cotton, stockpiled in Europe as a collateral and a basis for credit in the international markets where they had to purchase the supplies of war. That lack of sound finances bedeviled the South for much of the war.

*   *   *   *   *

When civil war erupted in 1861, the Union had a number of advantages that would help determine the nation's future. One underrated asset was its standing in the world community of nations. Recognized as a legitimate government, Washington had a long-established network of diplomatic relations. Lincoln placed one of his ablest diplomats in the post where he could best advance American interests. No one in the North ever doubted that any European involvement in the war would benefit only the South. So the major task of Charles Francis Adams in London and of his superiors in Washington was to forestall foreign adventurism in what they insisted on calling a domestic insurrection. For that task Adams possessed superb qualifications. Birth had given him a name nearly synonymous with the nation's diplomacy, especially its Anglo-American phases; his father, John Quincy Adams, had been in the forefront of the antislavery movement, and C. F. Adams shared many qualities of mind and outlook with Lord Russell. Despite a number of divisive issues that plagued these men throughout the war, they managed to stay temperamentally in tune. By any objective measure that one may devise, Adams was far better equipped for his mission to London than was his Confederate counterpart, James M. Mason. And, of course, Adams wanted to persuade the British *not* to do things, an easier task than that given to Mason, who sought British assistance.

*   *   *   *   *

The ineptitude of Confederate diplomacy cannot easily be exaggerated. Over seventy years ago, Owsley described the men

whom Jefferson Davis commissioned as his first European representatives as "about the poorest choices possible."[3] The Confederacy benefited greatly from the training and experience of
Southern officers in the United States military. In contrast, it
failed to find sons of the South comparable in talent who had
served prewar America overseas as diplomats and consuls. Of
course, experience was not everything. The diplomats of the
American Revolution learned their craft on the job and did so
successfully. Not so the Confederate diplomats. Their stock in
trade was naïveté, wishful thinking, rose-colored glasses, self-
deception, and golden illusions. The Southern failure overseas
was not inevitable. It came about in large measure because of
human foibles.

In 1861, selection of a secretary of state and foreign representatives owed more to domestic constraints — the need to placate
regional interests and to pay off political debts — than it did to
any understanding of the all-important foreign response to the
war. For the most important and sensitive diplomatic post in
Europe, President Davis selected a man who had neither talent
nor any qualifications. Apparently he made that choice because
he wished to rid himself of a powerful adversary by dumping
him on a foreign shore. William L. Yancey belonged to the most
radical wing of the secession movement, ardently defended slavery, and advocated reopening the transatlantic slave trade. Why
did Davis send an avowed partisan of the slave trade to London?
Leading Victoria's government were a prime minister and a
foreign secretary who considered the traffic in human flesh to
be one of the world's most despicable crimes.

The second (and final) Confederate representative to Britain, James M. Mason, scarcely was an improvement.[4] Mason's
petulant withdrawal from his London post in 1863 is but one
example of his maladroitness. For the most part — James Spence
would be a notable exception — the caliber of the so-called Confederate Lobby of British sympathizers left much to be desired,
and Richmond distrusted Spence's antislavery views. The efforts
of Henry Hotze as chief publicist for the cause have been much
exaggerated; they had no impact on the men who determined
British policy. One looks in vain for any evidence that anyone in

the cabinet read the *Index,* the official organ of Confederate propaganda. Nor did the Southerners organize the uncoordinated agitation in the churches and the peace groups on behalf of intervention.

It was more than hopelessly incompetent and inappropriate diplomats overseas. Richmond was the fundamental problem. In his initial instructions to his foreign representatives, Jefferson Davis paid more attention to the quality of stationery than to the cultivation of a broad base of mutual interests between the Confederacy and the great naval powers of Europe. Davis would not do those things which might have brought foreign support for his bid to create a new American republic. Or, rather, it might be more proper to say that he would not do those things until it was too late.

In his search for a new voice in foreign affairs (or to placate domestic critics of his military policy in the "terrible spring" of 1862), Davis appointed a longtime friend as Confederate secretary of state. Then and now, his appointment of Judah P. Benjamin to that post has been difficult to explain. Even Eli Evans's fine biography of the Jewish Confederate, who by birth was a British subject, has not resolved that mystery.[5] There can be no doubt whatever of Benjamin's intellectual qualifications for his new post. And in the prewar years he often had summered in Europe. Nor can there be any question of Benjamin's commitment to the Southern cause. But as an outsider his ability to shape policy was seriously circumscribed. Because he had no power base of his own — and in part because of his religion — his impact on the course of events depended on his skill in reading and reflecting the president's mind. (His position in Davis's cabinet might be described as analogous to that of Alexander Hamilton in George Washington's cabinet.) Benjamin could do nothing in affairs of state that did not reflect the will of a parochial-minded president. Moreover, the secretary of state had no safe and efficient means of communication with his diplomats in Europe and often had to depend on newspapers published in the North for information about changes in the policies of Britain and France.

Not even Benjamin had a firm grasp of the war's international ramifications or of the impact that Europe's response would have on its outcome. Often his cleverness was unproductive. Unable to free himself from the myth of King Cotton, he demonstrated a surprising misunderstanding of the South's weak international bargaining position, as when in 1862 he tried to play France against Britain. His 1862 note to Russell on British policy toward the Union blockade was devoid of the prospect of doing the Confederacy any good. How relevant was Benjamin's legalism? On one occasion the British foreign secretary told a colleague that the nuances of neutrality concerned him not at all: The "real" difficulty, he said, was "one of policy, not of right." In that instance he was speaking about British policy in China, but the words apply with equal weight to his attitude toward the Confederacy. Perhaps Benjamin realized that any attempt to orchestrate a concerted Confederate / European assault on what he denounced as a "paper blockade" was doomed to fail. Other initiatives while he served as secretary of state do not impress. The abortive Roebuck affair of 1863, a heavy-handed attempt to force Britain to recognize the Confederacy in conjunction with France, must rank as one of the supreme miscalculations of Civil War diplomacy.

Admittedly, in their pursuit of international recognition and support, the Confederate president and his diplomats faced formidable challenges. The world was hostile to slavery. Europeans were cautious about interfering in the affairs of other sovereign states, especially if they were powerful. In 1861, the new American rebels lacked an important advantage that their revolutionary forefathers had possessed in 1776: a natural ally in Europe. No European nation stood waiting in the wings to redress the balance of power, as France had done in the aftermath of the great eighteenth-century wars for empire that had led to her expulsion from North America. The enigmatic Louis Napoleon III's intervention in Mexico, his adventurism in Italy, his challenge to British sea power, and the shifting European configurations of power dictated a prudent French response in transatlantic events in the 1860s. Above all, Mexico determined the emperor's reading of American affairs.

When war came, there was only one European power in a

position to champion the Confederate cause, whether alone or as the leader of a European coalition. The rise or fall of Davis's government depended more than he knew on the ways the British government perceived his effort to create an alternative to Yankee dominance in America. To succeed in making a nation, Davis needed to weave a web of reciprocal interests between London and Richmond. He had to persuade Britain that it was in its interest to aid the Confederacy.

If Richmond really wished to weave such a web of mutual interests, it would have to teach itself realism. For a start, Davis and his colleagues would have to jettison their naïve faith in cotton's power to dictate Europe's response to the war. That faith, as we now know, was tragically misplaced. The assumption that Britain was a natural ally of the South also was dangerously wrong.

For instance, while the ministers of the Queen would see Southern representatives, they refused official intercourse with them. In the vast corpus of Russell papers in London's Public Record Office, this researcher can recall only one document in Mason's hand. That note was a pro forma "thank you" for a pass of admission to the House of Commons when an issue vital to the South was to be debated. There is nothing in that note to suggest that Russell or any of his cabinet colleagues had anything like a "special relationship" with either of the contending parties in North America. To suggest, as some students of the war have done, that Russell, in July 1862, tipped off the South's chief naval agent about British's impending seizure of the CSS *Alabama* is to indulge in fantasy.

*   *   *   *   *

The Confederacy's best hope was an Anglo-American war. It has been contended that on three occasions the United States and the United Kingdom stood on the brink of war. It is difficult to explain those confrontations in terms of rational interests of state. They are the famous *Trent* affair, which lasted from early November 1861 to mid-January 1862, the less famous but arguably more dangerous mediation maneuvers in September and October 1862, and the dispute over the Laird rams in the autumn of 1863. There is a consensus that the Laird rams controversy was the least important of the three crises, but historians are equally divided about the relative importance of the *Trent* imbroglio and the mediation maneuvers.

What vital interest — except national honor — was involved in the *Trent* affair? In November 1861, an impetuous and high-handed Union naval captain, Charles Wilkes, stopped a British mail steamer, the *Trent,* off the coast of Cuba and forcibly removed two Confederate envoys from its deck and the protection of the British flag.

In no time at all, the incident became a cause célèbre and nearly became a casus belli as well. Wilkes became a hero in the North, much feted for his initiative in capturing the Confederate diplomats, James M. Mason and John Slidell, who were the new and much-feared commissioners to Britain and France.[6] In the euphoric outburst that greeted his deed, it was overlooked in the North that Wilkes had committed a serious breach of international law. Nor did many people recognize that the incident might be regarded in Britain as an insult to national honor. All of this became clear, however, when the ramifications of the incident began to filter back from Europe. In truth, Wilkes had brought the two countries perilously close to war. The way the crisis unfolded sheds much light on the hidden dangers in wartime diplomacy. It also illustrates the roles that individuals play in creating and resolving crises in the affairs of nations.

The high level of emotion that the incident engendered in both countries was one of the most dangerous components of the crisis. In England the public and private response was all out of proportion to the significance of the event itself. The ham-handed naval officer was something of a stock figure in that age of gunboat diplomacy, but the tensions of war added explosive elements to the removal of the Confederate diplomats from a British mail packet. If the incident had come a year later — during the mediation maneuvers — the danger of international war would have been magnified. Adding the emotional intensity of the *Trent* affair to the arid cabinet debates in 1862 might have pushed Britain over the edge.

With some trepidation (and many apologies to those who

have studied this subject with great sophistication), let me suggest a simple way of thinking about the first great international crisis of the Civil War. Regard it as an aberration in wartime diplomacy. In a manner of speaking, the confrontation over the removal of the Confederate commissioners from a British mail steamer in the Bahama channel does not go to the heart of the ways the British monitored the war. That is to say, the issues raised by the *Trent* would have been the same, war or no war, in 1851 or 1871. British responses may be best gauged by regarding the crisis as an old-fashioned "affair of honor," an intolerable insult to the Union Jack and Britain's control over the sea-lanes. The British response to the Wilkes outrage—in the press, in the public, in Parliament, and with the prime minister—was an 1860s version of the Don Pacifico affair, an updated version of Palmerston's famous *Civis Romanus Sum* speech of an earlier era. No one with any knowledge of Pam's ringing affirmation that Victoria's flag protected *all* who traveled under its protection would have expected him to respond to Wilkes's "insult to the flag" in any manner other than the way he did: "Damned if I will tolerate this outrage." Preparations for war were set in motion, and if it came to that, the British public would have supported a vigorous defense of the flag. By his affront to British honor, Wilkes had stirred up that deep pool of anti-Americanism that lurked just under the surface of nineteenth-century Anglo-American relations.

The key points of the affair are two: first, it was a serious crisis that almost brought Britain into the war and, second, it was resolved peacefully by good sense on the part of both British and American leaders.

Many people deserve credit for that outcome which prevented a confrontation that in all probability would have destroyed the United States. But it does not go too far to accord the British foreign secretary the lion's share of praise for keeping the peace at a time of intense emotional clamor for war. It was Russell, after all, who devised the diplomacy that permitted a face-saving compromise in Washington. Others contributed. One was the prime minister, who retreated—or allowed himself to be led away—from his initial warlike response. Prince Albert, the Queen's consort, then on his deathbed, roused himself enough to tone down the British note to Washington. In turn, the minister there, Lord Lyons, allowed the bellicose secretary of state, William H. Seward, a little extra time to formulate a reply to the Queen's ultimatum and to accept a face-saving retreat. Without Seward and Lincoln's reluctant realism, British attempts to resolve the crisis peacefully would have failed. After deciding to release the Confederate diplomats and apologize for their capture, Lincoln and Seward had to sell the decision to the cabinet, congressional leaders, and the public.

Earlier I argued that the *Trent* affair did not reveal any British favoritism toward the South. Nothing in the crisis better captures its essence than the comment Russell made when Mason paid a courtesy call on him. The purpose of that visit was to present the Confederate's diplomatic credentials and to thank Her Majesty's government for its role in securing the release of the two commissioners. Russell remarked that no thanks were necessary; the British had done no more for Mason and Slidell than they would have done "for any two Southern negroes." That was a hard truth for the scion of one of the first families of Virginia to hear. Moreover, Mason never received formal accreditation to the Court of St. James's.

Successful resolution of the *Trent* affair had a number of important consequences.[7] First and foremost, it inoculated Britain and America against an unwanted war occasioned by a naval incident. "One war at a time," Lincoln said, as he released the men. The release of Anglo-American animosity brought each nation to a finer appreciation of the potential for danger inherent in the normal play of wartime maritime activities. The Confederates in Europe immediately noticed a decline in official sympathy. The outcome of the *Trent* affair did not advance the Confederate cause.

Russell soon took another important step to avoid war. In February 1862, he conditionally accepted Union, rather than Confederate, standards of blockade effectiveness, thereby neutralizing a dangerous source of friction between Britain and America. Three long-range consequences of Russell's note may be summarized here. It thwarted all Southern efforts to exploit those "evasions of blockade" by informing the British of the many ships that had slipped out of Southern ports through a mere "paper" blockade; the note lessened possibilities of an Anglo-American clash over arcane points of law and commerce between Yankee blockaders and British merchants, whether that trade was conducted from ports in the United Kingdom or from those in the British West Indies; and, perhaps most important, Russell provided a substantial leeway to his cabinet and Admiralty colleagues in dealing with future episodes akin to those of the Union captain Charles Wilkes which had brought the two countries to the brink of war.

Russell's decision turned out to be one of the most critical of the war, even if the literature of that subject rarely accords it the importance it deserves. Few scholars have recognized its role in the outcome of wartime diplomacy. Nor have they appreciated the context and consequences of that note. Even the correct place of that note in the chronology of wartime diplomacy has not yet been properly assessed. If, as Peter Parish has argued (correctly, I think), commerce and command of its sea-lanes provided the flashpoint of danger for Civil War neutrals, then Russell's note had long-range results.[8] It suggests that he had decided not to challenge Union efforts to strangle the South into submission. In effect, by tolerating a looser definition of blockade effectiveness than had been the norm in the nineteenth century, Russell was putting Her Majesty's seal of approval on Lincoln's Anaconda Plan to choke the Confederacy into compliance with Union conceptions of the nature of the Federal constitution.

Whether by accident or design — the record is unclear — Russell's explication of the fine points of blockade law undercut the arguments of his new Confederate counterpart, Judah P. Benjamin, even before that official could draft them. Soon after becoming Confederate secretary of state in March 1862, he challenged Britain's response to the war and castigated the Queen's indifference to the cause of Confederate independence. In his analysis, Benjamin took Russell to task for his interpretation of the 1856 Declaration of Paris, which had attempted to set out rules for neutrals and belligerents in future maritime wars. The precise relationship between that 1856 definition of neutral rights and the American war has never been properly defined, but it is not unreasonable that the British foreign secretary (who had helped draft it) understood it as well as the Confederate secretary of state.

Russell deserves to be better appreciated on both sides of the Atlantic as a Civil War peacemaker. After the resolution of the *Trent* affair, he confirmed this role by his decision to disengage Her Majesty's government from any active role in protecting those subjects who tried their hand at running the blockade, by his willingness to test the legal limits of neutrality in that still curious case of the *Alexandra,* by his "unforced" decision to prevent the escape of the Laird rams in late 1863, and by his little-known investment of substantial sums of government funds to neutralize what might have become the Confederacy's Chinese fleet.

*   *   *   *   *

Russell the peacekeeper has another, puzzling side. In the autumn of 1862, he almost single-handedly brought Britain into the war on the side of the South. Russell's conduct remains hard to understand. Someone once described him as an odd mix of "giant and child." Fortunately, when he crossed the line between humanitarian concern over a bloody war and the demands of national interest, he always had Palmerston's realism to correct his course. This second crisis was, I think, the only time that Europe seriously considered entering the war. In late 1862 there was a very lively possibility of a British intervention in the American Civil War. For reasons of its own — and without any pro-South proclivities — the government of Queen Victoria, in the fall of 1862, deliberately and unemotionally came to the brink of intervening in the war. Such an intervention, had it come about (and it very nearly did), would have destroyed the American experiment and gone a long way toward perpetuating slavery in the South.

Russell was the driving force behind the mediation maneuvers in September and October 1862. He masterminded a series of intricate moves to "do something" to end the war. It is clear that he had not properly considered the difficulties of his project. His maneuvers highlighted the complexity of the problems confronting European statesmen as they sought to work out a response to the war. The crisis of 1862 provides a useful test case of wartime diplomacy. Curiously, it shows virtually no input from either of the contending parties in America.

Part of the impetus for doing something to make the carnage stop had its origin in humanitarian impulses. This was the age of Victorian morality. The horrendous casualties and the apparent futility of the North's attempt to coerce the South back into the Union generated widespread sentiment for a cease-fire. Then, too, in late 1862 the shortage of cotton began to cause serious distress in Lancashire and Lyons. New leadership in the French foreign ministry and a restive emperor hinted at a readiness in Paris for cooperation vis-à-vis America. With Robert E. Lee's stirring September sweep into Maryland, the time seemed ripe for a vigorous European response to the war.

The reasons why Russell failed are instructive. They bring us close to the critical reason for the Confederacy's demise. First, there is the verdict of the battlefield. At the one moment it mattered most, Lee failed. His defeat at Antietam cost the South dearly. Antietam, not Gettysburg, was the lynchpin of Southern success or failure.[9] What makes a battle "decisive" is its connection with the larger context of a war. One of the most significant consequences of Lee's retreat from Maryland was the loss of Prime Minister Palmerston's support for the mediation maneuvers.

Wise men say that in the council of warriors, diplomats must remain mute. It restates the obvious to note that Europe's response to the American war was largely conditioned by military results across the Atlantic. Howard Jones's work on the intervention crisis, if I read it correctly, requires new ways of seeing the foreign response to the Civil War.[10] Jones has confirmed an old-fashioned (but accurate) assessment that the God of Battles spoke to the British cabinet in the fall of 1862, not in the summer of 1863, as conventional wisdom would have us believe.

When news of Antietam reached Palmerston, he immediately

reverted to his wait-and-see policy. Sooner than most of his cabinet associates, he recognized that there could be no intervention without going to war. The good sense of Palmerston, the supposed warmonger of nineteenth-century mythology, kept Britain at virtually the last possible moment from taking the fatal step that separates peace from war. From his perspective no vital British interest would be advanced by direct participation in the transatlantic war. Unlike his cabinet colleague, the chancellor of the exchequer, William E. Gladstone, the prime minister was not convinced that Jefferson Davis had "made a nation." Palmerston had no interest in helping him in that task. And Gladstone, as even he himself later admitted, did not know what he was talking about.

In addition, Russell faced several other formidable impediments. For one thing, he was not exactly clear about what he wished to do. To propose an armistice or cease-fire was one possibility, but it soon became clear that the North would resent and reject such a move, especially if it was tied to any implicit recognition of the Confederacy. It never became clear what form European intervention might take if it were to have any chance of success. Any unilateral approach by Britain would be unwise, so it seemed more expedient to mount a multilateral effort. When Russell canvassed that possibility, however, he ran into two problems: domestic politics delayed and ultimately destroyed any prospect for a joint Anglo-French venture in America, and the Russians, for reasons more anti-British than pro-American, refused to participate.

At home the foreign secretary's plan ran into intense opposition, especially in the cabinet. There, Russell and Gladstone could not overcome the determined resistance to intervention mounted by Palmerston and the secretary for war, George Cornewall Lewis. They recognized that any form of intervention in America, even if presented as the work of an impartial and "honest broker," would do no good as the war then stood. And any kind of involvement would mean Britain must join the fighting. Despite considerable distress in the cotton-manufacturing districts, there was no public outcry to get cotton at the cost of war. A newspaper caught a popular mood when it suggested that it would be cheaper to feed all cotton textile workers on venison and champagne than to go to war so that they might have jobs.

The intervention crisis illustrates two other aspects of the foreign response to the war. Both were deadly to Southern aspirations of statehood. Quite simply, the effort to establish an independent nation in America never impinged on a vital British interest, as David Paul Crook has brilliantly shown in *The North, the South, and the Powers.*[11] And it is rarely understood how abysmally the South failed in selling itself to the pragmatists who directed European statecraft in the 1860s. Continental politics concerned those men far more than did the domestic discontents of Americans. To be sure, European statesmen stood ready to take advantage of the transatlantic disruption, but not if it involved them in war.

Of course, the decision to step back from intervention in the American war was conditional, not absolute. Certainly, even after Antietam, the British still did not want to abandon the wait-and-see stance they had adopted after Fort Sumter. But, after a long career of studying the international dimension of the Civil War, it is difficult for me to believe that even a Confederate victory at Gettysburg would have brought the British back up the peak of interventionism that prevailed in the fall of 1862. The emotional climate had changed.

And what was the role of slavery in determining Europe's response to the war? Although in the decades leading up to the Civil War white racism grew stronger there, Europe remained decidedly hostile to slavery. Yet Lincoln's preliminary emancipation of the slaves after Antietam did *not* rally the forces of European liberalism to the Union cause. If anything, it strengthened opposition to the war's bloodshed. Victoria's ministers suspected that Lincoln's "real" reason for freeing Confederate slaves was to turn the American war into a "servile insurrection" of black slaves against their masters. To Russell and others in the British cabinet, Lincoln's proclamation was no more than a cheap political trick to incite a race war and transform the South into the hell of Haiti in the 1790s. So Lincoln's announcement did nothing to slow down the interventionism of Russell.

There is no clear answer to the question about the role that slavery played in conditioning the ways in which the British responded to the war. But it is surely a point of some importance to stress that on the two (or three) occasions when the British came closest to intervening, slavery played no role whatsoever in the debates on that question.

The third crisis that might have produced an Anglo-American war — over the Laird rams in the autumn of 1863 — was largely resolved before it began. As a casus belli, the Laird rams crisis of late 1863 has been much overrated. The innovative research of David Krein and others has made it clear that Russell and his colleagues had decided to take those "formidable ironclads" into custody long before the Foreign Office received the American minister's oft-quoted (but much misunderstood) "this is war" note of 5 September 1863.[12] Because so many historians follow the classic account of E. D. Adams, a simple mistake that ought to have been corrected years ago continues to color accounts of this contretemps. On a key point he is dead wrong: April 1863 had nothing to do with the ram crisis five months later. In fairness to E. D. Adams, it should be acknowledged that the abbreviated date on the C. F. Adams document is illegible: the initial letter of the month may as easily be read as "S" or as "A." Internal evidence makes it clear that the letter could not have been written in April, the month that Adams assigns to it.

E. D. Adams constructed his distorted interpretation on the basis of his misreading of the evidence. No student of the war needs to be reminded that between April and September 1863 the war took an unfortunate turn for the Southern aspirations of statehood. In the fall of that year the outcome of the war was clearer to the British than it was in the spring. The mistake of Adams in dating the "real crisis" of the rams suggests the need for a new chronology of wartime diplomacy.

*   *   *   *   *

Direct European intervention would have benefited the Confederacy the most, but if that was not to be, the South hoped to build warships in neutral British and French shipyards. Its imaginatively conceived and brilliantly executed plan to acquire a modern navy in Europe turned out to be the one indisputable success in the foreign affairs of the Confederacy. In June 1861, James D. Bulloch arrived in Liverpool as chief of foreign naval procurement. Georgia-born, he had served as an officer in the American navy and later as a New York–based merchant marine captain. Bulloch came to Britain with a three-part plan to redress the balance of power on the sea. Sooner than their adversaries, Southern navalists had grasped the implications of the nineteenth-century naval revolution. Recognizing their own limited ability to manufacture the new weapons of naval war, they turned to Europe to buy and build modern warships for the South. They wisely sent Bulloch to Europe to mastermind those efforts.

He had three objectives: to build a fleet of swift cruisers to sweep enemy commerce from the seas and to pressure the Northern mercantile community to sue for peace; to construct a squadron of ironclad rams to break the blockade of the Confederate coast; and, while these projects matured, to purchase large numbers of specially designed blockade-runners to keep the South supplied with the materials of war. In the first phase of the plan he achieved outstanding success. He built and sent to sea the most famous and effective commerce destroyer of all time, the CSS *Alabama,* whose life and death might stand as a microhistory of the Confederacy itself. She and her sister ships soon drove Yankee trade from the oceans of the world. The damage done by those vessels cost the British government more than $15 million in postwar damage claims.

The escape of the *Alabama* from Liverpool in July 1862 illuminates significant aspects of Britain's response to the American war. Some features of that story remain mysterious. Bulloch's papers have never come to light. The construction of the ship and Union efforts to prevent her escape posed complex questions of property rights, the legal limits of neutrality, the ambiguities of the Foreign Enlistment Act (Britain's antiquated defense against illegal shipbuilding for belligerents), and governmental responsibility for the proper enforcement of neutral obligations in wartime. Bulloch's success in getting that ship to sea offers a splendid example of what imagination, intelligence, and luck may achieve under daunting circumstances. The Confederacy had few who could match him in clarity of conception and virtuosity of execution. No story of the war's international dimension can be complete without acknowledgment of his superb achievement, of which the escape of the *Alabama* remains a supreme example.

His success in the ironclad phase of his mission was muted. Alas, the inept officer originally in charge of the ram plan contributed only a year's delay before Bulloch superseded him. Bulloch merits high marks for his innovative design for the famous Laird rams. These ships incorporated all the improvements in naval architecture that human ingenuity could devise in that era. They were clad in armor to make them nearly impervious to enemy fire. They carried large-caliber rifled shell guns to afford them range and formidable firepower. They incorporated turrets, revolving fire platforms that significantly increased their arc of fire. They possessed new standards of maneuverability because of twin screw propellers that enabled them "to turn like a duck in water." Their distinguishing feature, the ram, was a strong metal projection of the bow. It extended under water some six or seven feet in front of the ship. This device turned the vessels into immensely powerful mobile battering rams—hence their name. Such ships would pose a terrible threat to wooden Yankee blockaders off the Confederate coast. But, unfortunately for Bulloch and his cause, by September 1863, when the rams were ready to go to sea, London had changed the way it saw the responsibilities of a neutral power. The British decided not to allow such formidable vessels to join the Confederate navy. They became part of the Royal Navy by preemptive purchase in 1864.

The importance of Bulloch's work may explain why he was one of the very few Confederate officers to be denied amnesty at the war's conclusion. He died in England in 1901.

*   *   *   *   *

There can be few incidents in the diplomacy of any era to match the Alice in Wonderland quality of the Duncan Kenner Mission in the final year of the war. The Confederacy pathetically attempted to trade the abolition of slavery for foreign recognition.

In his biography of the Confederate president, historian William C. Davis (no relation) has allocated some dozen lines to this critical episode in Confederate diplomacy that point to President Davis's reluctance to come to grips with the problem of slavery (the Kenner proposal had lingered on his desk for nearly two years).[13] The thoroughly tawdry Kenner Mission exposed all the defects of Jefferson Davis's diplomacy and highlighted all of Mason's incapacity to conduct it. In fact, it encapsulated the defects of diplomacy that had plagued the Confederate cause from the beginning. The proposal was made too late, in the wrong way, by the wrong people, and for the wrong reasons. In Confederate diplomacy the timing was always wrong. Had it come sooner and more graciously, this offer of emancipation would have made friends of enemies.

*   *   *   *   *

Timing made the difficult task of obtaining European support even more difficult. Not only did the South represent a retrograde social and economic system but its bid for independence came at a time when European affairs distracted London and Paris from the epic struggle of the Blue and the Gray. Also, just as the cotton glut of 1861 blunted the power of that commodity to influence the course of foreign deliberations about the war, so, when the cotton famine began to bite, Gladstone as chancellor of the exchequer magically overcame the severe hiccup the war had caused to trade. He manufactured a budget surplus for 1862–63 of some 3.75 million pounds sterling, a sum that biographer Roy Jenkins has described as "massive for those days."[14] Just at the critical moment in 1862 when many in Europe were prepared to believe, like Gladstone, that Jefferson Davis had indeed "made a nation," Lee failed to validate that assumption on the battlefield. His retreat from the bloody field of Antietam deprived the South of European support at the very moment it appeared most likely. The narrowness of the margin that kept Europe out of the war is still not fully appreciated. The South had extraordinarily bad timing.

A central fact of the war remains: At no time were Southerners able to orchestrate that combination of circumstances which would have compelled a more favorable verdict from those who watched the war from an international perspective. What they saw did not move them to intervene. Their failure to do so shattered Southern aspirations of nationhood.

*   *   *   *   *

No account of the Civil War should ignore a work of fiction that has dominated popular conceptions of the war: Margaret Mitchell's *Gone with the Wind,* a novel both brilliant and wrong-headed. A native of Atlanta might be excused for considering the burning of that city as the *key* event of the war; a Georgia girl would require little justification for seeing the march of Sherman through that state as the death knell of a civilization. Nor does one need any sophisticated knowledge of antebellum Southern history to conclude that her account of the coming of the war has serious flaws. Yet her fiction hints at truths that the books by professional historians often obscure. For all the excesses of an overwrought romantic imagination, she has pinpointed a number of reasons why the South lost the war. Between the lines of her novel lie many historical insights. Careful readers — admittedly, always a minority — will discover there many reasons for the collapse of the Confederacy. No professional historian has better captured that inane but commonplace assumption south of Mason–Dixon, that "one Reb could whip ten Yanks," a serious misperception of the way the real world worked, as Rhett Butler was quick to point out.

More important, Mitchell has also isolated one of the supreme delusions of the South's ruling class: the misguided belief that the embryonic nation could go it alone. That assumption, as much as anything else, doomed Jefferson Davis's bid for independence. So, in the 1930s, a novelist intuitively knew that the lifeline of the South stretched to the quays, warehouses, and shipyards of Liverpool and beyond them to the corridors of power in Paris and London. The blockade-runners who kept open that lifeline rendered important service to the South, even as they enriched themselves.

Mitchell's portrait of the romantically roguish blockade-runner Rhett Butler has about it the stuff of genius. Her picture of that prince of runners, her conception of a cavalier of the sea, could not be bettered. The cosmopolitan and skeptical outsider has no burning commitment to the cause. When he gives that green bonnet to Scarlett, no one has to be reminded by a footnote that his object is not the advancement of the war effort.

But few readers or viewers understand the ways in which that scene has encapsulated an important historic truth, germane to any explanation of the South's failure to achieve independence. Of course, there is the obvious fact that bonnets were no substitute for bullets — or for medical and naval supplies. No amount of luxury goods brought into the beleaguered South would much enhance its chances for victory. The scene also suggests a higher historical truth: the government at Richmond was in error for allowing private profit to compete with public good, when supplying the South with the sinews of war was at stake. Rhett knew that the lifeline of the cause stretched from the Confederate coast to the waters that washed the shores of Britain and her Caribbean islands. He understood better than most that it was from those sources that the South might draw the weapons to weary the enemy into a military stalemate and a negotiated peace and thereby achieve its goals of independence and international recognition. In Rhett's pragmatic view, and it is one that most students of the war's foreign dimension would endorse, the business of blockade-running allowed the South to fight the war for four long years.

That point, an important if underrated one, takes center stage in one of the movie's most prescient scenes. Every fan of the film version of *Gone with the Wind* will remember that the transition from the war to its aftermath centers on Rhett in a Yankee prison, playing cards with his captors. Like many others in the defeated South, he is short of money, though his particular financial embarrassment stems from the fact that his funds were temporarily tied up in Liverpool.

In a flash of insight, the novelist or the moviemaker has captured another of the war's larger dimensions. To date, no one has adequately explained that odd juxtaposition in post-war Liverpool of the Confederacy's secretary of state, its chief naval agent, and substantial sums of Southern money in that British city on the river Mersey, where so much of the Confederacy's blockade-running and naval construction had been centered.[15]

TWO | TOWARD THE CSS *ALABAMA*

*M*Y STUDY of the CSS *Alabama* has a curious set of origins. It has a special set of objectives as well. This work does not seek to add one more romance of a rebel raider to the vast literature of the Civil War naval history. My aim, rather, is to disentangle fact from fiction in an important chapter of that history. The escape of that famous cruiser from England in the summer of 1862 has about it the stuff of legends. More than a few of them have clouded efforts to get at the truth of what really happened in Liverpool and London in July of that fateful year, when the chief naval agent of the Confederacy, James D. Bulloch, launched the most successful commerce raider of all time. In the circumstances of that escape and in the subsequent career of that ship is written a microhistory of Jefferson Davis's efforts to make a navy and a nation.

The germ of such a work first started in my mind in the mid-1960s. That version would have been a joint effort with my English friend, Tom Green, of Southampton. His untimely death ended that project, though I like to think that his spirit hovers over my present work. In any event, soon after Tom's death in 1967, I began to contemplate a different sort of book on the Confederate cruiser. That one would have focused on the postwar claims controversy that the ship's success in commerce raiding had engendered. Such a work seemed a natural follow-up to my study of wartime naval diplomacy. Its theme and subject matter fell comfortably into my area of expertise. That topic had the added advantage of giving me a head start with the literature, the sources, and the archives of that subject. Or so I supposed in the euphoria that followed publication of my first book in 1970. Of course, things did not go as planned, and my intellectual overreach soon received its just retribution. In all innocence I had unleashed a fury that pursues me still. In moments of despair it now seems to me unlikely that any one person will ever master the mountain of material that has accumulated around the *Alabama* claims controversy.[1]

My first book, *Great Britain and the Confederate Navy,* centered on the British response to the American Civil War. Despite its title's emphasis on naval affairs, it was, in essence, a study in diplomatic history.[2] Naturally, the overseas naval activity of the Confederacy played a prominent part in that book, and the *Alabama* affair received a proper emphasis in it. In the course of my research I had discovered new information on little-known aspects of her career in Liverpool, in the Caribbean, in South Africa, at Cherbourg, and in the Far East, but I could not fit that information into my diplomatic study. All but one of those items have now been published. That missing one will form a portion of this book. Of more importance for my future work, however, was my increasing fascination with the career of the man who had built that magnificent ship. At one point I even considered writing Bulloch's biography, but I was deterred by the absence of any private papers to fill out the details of his public life.

At any rate, in the early 1970s my research and writing interests began to tilt toward naval history. That change was more a shift of emphasis, rather than a new direction. I retained all the advantages of my graduate training in diplomacy and served as coeditor of the massive *Makers of American Diplomacy* in 1974. But, in time, as much by chance as by design, my work began to take on a dual focus, the double perspective of the diplomatist and the navalist. As things worked out, that bifocal vision proved to be a considerable advantage as I continued to wrestle with my principal preoccupation — the international dimension of the American war. Now, however, I could approach the problems of that war with the sharper perspective of two disciplines, using the insights from one to illuminate the other. Such an approach is rare, and I know of no others who practice it.

The next step in my journey toward the *Alabama* took place when, at a critical point in my career, the International Commission on Maritime History accepted my proposal for a paper on "The Confederacy's Chinese Fleet." In that strange story the South's most famous cruiser had played a significant role. My participation in that conference was to have significant consequences as well. Again by chance, I was in the audience when the French delegation announced that navy divers had discovered the wreck of the Confederate cruiser off Cherbourg. That discovery set off a flurry of renewed interest in the ship. The ripples of that excitement led me to volunteer my services to the *Journal of Confederate History* as guest editor of a special issue to commemorate that cruiser's career. The French discovery seemed certain to inaugurate a new era in Confederate naval history, and I wished to be part of it.[3] My task as editor of the *JCH* project was to clear away the encrusted barnacles of a century of misinformation. A second objective of my work was to provide other students of Confederate naval history with a reliable assessment of the *Alabama*'s career as it was seen in the late 1980s by a distinguished group of international scholars. Although the finished product fell far short of my expectations, the project yielded a number of beneficial results.[4] For one thing, it conferred on me a certain patina of expertise about the ship and her exploits. For another, it opened the way to my TV debut as an "expert" commentator on the *Alabama*—my fifteen minutes of fame had arrived, at last.[5] In short, that project provided a necessary prelude to my present one, though I did not know it at the time. Several intermediate steps on that road remained to be taken.

One important fringe benefit of the *JCH* project was that it introduced me to a wider circle of people interested in Confederate naval affairs. One was Renata Eley Long, an Englishwoman who set off the sequence of cause and consequence that culminated in this book. It did not happen at once, however, and we corresponded for several years before historical lightning struck. It should perhaps be noted that the two of us share a deep and abiding interest in the life of James D. Bulloch. We had arrived at our respective appreciations of his career independently of each other. By the time our paths had crossed, I had spent many years studying Bulloch's wartime exploits in England; my correspondent had spent nearly as much time in compiling material for a projected biography. With that common interest we soon fell into an easy exchange of views on all aspects of his career. At one point my correspondent casually mentioned that she was compiling a character sketch of one of Bulloch's most important English associates, one Matthew James Butcher. That man, as every student of *Alabama* affairs knows, was a vital link in Bulloch's plans to get his ship safely out of Liverpool. But beyond that, Butcher remained an enigma, even to us.

In reply to a query about him, I offhandedly mentioned that my files contained a nugget of information that she might find useful. But I cautioned that my "fact" lacked context and might be of small importance. To pique her curiosity about that mysterious fact, I promised to tell her the story of how it had come into my possession (another consequence of the *JCH* project). That story—it is one which skirts the outer limits of credibility—cannot fit within the boundaries of this introduction.[6] Suffice to say that my unusual tidbit of information about Butcher proved to be the vital clue that led my English friend to one of the more important documentary finds in more than a century of *Alabama* studies. All it took was a simple phone call—after one more trip to the Merli archives, one more double check on something we both thought we already knew, and one more look at the literature in our respective *Alabama* files.

And so serendipity in the search for sources led two transatlantic collaborators to the discovery of an "unwritten chapter" of Confederate naval history—and a valuable one, at that. Matt Butcher's postwar report of his part in the *Alabama*'s escape provides a unique angle of vision on that important event. He sheds new light on the always fascinating mystery of Merseyside, and he tells us things that neither Bulloch nor Raphael Semmes could supply in their respective accounts of her career. No one else could furnish the sort of detail about the cruiser's first weeks at sea as Butcher does. In addition, his account has another advantage: it provides a most useful double check on what we think we know about a well-studied event in Civil War naval and diplomatic history. This discovery came at an important point in the evolution of *Alabama* studies, and we hope that it will play a significant role in revising the history of that great ship.

As noted, major credit for this discovery rests with Renata Eley Long. It was she who located Butcher's granddaughter — after my clue had narrowed the search area. Her sleuthing confirmed the existence of the memoir (which I had inferred from a lot of old-fashioned historical detective work — and an extraordinary stroke of luck). But perhaps most important, she then convinced the document's owner that it ought to be brought to the public's attention. And finally, she secured permission for us to prepare an annotated copy for publication.[7] That task triggered my decision to write this book.

*   *   *   *   *

Our long experience in *Alabama* studies enabled us to recognize the potential value of what we had found. We also noticed its shortcomings. Chief of these was its date of composition, some fifteen years after the war. Moreover, it had been written without recourse to Butcher's "journal of that period," i.e., 1862, when the events recounted took place. Then, editing the document raised that tricky and fundamental question of reliability: How much credence could it command? It fell, after all, into that category of historical records that must be denominated highly suspect, the postwar recollection of Confederate naval personnel. These must always be used with extreme caution. I had become disenchanted with most of them, as readers of this book will quickly discover. This meant, of course, that we could not assume the document's reliability (even with its strong provenance). Like all such documents, this one required stringent tests of historical verification. As our task proceeded, we became aware that Butcher's account contained a number of defects, inaccuracies, and anomalies that might lead an uncritical reader astray. And it should be noted here that a significant feature of *Alabama* studies seems to be the ease with which even experienced researchers are led astray. On that point I am well qualified to speak.

Our long experience with the literature of this subject has alerted us to the pitfalls of defective sources and to the perils that followed from them. And so we made no premature rush to publication. We decided, rightly, it still seems to us, that the document's utility as a reliable historical source would be much enhanced if we could provide it with a correct context, put its subject matter in proper perspective, and give its readers an informed commentary on its contents. We had no doubts at all about our ability to do these things, but transatlantic editing posed peculiar problems. Those who know me and my penchant for procrastination will have no difficulty understanding that most of those problems occurred on the American side of the Atlantic.[8]

Constructing a proper setting for the gem we had discovered proved an arduous task, more time-consuming and more complex than either of us had anticipated. Our task, we soon learned, required a thorough review of all the relevant documents in this case; it also made necessary a detailed reexamination of the circumstances surrounding the *Alabama*'s escape from Liverpool. That work, in turn, dictated a comprehensive reassessment of the literature of that escape, going back to the war itself. We learned a strange thing: there were no accurate or fully reliable accounts of that escape in all the vast literature of that subject! Even my own youthful and pioneering 1970 commentary on the escape, careful as that work had been, was not free from error, as I now learned to my chagrin.

As my part of preparing the document for publication, I had undertaken an extensive and detailed comparison of Butcher with all the so-called standard accounts in the literature of diplomatic and naval historians. Here, my dual approach began to pay dividends. It soon became clear to me that many of those accounts were in error on critical parts of the story. It was equally clear that in many instances those mistakes had a common point of origin. To my considerable surprise, I traced many flawed accounts of the escape to an unimpeachable source — Ephraim D. Adams's monumental book on wartime diplomacy, *Great Britain and the American Civil War* (1925). Over the years since that classic work was published, any number of historians (and, alas, I must be included in their ranks) have allowed their accounts of *Alabama* affairs to be unduly influenced by Adams's work. The baleful influence of that master's mistakes forms a principal theme of my revision of Civil War naval, legal, and diplomatic affairs.

There can be no further doubt that Adams had made a number of serious errors in his account of the *Alabama*'s departure from Liverpool. Such things are easily done, as I now know to my cost. But my reading of that master's account of what happened in Liverpool and London during the summer of 1862 had more important results than the detection of my youthful error. That review exposed other "mistakes" in Adams's account of wartime diplomacy. And those errors are far more serious than incorrect dates and a garbled sequence of events. For one thing, my re-study of the escape convinced me of the critical importance of a correct chronology. The precise timing and the exact sequence of events are matters of importance. That simple fact has not been widely recognized, even now. No current work of which I am aware pays proper attention to that all-important matter of a correct chronology — partly, I now believe, because it is incredibly difficult to pin down and partly because its crucial importance has been overlooked.

The major error in Adams's account of the *Alabama*, however, is difficult to categorize. It flows, in part, from faulty dates and defective chronology, but is more insidious and has had more pernicious consequences. In a casual, curious, and most offhanded way, Adams implicates Her Majesty's government in connivance in the ship's escape. On the basis of evidence that must be described as insubstantial and unconvincing, he insinuates that high-level servants of the Queen "leaked" information about an impending detention of the cruiser to Confederate agents in Liverpool to allow Bulloch to get his ship out of harm's way. On the basis of incomplete and inaccurate information — and an out-of-context misreading of a key document — Adams laid the foundation for nearly a century of misrepresentation of a crucial event in wartime naval and diplomatic history.[9] Indeed, as I shall attempt to show, the mistakes that Adams incorporated into his 1925 study are alive and flourishing as we enter a new millennium and embark on a new era of *Alabama* studies. Surely, the time has come to set the record straight.

Unfortunately, current appraisals of that ship's career and captain compound the mistakes of a master historian. Sad to say, many contemporary authors have made matters worse. They take Adams's account — or its various permutations — as an expression of Holy Writ, a text set in stone, an interpretation to be taken on faith. In sum, Adams's version of wartime diplomacy and naval affairs has become virtually immune to critical historical analysis. In 1993 Bradford Perkins captured an essential feature of this approach. After noting the tendency of historians to retrace the trail blazed by that pioneer of wartime diplomacy, he notes that Adams's book is "one of those remarkable works that have stood the test of time, not impervious to attack but essentially above it."[10] A profession noted for revisionism has been painfully slow to revise one of the key works of nineteenth-century diplomacy. The profession has been loath to apply its basic tools of criticism to the work of one of its most distinguished practitioners. This study seeks to correct that lamentable state of affairs.

*   *   *   *   *

But my work has another objective, one that Adams failed to address. An important part of my task is to restore James D. Bulloch to his rightful role as the hero and mastermind of the *Alabama*'s escape. Although he is virtually unsung, even in the American South, he deserves to rank with Robert E. Lee as the best that region produced in its abortive search for statehood. Perhaps the recent discovery of his ship off the coast of France (and it must be stressed that the *Alabama* was Bulloch's boat) will reawaken interest in his contribution to the Confederate cause. Few worked harder than he did to ensure its success. Perhaps my study of that cruiser's life and death may allow him, finally, to reap some of the historical fame he so richly deserves. The biography of Bulloch that Renata Eley Long is writing should be another major step in achieving that goal.

Then, too, the estimable Bulloch has one additional claim on the attention of all serious students of Civil War naval history. That aspect of his career has also been neglected, though it too deserves greater and wider appreciation. This study of his ship has, as one of its subthemes, the task of stimulating an awareness of Bulloch's talents as a historian. His two-volume account of his European mission should rank as a classic. It is a glorious re-creation of his wartime work, and it stands head and shoulders above all other naval memoirs of the war. Scholars of a philosophic cast of mind may learn a good deal about the war and Confederate naval affairs by comparing Bulloch's memoir with that of the cruiser's captain, Raphael Semmes.[11] Such a comparison has much to teach the careful reader about the writing of history as well. Be that as it may, I have no qualms in asserting that Bulloch's book — his monument — is amazingly free of the defects one usually associates with retrospective reviews of one's work. In a genre of literature often described as history's most dangerous source, Bulloch reaches masterly levels of veracity and candor. He is, moreover, a model of fair-minded assessment of friend and foe. Both my wide-ranging and my microscopic reexaminations of his work undertaken for this study have re-affirmed my admiration for the man and for the way he carried out his mission. Rarely has a person so close to vital affairs of state spoken so modestly, so fairly, and so discreetly of his role at the epicenter of world affairs. In sum, his account furnishes a portrait of a man in full, warts and all. He compels admiration for his rectitude and for his generosity of spirit. We must, as Seneca advises, praise him for the great things he did. But, even more, we should admire him for those things he almost did.[12]

For almost eighty years, historians have been in thrall to E. D. Adams's flawed masterwork. Many of them have uncritically accepted his highly dubious charge of a government plot to assist Bulloch in getting his ship to sea. By giving credit for that masterstroke to "a spy at Downing Street," or to a "clerk in the Foreign Office," or to "a leak from the foreign secretary," those accounts falsify the story of what really happened in Liverpool and London in July 1862. They also distort history and do a serious disservice to the Queen's loyal servants. Moreover, they demean and downgrade Bulloch's contribution to the Confederate cause — in effect they deprive him of the credit he deserves as one of the South's most talented and imaginative heroes. He gave Jefferson Davis a navy, and if the president had had more men like him, he would have made a nation. A major purpose of this current work, then, is to put the story of Bulloch's wartime mission in proper perspective and to accord him full recognition as one of America's preeminent naval diplomats. That aim, of necessity, presupposes and encompasses other tasks as well. Chief among them is correcting Adams's flawed version of the British response to the American Civil War. It must not be presumed that errors on the *Alabama* are the only ones in his work.

My final objective in this work is to exonerate the ministry of Lord Palmerston and Lord Russell from the charge of complicity in the *Alabama*'s escape that Adams levied against it in 1925. As he admitted in his memoir, Bulloch had sympathetic Englishmen who were willing to apprise him of governmental intentions. To date, their identities remain shrouded in mystery. The generation that endured the treason of the Cambridge Five and the Rosenbergs should not be surprised that government servants sometimes betray their trust. But before Queen Victoria's prime minister or foreign secretary is condemned for connivance in the 1862 escape of a Confederate cruiser, more convincing evidence than we now have is needed. As of the time that I write, no one has produced any solid evidence to support those allegations. The charge of ministerial collusion in Bulloch's work rests on suspect assertions in the work of Adams. Until now, that charge has never been challenged. Any competent jury would throw it out of court.

Still, few historical verdicts are definitive, and it may be that the current renaissance in *Alabama* studies will stimulate fresh answers to old questions. New work based on more reliable evidence than we now possess may force even more revisions of the traditional story of wartime naval and diplomatic affairs. If my work clears the deck for such studies, if it clears away the myths and romanticism that have clouded the cruiser's story, and if it provides a finer appreciation of the work of James D. Bulloch, I shall be content in a job well done.

THREE | THE LAW OF
THE *ALABAMA*

*T*HE FULL story of James D. Bulloch's challenge to British neutrality during the American Civil War has never been told. His attempts to build a navy for Jefferson Davis in the United Kingdom raised complex questions of neutral rights and obligations in a new age of naval war. Those efforts brought on many disputes about the meaning of domestic and international law as it was practiced in the mid-nineteenth century. Confederate shipbuilding in the Queen's realm also soured diplomatic relations between Washington and London during the war and for long after it. So acrimonious did some of these quarrels become that on several occasions they threatened to disrupt relations between the two nations. Some historians even say that Britain and America teetered on the brink of war more than once. My own view is that those war scares have been exaggerated, but it is safe to say that much ill will grew from one of Bulloch's most successful challenges to the rules of the war game — the *Alabama*'s escape from Liverpool in July 1862.

That incident, along with its diplomatic and legal ramifications, has much to tell us about some of the larger repercussions of the war's international dimensions. Or, to put the case another way, the controversy over that ship — her last-minute departure from port, her challenge to the Foreign Enlistment Act, and the unresolved question of ministerial complicity in her escape — provides opportunities for seeing Anglo-American re-

41

lations in microcosm. This event also has enormous potential for lighting up a number of dark places in wartime naval and diplomatic history. Part of the difficulty in past studies of the *Alabama* stems from the false separation of these two approaches: The navalists do not know what the diplomatists do; the diplomatists do not see what the navalists see. But before these approaches can be unified, before these benefits can be realized, students of the war need to divest themselves of much of the received wisdom on those subjects. For it remains an unfortunate fact of life in Civil War diplomatic and naval studies that much of the story as it has been handed down to us is simply wrong. The mistakes, misperceptions, and misinterpretations of Ephraim D. Adams and Frank L. Owsley (and their disciples) have proved remarkably long-lived and resistant to correction. Even today they dominate the way we see the war's international dimension. Certainly, they furnish the conventional wisdom on that subject. Yet their accounts of the *Alabama*'s escape are fatally flawed, as is much else in their respective accounts of wartime diplomacy.

To be sure, the mistakes of the masters are not the only obstacle to a correct appraisal of what really happened in those mysterious days of July 1862. The controversy on that subject — it went on for a decade — has a built-in defect. Over the years the *Alabama* affair generated an enormous volume of documentary evidence of a peculiar kind. Not only did the controversy produce mountains of material (letters, speeches, pamphlets, special pleadings, legal briefs, treaty negotiations, and arbitration proceedings), but the special circumstances made certain that much of the evidence would be tainted, defective, dangerous, and difficult to evaluate. Almost from the moment the ship left port, charge gave rise to countercharge, and both sides began to produce expert testimony, special pleading, and retrospective accounts of what really had happened in London and Liverpool during those mysterious days of late July 1862. In practice, the enormous body of available evidence has rarely been investigated critically.[1]

There is another problem in getting at the truth of the *Alabama*. The lengthy, sometimes acrimonious negotiations leading to the Treaty of Washington in 1871 — and the subsequent

Geneva arbitration of American claims against Britain for the damage that Confederate cruisers had done to Union commerce during the war — did little to clarify the law of neutrality as it existed when Bulloch issued his challenge to it in 1861. The famous Three Rules of Neutral Conduct hammered out at Washington and incorporated into that treaty created entirely novel concepts of proper conduct in wartime, so those rules and the debates surrounding them do little to clarify the special circumstances that had confronted Her Majesty's government at the outbreak of history's first modern war. Of course, the animosity generated in Britain by the Geneva award was not conducive to clear thinking. To make matters worse, the Geneva tribunal could shed no light at all on the factual question of British ministerial complicity in the unleashing of the South's most deadly cruiser. In short, the ten-year controversy over Bulloch's masterstroke against enemy commerce did little to resolve the questions that still swirl around the *Alabama*'s challenge to British neutrality.

Surprisingly little has been written on the subject. In a pioneering article published in 1959, Rupert C. Jarvis drew attention to some of its salient features. No incident of comparable importance, he tells us, "has been so commonly misreported in the simple facts, or so commonly misunderstood in its wider significance."[2] Jarvis, chief archivist for Her Majesty's Customs and Excise Library at King Beam House in London, was the first person to draw attention to a significant fact of the law of the *Alabama:* The Treaty of Washington had changed the law. He correctly points out that in order to get to the heart of the ship's challenge to neutrality, one must discuss her case "in the light of the law as it then was." Here, my remarks are designed to supplement Jarvis's analysis and put it in the perspective of current research on that cruiser and the legal challenge she posed to the Queen's neutrality. All answers to such questions must remain tentative; a British court and jury never tested the legal status of the Confederacy's most famous cruiser.

During the nineteenth century, much ink had been expended on defining neutrality, but those efforts were largely unsuccessful. Many wartime complications flowed from the American failure to ratify the four principles or rules set out in the 1856 Declaration of Paris. Uncertainty over the status of privateers and the limits of effective blockade caused much grief in Anglo-American wartime relations. The technological innovations in naval war — shell guns, armor plate, steam power, revolving turrets, and the like — further strained those relations, for at the heart of Bulloch's mission was his intent to harness that technology for the South. The success of the *Alabama*, as Captain Raphael Semmes affirmed in his postwar memoir, remains a tribute to his skill in doing so, as does his imaginative and innovative design for the Laird rams.

In addition, there was a further complicating factor in transatlantic relations, for the Civil War reversed the traditional roles of the United States and Great Britain in control of the seas in wartime. Britain found herself a neutral in a war that had vast potential for raising distressing questions for the mistress of the seas. For the first time that anyone could remember, the Royal Navy and British Admiralty courts would not decide the proper limits of maritime law. Conversely, for the first time in its history, the American navy, its officers, and courts would determine the rules of contraband, blockade, continuous voyage, and myriad other things that had unlimited possibilities for creating disputes over neutral rights and free trade in wartime. Britain's role as the world's preeminent naval power, her concerns over unrestricted wartime commerce, and her insatiable need for cotton ensured that she had vital national interests to protect. Any serious or sustained threat to them might rupture Anglo-American relations and embroil Britain in the war. So, too, might Bulloch's efforts to build a navy in the Queen's realm. To forestall incidents that might escalate into war, Queen Victoria issued a Proclamation of Neutrality in May 1861. She also recognized the Confederate States as a belligerent power, although she did not confer international recognition on the new nation. Then, in a stroke of evenhandedness, she adopted a wait-and-see policy toward the Union's announced intent to create a blockade of the entire 3,500 miles of Confederate coast.

With his initial naval response to the Confederacy's challenge to national union, President Abraham Lincoln internationalized the war. He also set the stage for a major confrontation with the powers of Europe on three matters of vital concern to them: trade, cotton, and international law. Lincoln's proclamation immediately raised the question of a proper definition of an "effective" blockade. Nineteenth-century theorists of neutrality rejected "paper" blockades, established by decree without sufficient naval forces to prevent access to or departure from a specific port. A blockade of an entire coast by presidential fiat raised hackles in Europe. No one denied the president's right to establish a blockade (though there were quibbles about the utility and wisdom of doing so). To the pragmatic guardians of Europe's interests, the question immediately became the president's ability to enforce it, that is, to make it effective according to the standards established by the 1856 Declaration of Paris. To an objective observer in April 1861, it seemed reasonable to suppose that the Union navy did not have enough ships to establish and maintain an effective closure of the Confederate coast. If the blockade was not effective, the European powers had no obligation to recognize it. In turn, their merchants might attempt to evade it. These were explosive issues, and the Queen had ample reason to seek to stave off quarrels over the pursuit of profit by her subjects. Moreover, no blockade in history had ever been fully effective, and it soon became apparent that the South had a need for many things that Europe, and especially Britain, might supply. The South, conversely, had one thing that Europe, and especially Britain, needed. That was cotton. In time, a lucrative trade of immense profitability and danger grew.

In other places I have examined in detail some of the concerns that confronted Her Majesty's government when war broke out between the North and South in 1861: the general contours of Bulloch's challenge to neutrality; some fine points of the theory and practice of blockade; the British government's legal response to Confederate shipbuilding as reflected in the trial of the *Alexandra;* and the surprising variations on that theme occasioned by the Confederacy's Chinese fleet and the law officers' response to it. While all of that work has some immediate bearing on Bulloch's mission, here it is necessary to focus narrowly on the legal aspects of his construction of the

Alabama. Central to that story is the challenge that ship posed to the prohibitions of the Foreign Enlistment Act of 1819 and Bulloch's efforts to circumvent them. The Jarvis article mentioned above will serve as a starting point for a discussion of that complex subject. From time to time, the focus will widen to bring into the picture matters of significant detail. The bits and pieces that emerge from this microscopic examination will then be fitted into the larger mosaic of Bulloch's confrontation with British neutrality.

The object of our search remains what Jarvis has called "the law as it then was." In other words, our object is to see the *Alabama* case as it was *before* that ship became one of history's most effective commerce destroyers; *before* British ministers had to defend themselves in Parliament for their dilatory responses to Union complaints against her; *before* American diplomatic representatives began covering their own ineptitude by charging the Queen's government with connivance in the *Alabama*'s escape and responsibility for the extensive damage she did to the Northern merchant marine; and *before* the Geneva Arbitration Tribunal had presented Great Britain with a bill for over $15 million for that damage and for what her sister commerce raiders had inflicted. It would also be useful if one could see that case *before* it got caught in the distorting lens of historical interpretation. In short, one would like to create the circumstances of that case as it was *before* it became encrusted with myth, distortion, special pleading, the pride of those who sought to get the ship out of England, and the chagrin of those who tried to prevent her departure. Naturally, such purity of vision is impossible in this imperfect world. Few historic events have been as surrounded by misperception as the career of the *Alabama.* All aspects of her story should be approached with healthy skepticism.

We sometimes forget that Bulloch's program of cruiser construction on the Merseyside was barely under way in July 1862. Only one British-built cruiser, the *Florida,* had escaped, and she had done no damage to commerce while Bulloch prepared his second ship for sea. It is doubtful whether the Confederacy's first cruiser, the decrepit *Sumter,* had given rise to fears of what the future held when one more lone cruiser went to work as a maritime mugger. On the eve of her departure, the *Alabama* was an ordinary merchant ship — one strongly built, to be sure, one incorporating all the refinements of the shipbuilder's art. But she was (and it is difficult to remember the fact and to appreciate its significance) a simple item of commerce. Frederick S. Hull, a solicitor, told Bulloch that building ships in Britain for the Confederate navy was no offense, provided that such ships were not *equipped* in the Queen's realm. That interpretation of the law, however, was not universally recognized, and his Union adversaries soon proposed views of the law that were designed to halt his construction program. Between these competing views stood the majesty of British law, but in government circles no one — not even cabinet members — knew what that law was. In the years since its passage in 1819, the enlistment act had never been clarified in court. No precedents provided any clues to the interpretation of its imprecise language. Hence, both Federals and Confederates could wallow in the false comfort of their respective views.

Who was right? After the passage of well over a century, it is still difficult to answer that question. Much difficulty stems from the imprecision and ambiguity of the operative statute, the Foreign Enlistment Act of 1819. Officials charged with enforcing the act were loath to invoke it because they feared the heavy financial penalties that might be levied against them for false arrest or premature detention of suspicious vessels. Such difficulties were compounded by a merchant ship's status as a lawful item of commerce available for purchase by belligerents during wartime, a status recognized on both sides of the Atlantic. It should be noted parenthetically that many wartime disputes revolved around this simple point of maritime law. There was a corollary to it: Those ships must be unarmed and unequipped for war.

Jarvis notes that in the nineteenth century neither Britain nor America "sought to prevent the building of any ship for a belligerent by way of trade," including blockade-runners. Research subsequent to Jarvis confirms his view, though it might be amended to permit the sale as well as the building of such ships, provided, as Jarvis says in another place, they were not "equipped, furnished, fitted out, or armed." The act, as he points out, also contained a prohibition against recruiting or enlisting men in the Queen's realm for service on any foreign warship or other vessel "intended to be used for any warlike purpose." The act contained the usual stipulations covering penalties, enforcement, and special cases (for example, the force of a royal license to suspend some of the law's prohibitions). The fine for "recruitment" was £50 per person, and payment of that fine released a ship from the control of customs authorities. Proven violations of the act's provisions against equipping, furnishing, and fitting out might lead to a forfeiture of the ship and its stores.

This was the law as it applied to the *Alabama* in the summer of 1862. It was in no way adequate to the challenges that Confederate shipbuilding posed during the war. Before that became evident, the few stipulations of the act would prove capable of unimagined variations and flexible interpretations. The task of finding a proper balance between lawful commerce and the restrictions of the Foreign Enlistment Act would keep legions of lawyers busy for many years. That search, in the end, would require new definitions of proper neutral conduct. But that is to get ahead of my story.

So stately a ship as the *Alabama* did not long escape the attention of Bulloch's great adversary, the Union consul at Liverpool, Thomas H. Dudley. Having the ship under surveillance for some months, he succeeded in ferreting out information about the vessel and its mission. On 21 June he summarized his findings for his superior in London. He told the American minister that evidence against the ship appeared conclusive. In Dudley's mind there was no doubt of that ship's Confederate connection or of her hostile intentions against Union commerce. He reported (incorrectly) that she would carry eleven guns, and he correctly noted one of the distinctive features of her construction, a two-ton steam apparatus for lifting the propeller out of the water. He estimated that she would be ready for sea in nine or ten days. "When completed and armed she will be a most formidable and dangerous craft, and if not prevented from going to sea, will do much mischief to our commerce." It was widely believed in local shipping circles, he said, that "no better vessel of her class was ever built." This note and its context provide a prelude to the opening of the first phase of the *Alabama*'s confrontation with the law.

A number of observations about this note should be made, for it set the tone and direction for much that followed. All the information in it was hearsay and legally inadmissible in court. Much is asserted; nothing is proved. At this stage the burden of proof rested on the Americans. They had to demonstrate beyond reasonable doubt that Bulloch's ship was in violation of the enlistment act. That task proved to be exceedingly difficult. There was another feature of the case that was little noticed until Douglas Maynard brought it to our attention in 1954.[3] He pointed out that initially Dudley wanted to make a formal request for seizure of the ship directly to the Liverpool customs officials. He drafted such a proposal (a document that found its way into the American case against the *Alabama* at Geneva), but it was not sent. When Dudley broached the plan to Adams, the minister vetoed it and substituted a direct diplomatic appeal to the foreign secretary. According to Maynard, Adams apparently believed that Russell would detain a suspicious ship "on receipt of a note from him."[4] That did not happen. Whether the Dudley approach would have yielded quicker and more satisfactory results remains unknowable, but it was Adams's decision that set the stage for the delay about which the Americans complained so vociferously and for so long. It certainly is true that Adams's procedural choice caused much trouble and ill will in the months that followed.

He compounded his difficulty with another procedural mistake. He included Dudley's letter (which was essentially an in-house memo) in his own first "formal remonstrance" against the *Alabama*. Adams's note of 23 June marked a significant milepost in the unfolding of this tangled affair, and it may be described as the opening gun in a decade-long duel in Anglo-American diplomatic relations. This note and its enclosures largely determined the course that the controversy would take, especially in the all-important first month of exchanges between the two governments and between London and Liverpool. The first weeks of tension over the mystery ship of the Mersey, that is, the period from 23 June to 23 July, have generated much misunderstanding about the case, about what happened and when it happened. The story is complicated, and historians have not clarified the context of that story. An accurate chronology of events is therefore a precondition for any reconstruction of the events in Liverpool and London during those July days of 1862.

In his note to Russell, the American minister complained that Confederates in Liverpool, in violation of the enlistment act and the Queen's neutrality, were preparing a powerful warship to prey on Union commerce. He went further and charged that agents of the South were preparing that ship with the "manifest object" of waging maritime war against a nation at peace with Great Britain. They were doing all this openly and with a flagrant disregard for the law at one of the most prominent shipyards in the realm. Confederates were doing all this, Adams alleged, at "the dockyard of a person now sitting as a member of the House of Commons." (This was a sly reference to John Laird, senior member of the famous Birkenhead firm of shipbuilders, who had "retired" from business in 1861 to serve in Parliament.) He requested that Her Majesty's government halt "the projected expedition" or demonstrate that Bulloch's activity posed no threat to the people or property of the United States. Implicit in this note was Adams's view that Great Britain had an international responsibility to prevent rebels from carrying on a war against his country from British ports. In essence, he argued that the Confederates and their Liverpool associates were using Britain as a base for warlike expeditions against the United States. That, in his view, was both a clear breach of proper neutral conduct and a direct threat to peace between Britain and America.

Although he did not mention this decision in his letter to the foreign secretary, Adams also set in motion another long-range response to Southern shipbuilding in foreign ports. He authorized the USS *Tuscarora* to leave her post at Gibraltar (where she was blockading the first Confederate commerce raider, the *Sumter*) and come to England to intercept Bulloch's "warship" when she put to sea. That attempt did not succeed, but it was the beginning of a two-year seek-and-destroy mission that would culminate in the death of the famous Confederate cruiser off Cherbourg, France, on 19 June 1864. In bringing the *Tuscarora* to England, Adams was not seeking to beef up his diplomacy. He did not see her presence as an iron fist for his velvet glove. Nor did that ship's presence in Southampton create any serious tensions in Anglo-American relations or in any way influence the initial exchange of notes on Bulloch's Liverpool activities.

There was little in the note that hinted at things to come. Nothing in it differed in any important way from the routine matters that he and Russell had discussed on any number of occasions. There were no threats implied in it, there was no foreshadowing of storm clouds gathering on the horizon, and there was no whiff of impending crisis in its pages. If one sought a descriptive word for that note, an apt choice might be *innocuous*. But as events were to prove, its bland protestations contained much explosive matter.

There is another relevant feature of this initial stage of the quarrel over Bulloch's challenge to the Foreign Enlistment Act and to British neutrality. Aside from some smoldering resentment on the part of the Americans over Britain's "premature" recognition of Confederate belligerency, relations between Washington and London were relatively calm in the spring and summer of 1862. The *Trent* affair had been resolved earlier in the year, owing much to Russell's superb handling of his country's response to Union captain Charles Wilkes's heavy-handed and impolitic affront to Britain's flag and honor. Then, in February and March, Russell had made one of the most important pro-North decisions of the war by recognizing the Union's theory and practice of blockade, even if those practices and that theory did not quite measure up to the standards envisioned at Paris in 1856.

Russell refused to receive James M. Mason as a fully accredited diplomatic representative at the Court of St. James's, when that somewhat pompous and inept Confederate commissioner arrived in London after his removal from the *Trent*. He and his colleagues also had squelched parliamentary maneuvers for a more vigorous pro-South response to the war. His reply to

Adams's note on 4 July was courteous, considerate, and prompt, and it left that door open for the Americans to strengthen their case and repeat their appeal for redress. Before responding to Adams, the foreign secretary had done his diplomatic and legal homework. Because parts of those behind-the-scenes maneuvers of British officialdom have been left out of traditional accounts, they require some attention here.

Three leading authorities on this case — E. D. Adams, F. L. Owsley, and Mountague Bernard — fail to mention a significant feature of Russell's response to Adams. Their accounts convey the impression that the foreign secretary did not become "seriously concerned" about American complaints until very late in July. (Adams and Owsley date the concern to 26 July.) We now know that Russell took the American's complaint seriously enough to refer it at once to his highest legal advisers, the three law officers of the Crown. He also sent the complaint through the usual bureaucratic channels of the treasury and customs departments. In a word, he did everything appropriate to the circumstances as they existed in late June 1862. He did not bluster. He did not display a lack of serious concern. He did not delay, nor did he allow the complaint to wither in the nether regions of Britain's bureaucratic maze. Neither did he demonstrate any sense of compelling urgency about the case's potential for mischief. One infers that the complaint merely got its proper share of attention — no more, no less. In retrospect, it is difficult to find fault with Russell's processing of the American note or with the preparation of his response to it.

Because the matter of timing assumes such a critical role in latter parts of this narrative, it might be useful to examine the content and chronology of this initial exchange of notes. Such a procedure may provide a relatively objective benchmark for establishing the length of time it normally took to process an official complaint in a nineteenth-century bureaucratic state. As time went on, as tempers flared, as positions hardened in this tangled affair, the transmission of information grew less and less normal, more and more controversial. In the first weeks of the controversy there were periods of relative calm in which one might see the normal operations of a government on the eve of crisis, before the storm broke and destroyed all perspective. From such a vantage point, on the first occasion that the *Alabama* had been brought to his attention, Russell's handling of the complaint seems a model of efficiency (with, as we shall see, one anomaly).

The chronology of the exchange poses few problems, and its contours are easily ascertained. The foreign secretary, as one might reasonably expect, sought the advice of his legal advisers — and he sought that advice from two sources, one high and one low. He immediately sent Adams's note to the law officers of the Crown. Although there were three of them — the Queen's advocate, the attorney general, and the solicitor general — their opinions were usually rendered in the corporate voice of the Law Office. When the question of the *Alabama* arrived at that office, William Atherton, the attorney general, and Roundell Palmer, the solicitor general, considered the case and with commendable speed sent their reply to Russell on 30 June. This vital step in the transaction took less than a week, a period that would be about average for such an exchange of views at that level of government. Insofar as I can discover, there is no evidence of any sort of slowdown in the machinery of government in this particular case. On this occasion — and on many others during the war — the law officers worked with commendable dispatch. The absence of the signature of the third law officer will require special comment at a later point in the narrative.

The replies from the treasury and customs departments took somewhat longer, perhaps because there were many more steps in the bureaucratic chain of command that stretched from the lords of the treasury and their commissioners and the board of customs in London to the collector of customs and his subordinates in Liverpool. Each link in that command structure had its own legal adviser who had to be consulted in important matters. Despite the many steps up and down that chain, the system worked with all deliberate speed, at least in the case of Adams's initial complaint. In early July, Russell received a comprehensive review of the case, as it looked to those most competent to judge the law of the *Alabama*. As so often happens in legal matters, the lawyers did not agree on all points at issue, and so Russell faced his first dilemma in an affair that was to confront him with many undesirable choices in the future. The context of that advice will be examined in due course, along with the way he chose to respond to it. Here our focus on the chronology of the exchange (rather than on its content) requires us to note that by 4 July Russell was ready to answer Adams. The elapsed time in the exchange of notes—from receipt to reply—was a mere eleven days. That was not an unreasonable lapse of time, if one considers all the convoluted steps required by the structure of the Queen's government.

Many echelons of that government, from the highest to the lowest, had to be involved. Proper answers to the American allegations touched on many points of law. Some involved high matters of state; others concerned mundane details of ship construction and equipment. Those latter questions required a high level of technical competence, so they could only be answered by the lowly on-the-spot agents of the Crown who served in the Liverpool customs. Someone had to visit the ship, measure her dimensions, evaluate her equipment, consult with her builders, and assess her compliance with the law. All of this had to be done, and done well, before Russell could officially answer Adams. Such things would be done several times in the weeks that followed. From the documentary record thus compiled much of our knowledge of the case comes. Jarvis, for example, mined those customs records to prepare his article. They provide the bedrock of any investigation of the *Alabama* and the law. They also furnish a rich and unique angle of vision on that subject. And they are voluminous. For their part, the Americans compiled an equally impressive set of documents.

From this mass of conflicting information an answer to the American complaint had to be constructed. How then did the Queen's advisers assess the questions raised by Adams's complaints? One might describe the *Alabama*'s investigation as a legal feast. It furnished innumerable opportunities for a wide-ranging analysis of the law, as it was understood by those most concerned in its implementation. Even in the retrospect of more than a century, both the quantity and the quality of that legal discourse compel admiration. The range of argument and the acuity of intellect on display are of a high order — and that is so on both the American and the British sides, as it also is on the various levels within Her Majesty's government. If one factors in the quality of advice that the Confederates received in devising their counterstrategy, one is faced with a formidable array of legal talent and expert opinion. It is well to remember that those days in June and July 1862 were only the first stage of a decade-long controversy that would engage the best legal minds of the international community in the nineteenth century. These riches, alas, have gone largely underappreciated and unexploited.

The attorney general and the solicitor general had an opportunity to comment on the case when it was fresh and unencumbered by emotion or subterfuge. They faced no inordinate pressures from time constraints. In their first encounter with the case they had almost a week to evaluate the evidence and reach a conclusion. (Their second encounter was far less leisurely.) They faced no clamor in press or Parliament. They had no axe to grind, no official position to defend, no need for legalistic legerdemain — a situation that was soon to change. For all these reasons their initial views on the *Alabama* and the law deserve close attention and careful evaluation.

After taking the various papers of the case (especially the letters from Adams and Dudley) under careful consideration, they reported to Russell on 30 June 1862. First, they noted that if the "representation" made by Adams was accurate, the situation in Liverpool constituted "a manifest violation" of the enlistment act and "steps ought to be taken to put that act in force and to prevent the vessel from going to sea." Second, they pointed out that Dudley's letter of 21 June contained "grounds of reasonable suspicion" about the ship, and they noted that the letter also asserted that a foreman at the Laird yard had "stated" that the vessel was slated for the service of the Southern States. They told Russell that if the ship and her equipment were as they were described by Dudley, then "she must be intended for some warlike purpose."

Under such circumstances they thought it proper for Her

Majesty's government to take the necessary steps in cooperation with the customs authorities at Liverpool to ascertain the truth of the American allegations. If that investigation turned up sufficient evidence "to justify proceedings" under the Foreign Enlistment Act, then the government ought to act against the ship "as early as possible." In the meantime, the Americans ought to be notified that an investigation was under way. But they cautioned that Russell should make clear to Adams that any subsequent course of action by Her Majesty's government must depend on the "nature and sufficiency of any evidence of a breach of the law." They also suggested that Dudley turn over to the customs authorities at Liverpool any evidence in his possession.

Such was the advice Lord Russell received from two of the law officers of the Crown. Before making any comment on it, one should also look at the information that came from the lower reaches of Britain's bureaucratic structure. At the bottom of the chain of command for this incident was the surveyor of customs at Liverpool, Edward Morgan. Upon orders from his immediate superior — the collector of customs at that port, Samuel Price Edwards — the surveyor on 28 June "personally inspected" the vessel complained of and found that she was for the most part "rightly described" in the letter of the United States consul, except that Dudley had included some inaccurate information about her engines. He gave precise details of her measurements and noted the presence of "several powder-cannisters" on board, but he confirmed that no guns or gun-carriages were on the ship.

In addition, he reported that customs officials had had the ship under surveillance for some time but had seen nothing that might require "a special report." No efforts had been made by the builders to deny access to the ship or "to disguise what is most apparent to all — that she is intended for a ship of war." Nor had the builders, when questioned, denied that the ship was built for a foreign power. But the Laird brothers were not "disposed" to answer any questions about the vessel's destination after she left port. Without their cooperation, he concluded, there was "no other reliable source of information" on that vital point. He assured his superiors that any new develop-

ment concerning the ship would be "immediately" forwarded
to them. On the same day his superior started this information
on its way to the Foreign Office.

Before it could reach that destination, a number of other
government servants had to comment on it. On 30 June, Felix J.
Hamel, solicitor to the board of customs commissioners in London, assessed the documentary evidence he had received (the
American complaints and Liverpool's response to them). He
commended the careful attention that customs officials had
given the complaints, he found gaping holes in the American
case, and he alluded to some of the larger implications of the
situation as he saw it. In his view there was not adequate evidence to bring the ship under the seventh section of the enlistment act. There were insufficient grounds to empower customs
officers "to interfere in this case." A careful watch over the ship
should be continued, he advised, but no steps should be taken
"without the clearest evidence of a distinct violation of the foreign enlistment act." Such elements did not exist at the time he
wrote. He then went on to remind his colleagues on the board
(and in the customs services) that only the most compelling
emergency—he did not specify what that might be—could justify action. The terms of the act were highly technical, and its
requirements were "very rigid." Improper seizure, he warned,
might entail "very serious consequences" for any overzealous
officer and for his superior.

When the customs commissioners passed this report to treasury officials on 1 July, they expressed their "concurrence" with
Hamel's views, but they added a number of observations of their
own. Because customs officials at Liverpool could not act against
the ship without hard evidence "to warrant her detention," they
advised that the proper procedure would be for Consul Dudley
to furnish those officials "such evidence" as he had in his possession. They could then measure that evidence against the requirements of the law. The commissioners warned their colleagues: "Without the production of full and sufficient evidence
[under oath] to justify their proceedings the seizing officers
might entail on themselves and on the government very serious
consequences." They closed with a pledge that customs officials

at Liverpool would continue to maintain a "strict watch" of the vessel and keep the government fully apprised of Merseyside developments.

The next day, treasury officials forwarded these views to Edmund Hammond, one of the permanent undersecretaries at the Foreign Office, for the information of Lord Russell. The foreign secretary, in turn, sent this information to Adams on 4 July. He included in this communication the report that the customs commissioners had prepared for the treasury department, and he endorsed their suggestion that the American consul should submit whatever evidence he had to customs authorities at Liverpool to show that his "suspicions as to the destination of the vessel in question are well founded." Adams, in turn, thanked him and promised to arrange for Dudley to act on Russell's suggestion about the necessity for producing the evidence required by Liverpool officials. It was now 7 July.

It is now necessary to look at this exchange of notes in some detail. Each side had made its opening moves in a case that would grow enormously complex over the next decade. At this point, the chronology is clear. There was no discernible tension or ill will on either side, and relations were still cordial. No feathers had been ruffled; no emotions had been engaged. No one's amour propre had been wounded, no nonnegotiable demands had been made, and no vital principles had been announced. On the surface all appeared calm, and few could have foreseen any potential danger in this bland exchange of notes about an obscure ship on the river Mersey. Clearly, there had been no foot-dragging in the British camp, no inordinate delay in their handling of the American complaint.

Russell, however, had already made a fatal decision that would do much to alter the way events developed from this point on. Because of it, the case grew from an obscure difference of opinion about British law into a serious international crisis about the meaning of nineteenth-century neutrality. It became, in short, a multimillion-dollar brouhaha. Insofar as one can discover, Russell's decision had no secret or sinister purpose. It may have been the result of inadvertence, although, given his well-deserved reputation for mastery of detail, that seems unlikely.

When he sent Adams's note of the 23rd on its way through Britain's bureaucracy, he marked it in his own hand to convey his wish that it be sent to both the law officers and to treasury officials. There was no notation that one destination should take precedence over the other. When Hammond sent his covering instructions to those respective officers, they were couched in identical terms. In the normal course of events, the answer of the law officers would take precedence. During the entire course of the war, their advice often determined the direction of government action. Yet on this occasion Russell ignored their advice.

This anomaly remains puzzling. Long research in his private and public papers, in the official and private correspondence of his colleagues in the Foreign Office (especially the two permanent undersecretaries, Edmund Hammond and Austin H. Layard), and in the documents of the legal advisers has failed to explain why Russell, in effect, took the first step in compiling a multimillion-dollar lawsuit against Her Majesty's government. He did so by ignoring the advice of Atherton and Palmer for a government investigation of the American allegations. There is no indication whatever that he intended this move as a deliberate slowdown. There is even less reason to support that he intended the decision to aid the Confederacy or to involve Britain in the war on the side of the South.

It is therefore necessary to notice yet another aspect of that decision. It has been largely ignored in the literature of the foreign response to the war. Both of America's preeminent authorities on that subject have failed to appreciate its significance. For all practical purposes they ignore it. By so doing — and by seriously distorting the chronology of the case — those authorities have left an inadequate interpretation of the *Alabama* affair. There is no reason to support that those things were done in a deliberate attempt to muddy the waters of historical explanation. Their mistakes are the result of poor methodology, as best I have been able to ascertain.

The case is somewhat altered when one considers another classic defense of British neutrality during the war. Here the story is more complex and the evidence is more ambiguous. When he compiled his defense of government neutrality in

1870, Mountague Bernard omitted any mention of Russell's referral of Adams's note to the law officers and of his refusal to act on the advice they offered on 30 June. Although there is no explanation (that I have seen) for that omission, it cries out for one. We know that Bernard's reputation as an impartial expert on international law lent enormous weight to Britain's position. We know that he had access to secret archives in preparing the British case at Geneva. It seems reasonable to suppose that he knew (or, in that dread phrase, must have known) about the note, and yet he suppressed that information. I have reason to suspect that he was paid to do so — that he was a court historian, subsidized by the government to put the best possible spin on Russell's handling of the *Alabama* imbroglio. The records that lead me to that supposition are both imprecise and not in the public domain. They furnish a tantalizing clue, nothing more.

The anomaly of Russell's failure to follow the 30 June advice of Atherton and Palmer has yet another strange feature that requires mention here. In another part of this work I have drawn the reader's attention to the importance of Roundell Palmer's March 1863 parliamentary defense of the government's *Alabama* policy. In it he failed to mention the advice that he himself had helped draft at the outset of the affair, and, quite naturally, he says nothing of Russell's failure to follow that advice. In defending government policy, both Bernard and Palmer have by inadvertence strengthened the hand of those who make charges of governmental complicity in the escape. When rumors of the omission surfaced, the fact that information had been suppressed made it easier for those with an affinity for explanation by conspiracy to see plots and sinister government designs where none existed.

It seems unlikely that Russell was plotting much of anything when he made his official response to Adams in early July. Like most administrators, he went through proper channels. The customs service fell under the jurisdiction of the treasury. Moreover, the enlistment act and its enforcement were regarded as domestic concerns, falling within the purview of customs and treasury officials. It is possible — even probable — that Russell thought he was acting on the advice of his law officers when he reminded Adams of the requirement for stronger evidence. There is no way of knowing what impact a government investigation would have had on the course of events. The subsequent government investigation of the Laird rams in 1863 does not suggest that such things were better done in the nineteenth century than they are today.

Once they got their act together, Dudley and Adams procured enough evidence "under oath" to prod the law officers into issuing their detention order of 29 July — only they got that evidence too late to prevent Bulloch's escape. Much of the controversy over British policy toward the *Alabama* stems from the failure of Dudley and Adams to understand soon enough what the law required to justify a ship's detention. That misapprehension of the law led to a succession of procedural mistakes. These are difficult to understand because their failure to stop the *Florida* in March ought to have prepared them better. It is strange that they did not mount their campaign against the ship much earlier. After all, Dudley had her under observation from the start of his mission the previous fall. His detectives, especially the ubiquitous Matthew Maguire, had been feeding him full and accurate information about the condition of the ship and the people involved in her construction. Presumably, an earlier start would have led to an earlier awareness of the intricacies of the law and of the evidence needed to move British officials to action. It is important to stress that defects in the American approach had far more to do with the *Alabama*'s fortuitous escape than did any British delay or ministerial deviousness.

Still, Russell's decision to act in accord with the views of the treasury department was a crucial one, and it prepared the ground for an equally important American decision. This juxtaposition of mistakes had important consequences, and if one seeks a point at which things began to go wrong in Anglo-American relations over the *Alabama,* this is as good a place as any. Maynard, who has studied Union efforts to prevent the escape of that ship as closely as anyone and who was one of the first students of the war's international dimension to exploit the Dudley Papers, tells us that Russell, on that occasion, was "content to act" on the advice of the customs board in London.

He also notes a significant consequence of that decision: it "put the burden of proof on the American consul."[5] Maynard does not tell us why Russell was "content" to adopt the more passive approach of his customs commissioners, rather than the "positive investigation by British officials" envisioned by the law officers. My own research in Dudley's papers in California and in those of Russell in London also failed to provide any solution to this little mystery.

Although no one has plumbed Russell's motives, we do know that his decision put the ball back in the American court in early July. We also know that Dudley played it poorly. First, he was not in a position to return the ball to Russell's side of the net. He compounded that error by a further incorrect procedural call. Much of the information he had about the ship was accurate — but in a legal sense it was hearsay. Much of it had come to him in confidence, and he was anxious to protect his sources, many of whom were pro-Union Englishmen in a community rife with Confederate supporters. Especially he wished to keep secret the identity of his detectives. He elected to approach the collector at Liverpool with what he "knew." On this occasion (9 July) he did *not* include the names of his informants. More important, he did *not* furnish "legally certified affidavits from firsthand witnesses." (It might be noted that when Dudley finally put his own evidence in affidavit form on 21 July it was judged insufficient by the law officers of the Crown when they issued their detention order of 29 July.)

The result could have been predicted: The collector, S. P. Edwards, informed Dudley that no action could be taken unless his statements could be "legally substantiated." How that might be done he did not say, though he again referred the consul's note to his London superiors on 10 July. In the next dozen or so days, variations on this theme were played by the consul and the collector and by their superiors in London. Dudley, it appears, resented the burden of proof that was placed on him, and he remained reluctant to identify his sources. He somewhat smugly hinted that a "little inquiry" on the part of the government would easily "confirm" the truth of his information. Had a bit of pique begun to enter the correspondence? Edwards, for his

part, was equally adamant that the Americans were not producing proper proof of their assertions. Had an element of testiness
crept into his notes? It was too early to say: on the surface all was
still smooth sailing. For the moment, matters at Liverpool were
stalemated, a tad strained, perhaps, though not yet acrimonious.

As the July notes worked their way up and down the British
and American chains of command, other elements entered the
great game being played out in London and Liverpool. As the
Americans stepped up their efforts to halt the *Alabama*'s departure, the Confederates intensified theirs to get her to sea. Those
efforts, it hardly needs to be said, added new dimensions to
the Anglo-American dialogue and imbued it with a sense of
urgency, of impending danger. In the early weeks of July the
future raider took on coal, supplies, men. Those in control of
that ship seemed poised for flight. That possibility naturally
gave rise to concern in the American camp, and from mid-July a
new sense of apprehension began to creep into the correspondence. To be sure, there was cause for concern. Few who saw
that embryonic cruiser doubted her supreme fitness for future
tasks. But Dudley's spies and detectives had missed one vital
piece of information — the ship did not have a captain. Or, to be
more precise, the newly designated commander had not yet
arrived in Liverpool. And so the Confederates faced a problem
of their own making — one which led to serious delay in their
own plans to get the ship to sea. (It should be said that Yankee
convictions that Bulloch was to command the raider — hadn't
their spies and detectives told them so? — blinded them to the
Confederate contretemps over the change in command.)

Bulloch was aware of Dudley's net of surveillance, he knew of
the increased governmental interest in his ship by port officials,
and he had done everything humanly possible to circumvent
them. All the pieces for a quick and secret departure were in
place, and all situations were set to go — save one. Earlier in the
month he had received heart-wrenching news: Command of the
ship had been taken from him and given to Raphael Semmes.
But that officer was not in Liverpool, and no one knew when he
would arrive. How long could the departure be delayed in antic-
ipation of Semmes's arrival? Delay was dangerous; premature

departure might be more so. In mid-July the margin of safety for the ship was diminishing, but Bulloch's luck held as he opted to wait a few more days for Semmes. He knew that he did not have endless days to dally in port, but the gambler in his heart could calculate odds as well as anyone. And what was his mission if not a gigantic gamble? He elected to play one more hand, even though he felt the deck was stacked against him. Of course, he won.

Meanwhile, the Anglo-American exchange of notes continued. It would be tedious to examine them in detail, but certain persistent points in the British position must be emphasized, along with some modifications in the American procedures. Most of all, one must notice the conflict of legal opinion from 10 July until the 23rd of that month. New important elements began to develop in the American case; they altered and intensified technical aspects of their appeal; and they secured the assistance of a most important ally. Indeed, at one point, it appeared as if they were on the verge of winning their case. But a truly amazing set of circumstances came together to thwart their efforts. For these reasons one must trace those events of mid-July with some care, especially that all-important debate on the meaning of the law in its applicability toward Bulloch's ship.

In such cases the official documentary record at the top tends to be barren, uninformative, and dull. Even when one moves a notch down the scale, the tenor of discourse does not appreciably improve. But when one reaches the level of those who labored in the trenches (here that level is represented by the various government solicitors who provided the nitty-gritty opinions that their superiors passed along to their superiors), one gets a reasonably objective view of the law of the *Alabama* as it was seen at point-blank range in the initial days and weeks of the controversy. On the British side there was a rare consistency of viewpoint at all levels (save the highest), and that unanimity lasted for just about the entire duration of the debate. One is impressed by the consistency of views, the tenacity with which they were held, and the courage with which they were defended — even against some of the most expert legal opinion in the land.

For the usual reasons, it was not until 15 July that London's customs board answered Dudley's remonstrance of 9 July. Again, the record reveals no deliberate slowdown of this material in transit. The customs commissioners, after again consulting their own legal adviser, told the collector in Liverpool that he was to inform Dudley that his statement did not contain sufficient evidence "to justify the seizure of the vessel." In these few words Dudley's case was deemed unworthy of further action. The London authorities had been guided by the advice of their solicitor. On 11 July, F. J. Hamel had rendered a somewhat more detailed analysis of the points at issue. In Hamel's view there was "only one proper way" to regard the question. If the collector detained the vessel, he would have to defend that act in court and pay "damages and costs in case of failure." In the solicitor's view, the bulk of Dudley's statement, "if not all" of it, was "hearsay and inadmissible." No witnesses were to appear or even to be named. He closed with a strong affirmation of the weakness of the consul's evidence: "It is perfectly clear to my mind that there is nothing in it amounting to prima facie proof sufficient to justify a seizure, much less to support it in a court of law, and the consul could not expect the collector to take upon himself such a risk in opposition to rules and principles by which the Crown is governed in matters of this nature." The next day this information was sent to treasury officials.

At about the same time, that is, mid-July, Minister Adams began some slight alterations in his own approach. First, he took on the responsibility for transferring the *Tuscarora* to Southampton as "a last resource" to intercept the raider if she took to sea; then he asked the vice consul in Liverpool to send copies of all available evidence to London so that Adams could avail himself "of professional advice" about proceedings against Bulloch's ship in the courts. He also advised Dudley to prepare the required affidavits, and he gave him permission to increase his expenditure of funds to speed up that task. In addition, Adams authorized his consul to hire a solicitor to assist in preparing the evidence in proper form. He did all this, as he later reported to his superior, the secretary of state, "so that no mere omission of form could be made to avail against us." Despite all this preparation, all these resources, he remained apprehensive that his efforts would fail to move the British to detain the ship: "I am not sanguine of success," he told Seward in a later summing-up of his efforts.

Adams then made the crucial decision that proved to be one of the key elements in the preparation of the American case. Why he waited so long to do so is not clear, but one needs no clairvoyance to see that if Adams had consulted Robert P. Collier earlier, the course of the case would have been speeded up and in all probability would have unfolded in ways less damaging to Anglo-American relations. Collier was one of England's most distinguished authorities on maritime law and the meaning of the Foreign Enlistment Act. He was also a member of Parliament and active in the administration of Admiralty law. In short, he was an ideal person to assist in the preparation of the American case.[6] Adams submitted to him Dudley's 9 July resumé of the case, and on 16 July Collier rendered one of the significant pre-escape comments on the law and the *Alabama*. Let me stress that he did so on the basis of the consul's unsupported statement of early July, the same document that the legal advisers at the customs and treasury had deemed "insufficient." It is also important to remember that though Collier was a QC (Queen's Counsel), he acted for Adams in his professional and private capacity, not as any sort of government official.

Collier's first opinion coincided with that mid-month flurry of activity in American efforts to move Her Majesty's government to act against Bulloch's ship. Indeed, his views accelerated those efforts by infusing them with an enthusiasm and sense of purpose that they had not had earlier. His reading of the case was "most decided" in its impact and provided a strong endorsement of American contentions. It also may have played an important role in moving the British in their response to Dudley's allegations from customs and treasury solicitors back to the law officers of the Crown. But it is not known when Collier's first note (or news of its contents) reached royal officials. So one must be tentative in asserting conclusions when the documents are silent. If that opinion did no more than stimulate American efforts to secure proper evidence in proper form, that is, under oath — as Maynard tells us it did — that alone would have been a vital step in the way the case developed.[7] Under the impetus of Collier's views, Dudley and his solicitor stepped up their collection of hard evidence, and in three days they had prepared six affidavits. These were presented to the collector at Liverpool on the morning of 21 July, along with a "formal" request for the seizure of Bulloch's boat.

What had Collier said to speed up the case? His first opinion offered a low-key assessment of the law of the *Alabama,* which was all the more valuable for being so. It did not operate in a vacuum, however. His answer to the questions Adams had posed about the validity of the American case and the proper procedures for advancing it coincided with (and was part of) the minister's search for a new way to overcome British "indifference" to the justice of his contentions about Bulloch's work. That intensification of effort by Adams and Dudley took place primarily between 16 and 23 July, and it owed much to the dogged and skilled work of Dudley and his Liverpool solicitor, A. T. Squarey. The essential features of this counterattack on Britain's reluctance to move against the Merseyside mystery ship were these: consultations with Collier on the 16th and 23rd, formation of the Dudley-Squarey team in Liverpool, the infusion of large amounts of money into the campaign, the preparation of affidavits "under oath," and a long overdue system of closer coordination between the minister and consul. All of this preparation was a necessary precondition for the next phase of the affair. Much of this activity reflected what might be called the "spirit" of Collier's *Alabama* law.

Though brief, his first opinion requires extensive quotation and comment. He begins with the assertion that the evidence, that is, the information contained in Dudley's note to S. P. Edwards on 9 July, was "almost conclusive" that the vessel in question was being "fitted out" for the Confederates "in contravention of the provisions of the foreign enlistment act." Because of the "urgency" of the matter, he advised an immediate application to the chief customs officer at Liverpool "to exercise the powers" conferred upon him by the act "to seize the vessel, with a view to her condemnation." He suggested that if the collector required an indemnity, one should be given to him. He also advised that it would be "proper" for the Americans to inform the foreign secretary of what they had done and to request that the government seize the ship — "or ratify her seizure if it had been made." He then alluded to what was to become one of the case's distinctive features: it would take "some little time" for the government to determine "what course to pursue." He closed on a note of unconscious irony when he told his client that he had recommended "the more prompt remedy." But even Collier, experienced as he was, could not foresee the glacial pace of Her Majesty's government on this critical question. Still, however one reads his opinion of 16 July, it conveys the impression that there was merit in the American case. That did not prove to be the dominant view in the British camp as the pace of events speeded up in the immediate aftermath of Collier's note.

As mentioned, Dudley and Squarey intensified their efforts to put their evidence in proper legal form. In a few days they had drawn up half a dozen affidavits, and on 21 July they took these to the collector's office and had them properly notarized. Squarey then made a "formal" request for seizure of the ship. Collector Edwards said that he could not act on that request without instructions from his superiors in London. Even at this late date, the customs commissioners "declined to sanction the detention of the vessel." In effect, the London customs board, with the approval of their treasury counterparts, had nullified the evidence of six witnesses who had sworn under oath that they had firsthand knowledge of "unlawful" activities on the Merseyside. There is no need to cross-examine those witnesses here, though it might be useful to mention their names for the benefit of future students and to note that the numbering of their affidavits may vary from source to source. Only one of this set, number six, has any claim on our attention. Rightly or wrongly, the evidence of the other five was discarded as legally deficient: (1) Dudley, who was a Quaker and could not "swear" an oath, affirmed his information, (2) J. deCosta, (3) M. Maguire, (4) H. Wilding and M. Maguire, (5) A. S. Clare, and (6) William Passmore. (In the view of the law officers of the Crown, when they finally got the case for the second time on 28–29 July,

five of these depositions were deemed invalid and only Passmore's figures in their ruling. Palmer confirmed this fact in his
March 1863 parliamentary defense of government policy.)

As might be expected, the London customs board's wholesale
rejection of evidence so painstakingly assembled stunned the
Americans, but they did not give up. Once again the intensity of
activity ratcheted upward; the pace of events on the 22nd and
23rd was particularly hectic, as even a cursory check of the record will reveal. And again, the chronology remains a key concern. Although one cannot pinpoint it with the accuracy it deserves, the all-important decision to "suggest" a return of the
case to the law officers of the Crown occurred during the frantic
to-ing and fro-ing of 22 and 23 July. That activity culminated in
Collier's second, more famous comment of the latter date.

After delivering their affidavits to Edwards on the 21st, Dudley and Squarey went to London to consult Adams and coordinate their drive to convince the British to move against Bulloch's ship, which now appeared ready to go to sea at any
moment. Time was running out, and anxiety mounted. They
had one more card to play. Soon after their arrival in London,
Dudley and Squarey had received two additional affidavits from
the vice consul in Liverpool: number 7 by Edward Roberts and
number 8 by Robert Taylor. These were presented directly to the
London board of customs on the 23rd as part of the stream-
lined effort to increase pressure and efficiency. It was at this time
that the Americans learned that their earlier application for a
seizure order (the one backed up by the first six depositions)
had been rejected on the 22nd.

Again, the Americans consulted Collier, but this time they
asked for his opinion based on the evidence of the eight affidavits so far accumulated. Henry Reddin produced a ninth document on 24 July, but its content merely corroborated the evidence in the papers of Passmore, Roberts, and Taylor. Collier
then produced his well-known opinion of 23 July, one of the key
documents of the case. He supported the American position
even more strongly than he had on the 16th. He had been asked
whether the information of these affidavits "would justify the
collector of customs in detaining the vessel under the act in

question." In Collier's considered judgment, the collector in Liverpool would be "justified " in detaining the vessel. More than that, he had a "duty" to do so. And if, in light of the present evidence, he allowed the ship to depart, he would "incur a heavy responsibility," one which would have to be shared by those superiors "under whose directions he appears to be acting." If that ship were allowed to escape, that event would give rise to "consideration" of whether the federal government "would not have serious grounds of remonstrance." After noting that it would be difficult "to make a stronger case" of violation of the enlistment act than the available evidence presented, he made a prescient observation: if the act was not enforced on this occasion, it was "little better than a dead letter."

My reconstruction of the chronology of this tangled affair suggests that the defining moments of the case occurred in the twenty-four hours after the late evening of 22 July. The records, because they do not contain hourly notations of receipt and dispatch, do not permit dogmatism on this point. The defining moment of which I speak was the decision by London customs and treasury officials to suggest that it might be wise to bump the *Alabama* dossier back up to the law officers of the Crown. That was done, we are reasonably sure, in three stages: twice on the 23rd and again on the 26th. But before that decision at the upper echelon could be set in motion, the lower-level officials in the customs and treasury had to be persuaded that the time had come for an appeal to a higher authority. Beyond any doubt, the second appeal to the law officers on 23 July was promoted by Collier's second opinion and Dudley's depositions number 7 and 8. (It will be remembered that on the 22nd London authorities had rejected the first six depositions and had refused to take any action against Bulloch's ship.)

The question now becomes what triggered the first referral to the law officers early on the 23rd? We know the sequence of days, but in only one or two instances (that I have been able to discover) has the hour of receipt been recorded. Here a bit of backtracking is required. Maynard tells us that on the 23rd Dudley and Squarey personally delivered the affidavits of Roberts and Taylor to London customs officials. They then learned that their earlier application for a detention order "based on the first six affidavits had been rejected." At this point the precise sequence of events becomes fuzzy. They immediately consulted Collier, who rendered his second opinion. That document, along with the two new depositions, went to the board of customs, with a request for a reconsideration of the rejection of the American petition against the ship. After this was done, Squarey visited the undersecretary for state, A. H. Layard. On the subject of Squarey's visit — action against the *Alabama* — Layard was not forthcoming, or, as Maynard phrases it, he "was not disposed to go into the matter." He did, however, provide a useful clue: he told Squarey that "the first papers" (depositions 1–6) had already been submitted to the law officers, but no answer had been received.[8] Because of the extreme urgency of the case — the vessel's departure seemed imminent — Squarey asked Layard to expedite that review, if possible. No such special request by Layard to the law officers has been found, though we know that he and Russell forwarded a second request for law officer action at some time after 5:30 P.M. on the 23rd.

At that hour, Hamilton of the treasury sent to Layard at the Foreign Office the depositions of Roberts and Taylor and the second opinion of Collier, which had just arrived. He then suggested a bureaucratic innovation that might save time: "You may probably like to send the opinion of the law officers direct to the commissioners of the customs, if it is an object to save time. We can put the matter right afterwards." The hour — 5:30 P.M., 23 July 1862 — permits us to freeze the chronology for a moment and to fix with some precision an important step in the transmission of information on that key day in the drama. Hamilton's note included two enclosures (in addition to depositions 7 and 8 and Collier's opinion of that date). One was a letter from Squarey, transmitting this new American evidence and noting that he had learned that *morning* of the decision not to "exercise the powers of the [enlistment] act" because the evidence of depositions 1–6 had been judged "not sufficient" to justify a seizure of the ship. He requested that the matter be reconsidered in light of the new evidence "now adduced," and he added two warnings: The ship "may sail at any moment," and the matter involved "consequences of the gravest possible description." In conclusion, he asked to be excused for sending this material directly to the London board of customs (instead of going through customary Liverpool channels) by a reference to the "urgency of the case." The second enclosure came from the customs solicitor. J. G. Gardner, secretary of the customs board, relayed that the new evidence of Roberts and Taylor did not "materially strengthen the case." The solicitor added that he could not "concur" in Collier's opinion, but wondered whether his superiors wished to consult the law officers.

This material and Hamilton's covering letter reached Layard later in the evening of the 23rd at the House of Commons. With Russell's written approval, he sent "a further letter" forwarding the documents to the law officers. His note of transmission confirms that earlier in the day he had sent another packet of papers to the Crown's legal advisers — a fact that may be confirmed by a careful reading of the law officers' opinion that finally endorsed a seizure order later that month. On the basis of this detailed examination of the relevant documents, it is possible to say that at no point between Adams's first remonstrance against Bulloch's ship on 23 June and the time of Layard's second submission of documents to the law officers late in the evening of 23 July did Her Majesty's government act with anything less than admirable efficiency. All documents were transmitted with commendable speed, all complaints were carefully investigated, and all the opinions of customs officers and their legal advisers were conveyed with dispatch and given proper and timely consideration. It is difficult to see what the administrative machinery of the British state could have done that was not done to expedite a competent consideration of all aspects of the American complaint.

Several other features of the first month's contretemps over Bulloch's ship ought to be noted. First, it soon became evident that initially Adams and Dudley were woefully out of touch with the workings of the English legal system. In retrospect, it took far too long to get the kind of evidence that British officials could consider sufficient to justify proceedings under the enlistment act. Not until after 16 July did they *begin* to accumulate such evidence — and it was not presented to customs officials until 21–23 July (with a supplemental submission on the 26th). Part of the delay, of course, stemmed from Dudley's commendable concern to protect his English witnesses and his network of detectives. It cannot be coincidence that the efforts and efficacy of the Americans picked up in significant ways only *after* Squarey and Collier joined their team. In contrast, Bulloch had had himself fully briefed on the intricacies of the enlistment act shortly after he arrived in England. That head start was a vital component in his success in getting the *Alabama* to sea. It is seldom mentioned — or even known — that part of Dudley's problem in procuring evidence has a simple explanation: There was no evidence of any violation of the law because Bulloch did not violate it. As he pointed out in his postwar memoir, no one was ever convicted of, or even prosecuted for, any violation of the law in connection with the *Alabama*. No one has ever been able to contradict that statement. And, as Rupert Jarvis has shown, the assessment of damages at Geneva for her wartime destruction of Union commerce stemmed from an alteration in the law that was then applied retroactively to the circumstances of 1861–65.

In earlier pages I drew attention to another aspect of the case, one that perhaps slowed down Dudley's handling of it. He resented the need for him to produce evidence. (Adams suffered from a similar delusion — that a mere request from the American camp would be sufficient, in and of itself, to move the British to a radical departure from their legal procedures and into a dicey interference with traditional concepts of property rights. This aspect of the case emerges clearly when one compares the "law" of the *Alabama* to that of the *Alexandra* in the following year.)

One does not wish to push this charge too far, but on at least one occasion Dudley let slip a few hints about this facet of his character. Writing to Seward on 25 July, he said that the evidence of Passmore, Roberts, and Taylor furnished "as strong proof as can ordinarily be made" in such cases. To his mind that information ought to have been "strong enough" to issue a detention order, *"if there was any disposition to do it"* (italics added).

He went on to assure his superior that everything possible had been done to stop the ship. Indeed, he lamented, he had done much more to stop her "than this government ought to require [of] any friendly government." Matters were now out of his hands, and his legal advisers were convinced that they had a case against the ship that was strong enough to ensure "her condemnation before any court." So he was flabbergasted when the board of customs rejected this evidence. Dispirited, he complained that he could do no more; he had no power to stop the ship. That power was lodged with the collector of the port, who refused to act without authorization by his London superiors, and those superiors had again rejected the American request for a detention order. No wonder the consul found himself despondent. At this point he did not yet know that the case had reached a critical point, that it had moved out of the jurisdiction of those lower-echelon bureaucrats who had frustrated all his efforts to move the government to action against the mighty ship that each day seemed ever nearer to slipping beyond his reach. News of the referral of the case to the law officers may have cheered him up somewhat. But that referral was eventually to result in even more complications and higher levels of frustration. Over these he had no control, nor, as things turned out, did Her Majesty's government.

We know with some certainty that Russell referred the case to his law officers in two stages on 23 July. In most accounts of these proceedings, Collier's second opinion of that date receives credit for bumping the case upstairs. What we do not know in any detail or with any precision is how the case got from the lower to the higher level on that morning. Fortunately, we know that Collier's second opinion and depositions 7 and 8 did not leave the treasury until after 5:30 P.M. on 23 July. We also know that Layard had sent the "first papers" on the case to the law officers that morning. He reported that information to Squarey in the afternoon, and his second transmission confirms that other material had already been sent earlier in the day. Obviously, Collier's second opinion could not have triggered that first transmission on the morning of the 23rd. What, then, did? Alas, we do not know, for the documents do not permit a firm answer. They do, however, allow an educated guess or fair inference from the evidence.

One of the compelling features of the case during its first month was the consistency with which customs and treasury officials rejected American allegations of unlawful activity on Merseyside. S. P. Edwards, collector at Liverpool, did so from the first. Some historians have claimed that investments in cotton made him a Southern partisan and led him to be out of the way on purpose when the *Alabama* sailed. (The evidence for such charges is insubstantial, and Bulloch specifically exonerated him from any charge of complicity in the escape.) Too many other officials objected to the American allegations to give any credence to a charge of Confederate bribery or sympathy as a causative factor in the escape. The fact remains that a significant number of well-informed British lawyers simply could find no merit in American arguments and evidence. They never, to my knowledge, ever said, "These Yankees seem a little dense in not understanding basic rules of evidence," but I cannot escape the impression that such thoughts may have crossed their minds.

Even late in the evolution of the controversy, on 25 July, the assistant solicitor to the board of customs in London, James O'Dowd, could argue that the "last, final" piece of evidence in the *Alabama,* that allegedly magical ninth affidavit of Henry Redden, weakened rather than strengthened the American case and demonstrated their inability to produce legally valid evidence. In a word, the case lacked substance and could not justify any proceedings under the enlistment act. All of this suggests that, if left to their own devices, these lower-echelon legal advisers would have continued to argue that the American case was too insubstantial to require any review by the law officers of the Crown. But a decision was made by these same officials to "suggest" a referral of the case to those officers.

In a narrow, technical sense, that step could be taken only by the foreign secretary, Lord Russell. And he did so twice, once early in the day and again late in the evening of 23 July, while he was preoccupied by parliamentary business. To Layard's cryptic request to refer the *Alabama* dossier to the law officers, Russell had hurriedly scrawled, "Yes, at once," and initialed the order.

Of course, he did so a third time on the 26th, when the final deposition was referred to the law officers. Even if the sequence of events suggests that Russell probably had little opportunity for deep, reflective thought over where this case might be taking him and the Queen's government, the documentary record certainly does not support the E. D. Adams and F. L. Owsley claim that he showed "no serious concern" until that last deposition arrived on 26 July. At that point it was doubtful whether he had spent much time mulling over the consequences of that act. The future would provide ample opportunity for him to do so.

In the nature of things as they were in the nineteenth-century British bureaucratic state and because the American Civil War was not the only problem confronting him, Russell relied on his two capable and experienced undersecretaries, Hammond and Layard. These men served him long and well and with complete loyalty. He trusted them and relied on their integrity and judgment. They, in turn, depended upon their subordinates to filter the commonplace from those things that needed decisions at a higher level. As it turned out, in the summer of 1862 the key person in the chain of command handling American complaints about Confederate shipbuilding in Liverpool was George Hamilton, secretary to the London-based lords commissioner of the treasury. Only that group, acting in its corporate capacity and through its secretary, could "suggest" to the Foreign Office a review of a case at a higher level. The secretary operated under orders of the commissioners and with the advice of the board's legal advisers. The treasury board, in turn, cooperated with their counterparts in the board of customs commissioners, who could also suggest that a review at a higher level might be advisable. And so, on 22 July, when a suggestion (that was all it could be) for a consultation with the law officers had been made at the proper place in the chain of command, it came in due course to Hamilton's attention.

Sometime that day, probably near the end of official business (no times are listed on any of the documents), he received from his customs counterpart, J. G. Gardner, an important message and some critical information about developments in the case. Again, at the risk of some tediousness, the content of this transmission requires our attention. First, there was a report from the collector at Liverpool, S. P. Edwards. In it he alluded to two aspects of the case: (1) that the evidence of Passmore's deposition might have some "importance," and (2) that he desired telegraphic orders with respect to Bulloch's ship because she appeared "ready for sea and may leave any hour she pleases." A new element of urgency had entered the case. Did the government wish to prevent the departure of that ship? If so, the collector must receive an immediate and unambiguous order to do so. By this late date Edwards felt himself powerless to act against the ship without clear and unequivocal authorization from his London superiors. By that same date those superiors were still not willing to issue such a directive. (Sympathy for the South had no bearing on Edwards's conduct. The ship got away, not because Edwards wanted to help the Confederate cause but because his superiors in London vacillated until too late.) Like good bureaucrats, the Londoners decided to kick that decision upstairs, which cost time. In the material that reached Hamilton on the 22nd was an extended commentary by Gardner. That information provided a synopsis of events surrounding the case, and it contained a "suggestion" for its resolution.

Among other things, Gardner noted that the contretemps had been going on for three weeks. He also made reference to the new evidence of the first affidavits (now enclosed for treasury officials), and he told his superior that this new information had been referred to the solicitor of customs. That official had ruled that the evidence of depositions 1–6 was "not sufficient to justify any steps being taken against the vessel under either the sixth or seventh section of the act 59 George III, cap. 69." That decision, Gardner told Hamilton, had been sent to Collector Edwards at Liverpool with a suggestion that if enough evidence of enlistment existed, the individuals involved in it might be prosecuted and fined. Customs might then detain the ship until those penalties were paid, but direct action against individuals could not be taken by customs agents themselves, for there was insufficient evidence of enlistment "to require the customs to prosecute." And while the solicitor himself did not think any such enlistment violations could be sustained in a jury trial, he noted that the American consul, or any other person, might bring such charges into court "at their own risk, if they see fit." Then, in what seems an afterthought, Gardner mentioned that if "the lords commissioner of Her Majesty's treasury have any doubts upon the subject, [they might consider] whether it may not be advisable that the opinion of the law officers of the Crown should be taken."

That same day, Hamilton relayed this information to Layard at the Foreign Office. In his cover letter, the treasury secretary remarked that the enclosed material might require urgent attention, so he was sending it unofficially "to save time." He then made a significant contribution of his own to the course of events by making the requisite suggestion: "Perhaps you will ascertain from Lord Russell whether it is his wish that we should take the opinion of the law officers as to the case of this vessel. It is stated that she is nearly ready for sea." Careful readers will notice how this last sentence echoes the urgency of that lowest-level bureaucrat, the collector at the port of Liverpool. And it seems to me — I hope that I am not alone in this reading of the evidence — Edwards's sense of urgency found a further echo when, some twenty-four hours later, Russell scrawled, "Yes, at once" on that second set of papers, the one he received in the House of Commons. Be that as it may, the information that Hamilton had received late on the 22nd went to Layard early the next day and was immediately sent to the law officers.

Later that day, the transmission sequence repeated itself with variations. Squarey presented deposition numbers 7 and 8, along with Collier's second opinion; the assistant solicitor to the London board of customs, James O'Dowd, upon considering the new material, rejected the two depositions and declined to "concur" in Collier's second opinion, though he submitted that the customs board "might act judiciously in recommending to the lords of the treasury to take the opinion of the law officers of the crown." Even Hamilton caught the soft inflection of urgency, for when he sent this material to Layard at 5:30 P.M., he suggested that the opinion of the law officers might be sent directly to the commissioners of customs, "to save time." Such an unofficial bypass of his office, he said, could be "put right" afterwards. As noted, this second transmission of the 23rd is the one that contained Russell's scrawled authorization to send this material to the law officers. And in his letter of transmission to those officials, Layard clearly referred to his "letter of this morning," which contained papers about the vessel "preparing for sea at Birkenhead." He noted that on instructions from the foreign secretary, he was sending "a further letter" from customs on that subject, and he requested that the law officers "favor" Russell with their opinion about "the steps which ought to be taken by Her Majesty's government in the matter." They should do so at their "earliest convenience." This sequence makes clear that it took only two days — from the 21st to the 23rd — to transmit Dudley's first six depositions from the lowest to the highest echelons of Her Majesty's government. It should be noted in passing that it took "some eighteen days or more" for Dudley to produce that evidence in legally binding form. One may therefore conclude that whatever "delay" occurred in the first month of this controversy had its origins in American mismanagement rather than in any British bureaucratic inefficiency or foot-dragging.

But that assessment still leaves one small mystery in the sequence of events for that first month. What triggered that "bump" from the lower reaches of the bureaucracy to the higher ones? In his fine article summarizing Union efforts to prevent the *Alabama*'s escape, Maynard gives proper credit to Hamilton's role in sensing danger in the stalemated situation on the 22nd, alerting Layard to it, and suggesting ways to speed up government responses. Of that work, Maynard rightly remarks: "Documents that were received late in the afternoon of 23 July, after going through two intermediate agencies[,] were dispatched to a fourth office on that same day — an enviable record for any bureaucracy."[9] That, it seems to me, fairly assesses the process that moved the ship's dossier out of the treasury and into the hands of the law officers. One step in the proceedings still is not clear, however: What caused the customs authorities in London to have second thoughts about the validity of their reading of the law of the *Alabama?* What led them to "suggest" to their superiors in the treasury that a referral of the case to the law officers might be expedient?

My own reconstruction of the case suggests that, if left to their own devices, those low-level legal advisers to the customs would have continued to insist that the American case did not merit any review at a higher level. Indeed, some of them continued to do so right up to the eve of that ship's departure. Still, as we know, solicitors in the customs service eventually saw the wisdom of referring the case to the law officers. Of course, that suggestion may have been no more than the built-in defensive mechanism of all bureaucrats from time immemorial. There may be another explanation, though there are gaps in it and it must remain somewhat speculative. As noted, the documents generated by the customs chain of command show a consistent reluctance to see any validity in Dudley's charges of illegal activity at Birkenhead. From first to last, those advisers seem to have convinced themselves that the Americans had produced no evidence of any violation of the enlistment act. In time, they reluctantly acknowledged the utility of sending the case to a higher authority. What catalyst, one wonders, set off that reaction?

There are not many clues for that change in tactics. As far as I have been able to ascertain, only one variable was factored into the *Alabama* equation in the first month — and that was Collier's original review of the case on 16 July. Unfortunately, we do not know if that opinion was part of the material submitted to the government from the 16th to the 22nd. But we do know that part of the *Alabama* dossier reached the law officers *before* Collier's second opinion was written. It is also known that the British received a copy of that first opinion at some point, though no one has determined when that occurred. And although Maynard quotes Collier's note of 16 July, he does not assign it any role in moving the case up the chain of command. But there is no doubt about that note's electrifying impact in the American camp. Almost overnight it revitalized their efforts to get the case out of the doldrums of inaction. Of its impact on moving the British to operate on a higher plane, one may only speculate. We know that Collier's second note galvanized movement in the upper echelons of the Crown's legal advisers, so it takes no great stretch of the historical imagination to see his first note as a trigger to sober second thoughts at a lower level.

The initial July "suggestion" to consult the law officers about the *Alabama* had its origins well down the chain of command. It had its impetus in the London board of customs. In turn, that body bumped the suggestion up to their superiors in the treasury. There, Hamilton had the good sense to relay it to Layard. He, in turn, consulted Russell, who decided to return the case to his legal advisers. And he did so before Collier's second note could have played any part in his decision or those of his subordinates. (It should be remembered that on his own initiative Russell had already consulted them about the case a month earlier.) And so we can only guess what triggered the decision of the customs board to suggest that the law officers review the case. For what it is worth, I believe that Collier's views of the 16th had made their way into the legal maze of Her Majesty's government. Once there, they shook the confidence of junior advisers just enough for them to think that some bureaucratic backside-covering action might be in order. So they suggested letting the boys upstairs have the final word. They did not surrender their own views. Indeed, they clung to them with amazing tenacity. Late on the 22nd, Hamilton acted on their suggestion and conveyed it to Layard, who acted on it early the next day with Russell's approval and set in motion that famous referral to the law officers early on the morning of 23 July. And if a perverse twist of fate had not intervened, that sequence of events would have ensured that the *Alabama* had a proper confrontation with the law of foreign enlistment. But that was not to be.

One must now confront the fate of the *Alabama* dossier from the morning of 23 July, when it was sent to the law officers, until 29 July, when those officers advised Russell to issue a detention order for Bulloch's ship. In that period, two supplementary sets of papers were also sent to the law officers. By now it should be clear that all officials concerned in the case considered it to be serious, a matter requiring prompt, if not immediate, action. Several close reviews of the sequence and speed of the transmission of documents in the first month of the case confirm my views that all concerned in it acted as promptly as possible to resolve it. There is no evidence of malingering or skulduggery by any official in any chain of command. That assertion can be verified by anyone willing to check the documentary record and establish an accurate chronology of the events from 23 June to 23 July.

And yet the *Alabama* dossier disappeared for nearly a week. Meanwhile, on this pressing matter of international business, the machinery of Her Majesty's government ground to a virtual halt. How did that happen? Who was responsible? What explanation can be advanced for this curious state of affairs? To put such questions in their proper perspective and context, they may be rephrased somewhat: Was the delay manufactured by royal officials to assist the Confederates in getting their ship out of Liverpool? And when mere delay no longer served the purpose of those crypto-Confederates in government service, did they then warn Bulloch to leave port before a restraining order could be issued and executed against his ship? In short, can this mystery be solved only as an explanation of conspiracy in high places? Such explanations remain alive and well in current literature. But there is not a shred of viable historical evidence to give them credence. To charge the prime minister or the foreign secretary with complicity in a plot to aid Confederate shipbuilding in the Queen's realm would require strong evidence, but to date no one has produced any. If there was no complicity by royal officials, how can that strange hiatus in the *Alabama* affair be explained?

That explanation is a simple one. It tells a sad, human, and tragic story. The last days of that cruiser's presence in Liverpool coincided with the final madness of the chief law officer of the Crown, Queen's Advocate Sir John Harding. It is not known precisely when he became completely incapacitated. It is surmised that his malady reached its final crisis stage in mid- to late July. (Harding was not actively engaged in government business for some time before the complete loss of his faculties, for he did not sign the 30 June opinion of his colleagues on the *Alabama.*) The state of his health was apparently not a concern

when Russell decided to refer the case to his legal advisers. Once
again, bureaucratic structure and practice impinged on the
case. As a matter of course and courtesy, those papers went first
to Sir John as chief law officer, and in the normal course of
events they would have circulated among the three legal advisers until a consensus was reached and they offered their official advice to the Crown. At this critical moment Sir John was
incapable of any sort of professional work.

The great drama of Bulloch's struggle to get his ship beyond
the reach of his implacable adversaries now gave way to a woman's confrontation with her husband's madness. Like Woodrow
Wilson's wife during her husband's illness, Harding's wife held
the nation's fate in her hands. Only she knew the true state of
her husband's malady. The papers of that case arrived in two
batches at Sir John's residence on the 23rd. He was in no condition to attend to them, and a few days of silence on his part
apparently rang no alarm bells for his colleagues. Then, on the
26th, a further set of papers was sent to Harding. Still, no opinion came from that tormented soul. And finally, on 28 July, the
attorney general, William Atherton, retrieved the documents.[10]
That night and the following morning he and the solicitor general, Roundell Palmer, took those papers and the questions they
posed under consideration and rendered their famous opinion.
Writing to Russell seven years later, Palmer recalled that he met
with Atherton "about 4 or 5 o'clock P.M. on Monday, the 28th of
July." Before that, he had not known about the existence of the
documents that he was obliged to evaluate. Surprisingly, he did
not learn about Harding's mental illness until still later.[11]

The Atherton-Palmer memorandum was dated 29 July 1862.
This advice did not reach Russell until that afternoon—a few
hours after the *Alabama* had departed the dockyards at Birkenhead for the Atlantic. The detention order that the treasury
authorized did not reach Liverpool until late evening on the
31st, some fifty-five hours after Bulloch took his most famous
raider to sea. That escape, one of the most dramatic events in
Confederate naval history, was a damn close-run thing. To succeed, it needed a unique combination of circumstances.

Over the years many fanciful tales have been told to explain that success. No one, however, has given proper credit to Lady Harding. Her failure to inform her husband's superiors and colleagues of his mental distress gave Bulloch an extra period of grace — and those few precious days provided all the margin he needed to engineer the escape. In all probability, had they received the dossier on the 24th or 25th, Atherton and Palmer would have ruled the same way they did on the 29th. All the information they needed for a firm ruling was available to the government from the 23rd onward. It should also be remembered that a month earlier they had already found the circumstances of the ship suspicious and had advised their superiors to detain the vessel if proper evidence against her could be procured. Therefore, there is no reason to suppose that they would have found depositions 6, 7, and 8 any less compelling if they had received them a week earlier. One does not indulge in counterfactual history by saying that a detention order issued on the 24th or 25th would have caught the *Alabama* in her Birkenhead dock.

Nor does one diminish the work of Bulloch by acknowledging the contribution of Lady Harding. It is most unlikely that he knew of her predicament, but her fears for her husband's fate gave Bulloch just the cushion he needed to complete his task. Why she neglected to report her husband's condition has never been explained. Some say she feared for a loss of her husband's professional reputation. Others say she feared a loss of her husband's pension. In all probability we shall never know what went on in that poor woman's mind as she confronted her husband's distressed state. But we may safely infer that she wasted no thoughts on the case she had entombed on her husband's desk — one that was to cost his superiors millions of dollars.

Nor do we need to give credence to those tall tales which tell us that while the *Alabama* dossier was in the possession of Lady Harding unknown Confederate agents succeeded in copying its contents and used that information to warn Bulloch of danger to his ship. The proponents of explanation by conspiracy have been most fertile and ingenious. They just have not yet produced any viable evidence of a plot by British officials to aid the escape of the *Alabama*.

It is now necessary to look in some detail at the reading of that law given to Russell on 29 July. Due to Harding's illness, that opinion was signed by Atherton and Palmer, the same two men who had signed the preliminary assessment of the *Alabama*'s status on 30 June. These two law officers represented the best talent available to the government, and even though their second reading of that ship's status was produced under great pressure and in near record time, there is no reason to suspect that the less-than-ideal conditions under which it was produced in any way weakened their exposition of the law as they understood it at the time of the *Alabama*'s escape. To understand the law "as it then was" (to use Jarvis's trenchant phrase one more time), one must compare the views of Atherton and Palmer on two separate occasions; then one must contrast those views with the two readings of the law provided by Collier. Of course, any analysis of this complex set of views remains handicapped by the absence of a jury trial and verdict on the status of the ship on the eve of her departure. That latter defect, however, can be partly compensated for in a small way by a careful comparison of the circumstances of the *Alabama* with those of the *Alexandra,* a ship of similar design, purpose, and challenge to British law. We cannot know in any meaningful way how a trial of the *Alabama* would have gone had she been detained in July 1862. Still, her situation has many analogies with her sister ship, which did stand trial in the summer of 1863. In other words, the law of the *Alexandra* should illuminate several facets of the probable legal status of the *Alabama.* The two ships had enough in common to make such a comparison useful.

But first the law of the *Alabama* as it was pronounced by Atherton and Palmer on 29 July 1862. Like all legal documents, their opinion requires careful reading, and it does not easily lend itself to paraphrase or summation. Its glory is in detail and argument, not in its prose, though that is clear enough, all things considered. When read by its four corners, it can still tell us a good deal about a much-disputed aspect of neutrality and maritime law in a period of rapid change in those areas. As was the customary procedure, they acknowledge receipt of Layard's "first papers" on the 23rd. They specifically refer to "a further letter" of that date and to "additional papers" about the vessel under discussion. In addition, they confirm receipt of the letter of 26 July, which Russell "had received that morning." This refers to that "last and final" disposition of Henry Redden, the one designated as number 9 in these pages. The preliminary, formal review of the question under discussion notes two other items that might have a bearing on their deliberation of the case: their own opinion of 30 June and "the former papers on this subject." This last reference is to the material included in Russell's initial submission of the question to his chief legal advisers in June. In short, on the night of 28 July and the morning 29 July, when Atherton and Palmer hammered out their recommendation for Russell, they had a full dossier of all relevant material with any bearing on the case. Only one question about that material cannot now be answered with precision. It is not clear whether Collier's opinion of 16 July had found a place in the dossier. (The reader is reminded that the answer to that question assumes added importance for the discussion of Palmer's subsequent defense of government *Alabama* policy in Parliament in March 1863.)

"In obedience to your lordship's commands," the law officers told Russell in ritualistic formality, "we have taken these papers into consideration, and have the honor to report": (1) The depositions of Passmore, Roberts, Taylor, and Redden (numbers 6–9), "coupled with the character and structure" of the ship, made it "reasonably clear" that she was intended for the "so-called" Confederate States and for "war like use" against the United States. That aspect of the case could not "be denied," they said. All the details of construction, the builders' acknowledgment of her foreign destination, and their refusal to identify the government for whom the ship was destined — all these things strongly suggested that the vessel at Liverpool was to serve as a ship of war. "It is not, and cannot be denied that the vessel is constructed and adapted as a vessel of war; being pierced for guns, the sockets for the bolts for which, Passmore states, are already laid down, and having a magazine, and shot and canister racks on the deck, and a certain number of canisters being actually on board." This part of the opinion takes up approximately two-thirds of the document, some fifty lines of the seventy-five given over to their ruling in the case.

But the last third of that ruling has far more interest for those concerned with the law of the *Alabama* "as it then was" in the summer of 1862. Neither quotation nor paraphrase does full justice to that part of their review. So perhaps a layman's free translation of legalese may serve our purpose here. Although portions of this opinion occur frequently in secondary accounts of Bulloch's work, such quotations seldom do justice to the nuances incorporated in this reading of the law. And yet, because of its timing and the circumstances under which it was produced, the views of Palmer and Atherton take on a peculiar resonance. Selective quotation (and here I speak from personal experience) gives us that famous reference to the enlistment act as a dead letter,[12] but it deprives the reader of the richer context in which that phrase appeared.[13]

Atherton and Palmer acknowledged that a court of law might ultimately find the ship blameless of violating the neutrality law: "neither guns nor ammunition have as yet been shipped," conceivably the cargo might be classed as military or as "mercantile," and "in terms and form at least" the crew had not been signed on "as a military crew."[14] Yet Atherton and Palmer believed that the ship should be seized "without loss of time" on the basis of what was known. "Previous to condemnation," interested parties could challenge the facts and "show an innocent destination." Given what the facts appeared to be, the owners and prospective purchasers had a burden of proof. "In the absence of any such countervailing case, it appears to us that the vessel, cargo, and stores may be properly condemned."

In language that parallels Collier's two opinions, Atherton and Palmer disputed the appropriateness of a narrow interpretation of the words *equip, furnish, fit out,* or *arm* in the seventh section of the Foreign Enlistment Act as applicable "only to the rendering a vessel, whatever may be the character of its structure, presently fit to engage in hostilities." Atherton and Palmer advised Russell that "such a narrow construction ought not to be adopted; and, if allowed, would fritter away the act, and give impunity to open and flagrant violation of its provisions." The absence of guns did not protect the *Alabama* from seizure.

Seizure did not mean that a jury would decide that the ship should be condemned. That jury trial never took place, so the nature of its verdict is unknowable. With the help of Harding's nervous breakdown, Bulloch had avoided the risk that a jury might agree with the law officers. It was a risk, not a certainty.

In April 1863, the British government seized the *Alexandra,* a steamer under construction at Liverpool, on the argument that it was intended for service as a Confederate warship. In June, Palmer represented the government in the trial. His arguments, justifying the government's action, failed to persuade. The presiding judge asked the jury whether it was lawful to furnish ships "to be used against a power with which we are at peace?" and answered that it was. In his charge to the jury, he declared that, to violate the law, the ship had to be armed in British waters.[15] Predictably, the jurors ruled in favor of the rights of private property and against the government's seizure of the ship. The same might have been true if the *Alabama* had been seized in 1862. A jury, not the law officers, had the final say in interpreting the law.

It was not the law but political reality — the recognition, after the South's defeats at Vicksburg and Gettysburg, that the North was winning the war — that persuaded the British government to thwart the Confederate naval building program. "Lord Russell, in opposition to his legal advisors, felt compelled to go behind and beyond the law" to prevent British-built ships from becoming Confederate warships.[16]

FOUR | E. D. ADAMS, ROUNDELL PALMER, AND THE ESCAPE OF THE *ALABAMA*

*I*N THE late 1990s, a British colleague and I discovered a memoir of the escape of the *Alabama* written by its English first captain, Matthew James Butcher.[1] In preparing that piece for publication, I needed to reexamine how the Confederate raider escaped from Liverpool on 29 July 1862. Two aspects of that story dominated my attention: the precise chronology of its sudden departure and the question of whether British officials had aided or abetted that escape.

I undertook to do at least three things: first, to reconstruct from primary sources in minute detail how the escape had been managed; second, to see how accurately that tale had been told over the years; and, third, to determine the sources of the errors about the escape that had crept into the literature of Civil War naval and diplomatic history.

That event, the escape of the *Alabama,* is in itself a fascinating affair, rich in human drama, filled with international intrigue, and fraught with consequence of grand importance. Among other things, it accounted for nearly half of the more than $15 million in postwar damage claims that the British government reluctantly paid. It deserves greater emphasis and a more nuanced treatment than I gave it in my 1970 book, *Great Britain and the Confederate Navy.*

I undertook afresh a critical review of *Alabama* scholarship. In

89

the years since French divers discovered the remains of that famous warship off Cherbourg in 1985, there has been a revival of interest in the cruiser, her captain, and her career. I myself edited a set of *Alabama* essays and reviews in 1989 in a special issue of the *Journal of Confederate History.*

My critique of the literature began with the works of the two preeminent authorities on Civil War diplomacy, Ephraim D. Adams and Frank L. Owsley. Adams (1865–1930) wrote *Great Britain and the American Civil War* (1925), and Owsley (1890–1955) published *King Cotton Diplomacy* (1931) shortly after the death of Adams. My rereading of these masters made it clear that both had made serious errors in their accounts of the *Alabama*'s escape. Not only did they get many of the dates wrong but they also put in a false perspective the entire sequence of events surrounding the escape. Most important, these classic accounts misrepresented the role of British officials in the escape. In fact, Adams indicted the British foreign secretary, Lord Russell, as an active participant in that vessel's departure. In suggesting that British governmental officials cooperated in the escape, Adams and Owsley wrongly diminished the role of James D. Bulloch, the Confederate naval agent. It is Bulloch who deserves most of the credit for the *Alabama*'s successful flight from British territorial waters.

As my survey of the literature expanded, I soon noted that the nebulous charges of Adams had been picked up by other writers who were, if anything, less careful and circumspect than he had been in leveling attacks at British officials. In time, the distorted chronology and unsupported charges of complicity that had their origins in Adams's work had, in the hands of less skillful historians, become matters to be taken for granted. The unproved accusation of Adams against Russell had soon been enlarged to include the prime minister, Lord Palmerston. This mythical history had two salient features: It was derived in large measure from E. D. Adams (usually via George W. Dalzell's *Flight from the Flag* [1940]), often in books that do not even afford Adams the courtesy of citing him, and it was supported by no convincing evidence.

As a disciple of E. D. Adams — in graduate school I had learned the rudiments of the British response to the Civil War from him, and it is no secret that my first book owes a heavy intellectual debt to him — it was exceedingly difficult for me to acknowledge how defective his account was. The point of the following pages is not that Adams made mistakes — what historian is free from error? My purpose, rather, is to draw attention to the persistent influence of these errors and to offer an explanation why Adams made them.

*   *   *   *   *

The account by E. D. Adams of the escape of the *Alabama* covers less than four pages in the second volume of a two-volume work.[2] Some nine notes are used to document his interpretation, but only one can be described as archival, though three citations are to printed primary sources. In passing, it might be mentioned that Adams both misspells Bulloch's name and mistitles Bulloch's postwar memoir. The information derived from that book is literally correct, but the significance of what Bulloch said did not properly catch Adams's attention. It is a point of importance. In his own book, Bulloch says that he never violated British neutrality law and that prevailing legal opinion in England supported him in this view. Both parts of that observation are true, though one would not know this by reading what Adams says about the Confederate's memoir.

One of the great gaps in Civil War diplomatic historiography is that no one has fully studied the legal dimension of the British response. A comprehensive view of legal problems connected with the war requires detailed analysis of the way the law officers of the Crown responded to a wide array of legal issues over the entire course of the war and even beyond it. No one case in isolation, not even the *Alabama* or the Laird rams, contains an interpretive key to unlock a magic cabinet of solutions to the still mysterious features of wartime diplomacy.

The second footnote in Adams's account of the escape also requires mention. Again, Adams uses his source correctly, though why he used a secondary source when a primary one was easily at hand is not clear. What remains puzzling in his use of that secondary source is that he did not warn his readers that a measure of caution should be used in reading Mountague Bernard's *Historical Account of the Neutrality of Great Britain during the American Civil War* (1870). Use of this source, however, leads Adams to an important gap in his own account. Bernard, for reasons unknown, had neglected to mention that on 30 June 1862 — a month before she escaped — the law officers had urged Russell to undertake a rigorous investigation of American charges against the *Alabama* and, if customs agents substantiated them, to detain the ship for legal proceedings. Even more strangely, Bernard — and consequently Adams — does not mention that Russell ignored the advice. It is difficult for me to believe that Bernard did not know such things, for he was a top-level adviser to the government and had access to materials that were long closed to others.

Several aspects of the way Adams used his sources should be emphasized at the outset. In his use of Bulloch's postwar memoir, *The Secret Service of the Confederates States in Europe; or, How the Confederate Cruisers Were Equipped,* he misunderstands its utility for the story he seeks to tell. He ignores parts of Bulloch's account that are central to establishing a correct chronology of events and to the more important task of evaluating the question of British complicity. In a second instance, he misses a number of salient features of the *Alabama*'s departure from Liverpool because of his reliance on Bernard. But much of his error stems from his misreading and misinterpretation of a central document in the case: Sir Roundell Palmer's 27 March 1863 defense of government policy in the House of Commons.

Then comes the matter of that all-important chronology. In 1861 the newly formed Confederate States of America had sent Bulloch to Europe to make a navy for Jefferson Davis. An important component of that mission was the construction of a fleet of commerce raiders. In March 1862 Bulloch had succeeded in getting one such ship, the *Florida,* out of England, to the intense chagrin of his Northern adversaries. And by June of that year he had a second, more powerful sister ship almost ready for sea. The American minister in London, Charles Francis Adams, and the Union consul at Liverpool, Thomas H. Dudley, began a coordinated effort to prevent that vessel from leaving port. Construction of the vessel had been completed in mid-May; her trial trip had taken place in mid-June; and by the end of that month she appeared ready to depart at a moment's notice.

Because the E. D. Adams account has assumed an independent life in many subsequent versions of the escape, it requires extensive quotation.

> From June 23 to July 28, when the second ship, "No. 290" (later christened the *Alabama*), left Liverpool, Adams and . . . Dudley were busy in securing evidence and in renewing protests to the Government. To each protest Russell replied in but a few lines that the matter had been referred to the proper department. It was not until July 26, when he received from Adams an opinion by an eminent Queen's Counsel, [Robert P.] Collier, arguing that the affidavits submitted were conclusive against the "290," that Russell appears to have been seriously concerned. On July 28, the law officers of the Crown were asked for an immediate opinion, and on the thirty-first telegrams were sent to Liverpool and to other ports to stop and further examine the vessel. But the "290" was well away and outside British waters. . . . [That] escape from Liverpool had been winked at by the British Government. What further evidence was necessary of bad faith in professed strict neutrality? . . . At the last moment it had appeared as if the Government were inclined to stop the "290." Was the hurried departure of the vessel due to a warning received from official sources? On November 21, [C. F.] Adams reported that Russell complained in an interview of remarks made privately by [John] Bright, to the effect that warning had come from Russell himself, and [it] seemed to me a little as if he [Russell] suspected that Mr. Bright had heard this from me. Adams disavowed . . . any such imputation but at the same time expressed to Russell his conviction that *there must have been* from some source a "leak" of the Government's intention. The question of advanced warning to Bulloch, or to the Lairds who built the *Alabama,* was not one that was likely to be officially put forward in any case.[3]

What should a careful reader notice about this passage? In the first place, Adams, usually a careful scholar, makes an elementary mistake in dating the escape, and it is an error that many have repeated. For the record, the *Alabama* left Liverpool on the morning of 29 July—not on the 28th, as Adams has it. If that were his only mistake, it might be excused as a typo or uncorrected printer's error. Such is not the case.

Even the way that Adams links the dates 23 June to 28 July distorts the chronology of the story in a simple way. The American minister made his first formal remonstrance to the Foreign Office on 23 June. That complaint immediately went to the law officers of the Crown and to local customs officials at Liverpool. As mentioned, the Queen's highest legal advisers, on 30 June, had recommended a thorough investigation of the allegations against the ship and—be it noted—they had done so with no delay whatever. And so, while the foreign secretary had been "concerned" enough to request an opinion from his legal advisers, he did not feel compelled to act on that advice. In consequence of Russell's failure to follow his legal advisers, the complaints against the *Alabama* bounced around the lower echelons of Britain's bureaucratic maze until 23 July, at which point the law officers of the Crown again got the case.

Next, one should notice the opinion of Collier on the ship came in two parts, one on 16 July and one on the 23rd. The first of these apparently got some of the low-level bureaucrats seriously concerned because on 22 July they were suggesting that perhaps it would be wise to consult the Crown's highest legal officers again. The second Collier opinion, the one arguing that American evidence was conclusive, had reached Russell on the 23rd (not the 26th), when he authorized his undersecretary to forward it to the law officers. In fact, two sets of *Alabama* papers went to the law officers on that day. But because the chief law officer, Sir John Harding, had suffered a nervous breakdown, the ship's dossier was in limbo from the 23rd to the 28th, when the papers were retrieved and the two remaining legal advisers considered them. In the early afternoon of 29 July their advice reached the foreign secretary. He then authorized a detention order, though for reasons no one has ever explained that order was not sent to Liverpool until 31 July, long after the *Alabama* had left her Merseyside berth. She had departed even before the advice of the law officers had reached Russell.

So far the question of British complicity in the escape revolves around timing and whether there had been inordinate delay in processing American complaints. My own review of this charge—after a detailed reexamination of all present evidence—convinces me that it cannot be sustained. If one makes reasonable allowances for the normal delays of bureaucratic machinery and if one factors in the all-too-human propensities for underlings to avoid antagonizing their superiors and do nothing not specifically authorized, then it is difficult to find any sustained or systematic delay in the British response from 23 June to 23 July. The delay occasioned by Harding's illness falls into a different category, but even then it was rectified faster than the Americans compiled their evidence.

Now one must confront the most serious charge against the British government and E. D. Adams's role in originating and spreading it. The charge he makes is that the escape from Liverpool "had been winked at by the British government." He asks the rhetorical question: "Was the hurried departure of the vessel due to a warning received from official sources?" He provides no answer. Farther along in the passage E. D. Adams the historian has C. F. Adams the diplomat expressing to Russell a "conviction that *there must have been* from some source a 'leak' of the government's intention." Minister Adams hints that the charge may have originated with John Bright, a champion of the Union cause in Britain.

From whence comes this strange tale, this serious charge of British complicity in the escape, these insubstantial rumors of leaks from the highest levels of Her Majesty's government? Can the charge be substantiated? Or, more properly, does E. D. Adams provide proper evidence for it? Insofar as I can ascertain, the quoted passage is the first scholarly mention of the charge (except for the article from which it is derived). It is also my impression that all subsequent variations of it derive from E. D. Adams, whether or not his paternity is acknowledged. I am unaware that the charge has ever been scrutinized with any scholarly sophistication. A look at the evidence E. D. Adams used to buttress the charge may be instructive. The sentence referring to a "leak" carries a note, citing Brooks Adams, "The Seizure of the Laird Rams," in volume 45 of the *Proceedings* of the Massachusetts Historical Society. In this otherwise forgotten article, published in 1912, Brooks Adams (son of the American war-time minister to London) reported that in 1865 his father had seen a copy of *what purported to be* a letter from one Victor Buck-ley, a clerk to the British Foreign Office, to Caleb Huse, a Con-federate army agent, warning of some unspecified danger to the latter's "protégé."

How should one evaluate the charge and its evidence? What do we know, and when do we know it? First, the charge origi-nated with the American minister, not perhaps the most objec-tive witness, especially if one keeps in mind the little-known fact that the escape of the *Alabama* resulted as much from American mismanagement as it did from British delay.

Next, one should bear in mind the testimony of another vital witness. The man in the best position to know whether or not British officials leaked information to the South denied receiv-ing any. Of course, Bulloch, the chief Confederate naval agent, like Adams, the chief Union diplomat, cannot be taken on faith. In his postwar account of his work, he had good reason to be discreet. Yet his account achieves a high level of accuracy with a minimum of self-justification. The circumstances in Liverpool on the eve of his ship's escape were much as he described them. In essence, he says — and I think says correctly — that there was so much evidence of increasing government interest in the ship and there were so many hints of impending danger that he didn't need governmental leaks to get the ship away. He does acknowledge, however, the receipt of a warning telegram on 26 July. Of its sender he tells us nothing. And he denies that any British official, high or low, ever passed on confidential informa-tion to him. Many may find his account just a tad too disin-genuous, but no one has yet supplied a better one.

There is one other small point to be noticed about that tele-gram and its date. If my reading of the evidence is correct, and if my reconstruction of the chronology is accurate, then it might be said with some assurance that on 26 July no one in Her Majesty's government knew what action would be taken against the *Alabama;* they only knew that some action was brewing. That fact — a growing awareness that Her Majesty's government would have to respond to American allegations of unlawful activity in Liverpool—was known by the top echelon of the Queen's advisers as early as the morning of 23 July. Or, to put the matter another way, if someone in the innermost circle of British maneuvers against the *Alabama* had wanted to warn Bulloch of danger to his ship, why wait until the 26th to do so?

The logical time for such a warning, surely, would have been as soon as possible after the foreign secretary and the law officers had received the second batch of American evidence and Collier's strong opinion in support of it late in the evening of 23 July. In other words, one should note that E. D. Adams's way of constructing his chronology has diverted attention from a crucial date in the unfolding drama to a peripheral one. Another aspect of the altered chronology should also be borne in mind. The dispatch of the warning to Bulloch on the 26th makes it a little less likely that it came from the inner sanctum of British officialdom. If Russell had wished to alert a Confederate friend in Liverpool to impending danger, would he not have done so as soon as he sniffed such a threat in the American documents? After all, he was one of the few people in Britain who knew what the law officers had advised a month earlier. He was in a position to know what their advice was likely to be in light of stronger evidence of what was going on in Liverpool shipyards. In such matters it is always useful to distinguish between facts and fictions, between suppositions and actions. It is also important to evaluate the evidence for each step in the sequence of cat-and-mouse maneuvers on the Mersey.

The rumor of government complicity in the *Alabama*'s escape originated with the 1912 Brooks Adams article on the rams. But it did not gain a wide audience until E. D. Adams embedded it in his massive and influential work of 1925. With that authority behind it, it began to take on greater credence.

*   *   *   *   *

The first important work on Civil War diplomacy to incorporate portions of the escape story as told by E. D. Adams gave that version an additional patina of scholarly acceptance. Although Frank J. Owsley, the author of this 1931 work, altered the general mode of interpretation in significant ways, the new version brought the essential elements of Adams's views to an audience it might otherwise not have reached. This work provided one of the major conduits for the flawed story that originated with E. D. Adams.

Although Owsley devoted a chapter of *King Cotton Diplomacy* to the building of the Confederate navy in Europe, his treatment of the *Alabama*'s escape is more superficial and more error-prone than that of Adams. It may simply be that his mistakes loom larger because they are concentrated in smaller space — less than a page covers one of the most dramatic incidents of Confederate naval affairs in Europe. Because Owsley's account has frequently been incorporated on faith into subsequent works, it should be tested for accuracy. On that score, it must be judged as wanting.

Again, as in Adams, many mistakes arise from a distorted chronology. Owsley begins with a slight ambiguity. He tells us that when the American minister first complained to Russell about the cruiser on 23 June, that ship "began to approach the final stages of construction." Fair enough, as far as it goes. But that ship had been under construction since the previous summer; she had been launched in mid-May; she had been put under command of an English captain soon thereafter; she had completed her trial trip in mid-June; and at the time Owsley picks up the story, Bulloch was doing everything humanly possible to get his ship to sea. At that time he himself expected to be her commander, with a target date of departure in mid-July.

Like Adams, Owsley does not mention that the foreign secretary had taken the American minister's complaints seriously enough to forward them to his chief legal advisers as well as "to the customs officer at Liverpool who declined to act on the evidence." Nor does the author note that the Americans themselves slowed consideration of their complaints by the way they presented their case to the British authorities. Neither does he tell readers that, for all practical purposes, Adams and Dudley did not yet have very much in the way of legally binding evidence of any violations of British law, a fact that accounts for much of the so-called delay in British responses. The Americans did not construct even the rudiments of a legal case against the *Alabama* until mid- to late July — and even then, there were many in the British chain of command in the customs and treasury departments who considered such evidence as the Americans were able to produce as hearsay and unconvincing. An impartial observer who studied the thrust and parry of the legal duel from 23 June until 23 July might even hazard a guess that if the Crown had detained the ship in early July, any competent jury would have thrown the case out of court. But that is speculative history. Next, Owsley notes that Minister Adams and his "henchmen" secured additional affidavits and submitted them to a Queen's Counsel, Robert P. Collier, and he quotes the advice Collier gave to the Americans: "The collector of customs would be justified in detaining the vessel." A few lines later, the author relates that Adams sent this opinion and its supporting documents to Russell on 22 July.[4]

A number of observations need to be made about this passage. For one thing, the opinion quoted was written by Collier on 23 July and so could not have been sent to Russell the day before. Of course, Owsley's passage omits any reference to the slow building of the American case, to the full, frequent, and prompt replies by customs and treasury officials refuting American allegations throughout July, and to an earlier opinion by Collier about the merits of the case against the *Alabama*. Owsley, like E. P. Adams, also omits a vital piece of information. As a paid legal consultant to the diplomats Adams and Dudley, Collier acted as a private citizen, not as any sort of official agent of the government. As a distinguished authority on maritime law and an influential member of the legal profession, his words carried great weight in and out of governmental circles. Indeed, his earlier opinion on 16 July was influential in breaking up the logjam that had prevented any British action vis-à-vis the *Alabama* in early July. That opinion is not quoted by Owsley. Nor does he convey any awareness of its importance.

More important, Owsley once again gets the sequence of events badly out of sync. Because his account is cited almost as often as E. D. Adams's, it requires a critical evaluation. The precise dating of all exchanges between the government and the Americans and within the British bureaucracy, as well as between London and Liverpool, assumes critical importance in the period from 23 July until the end of that month. And from 1862 until the present, that chronology has been much distorted. What follows is an attempt to determine what actually happened — and when.

As noted, Owsley tells us, incorrectly, that C. F. Adams sent Collier's opinion of the 23rd to the foreign secretary on the 22nd. Then he says: "Russell received the new evidence July 26 and on July 28 asked the law office of the crown for an opinion. On the basis of the opinion of the law officers of the crown Russell on July 31 had telegrams sent to Liverpool and neighboring ports to stop the 'Alabama.' But the bird had already flown."[5]

Careful readers will notice affinities with the account of E. D. Adams, which, in fact, Owsley cites. At the risk of repetitiveness, I must draw attention to their common errors. Notice in particular the emphasis that both authors assign to 26 and 28 July. Both accounts are, of course, incorrect. What then might a proper chronological sequence look like? First, one should note that the initial stage of the *Alabama* affair stretches from 23 June, when C. F. Adams made his first formal complaint against that ship, until 23 July, when the law officers of the Crown received for the second time that ship's dossier and a request for official advice about her status. It should be noted again that Russell, for reasons unknown, had refused to act on the advice that they had given on 30 June. Another aspect of the case must be stressed. On 23 July the law officers received *two* sets of papers from the Foreign Office. The first was sent fairly early in the day. It included (and here one must be tentative) the bulk of American evidence against the ship, some depositions against the vessel, plus Collier's first opinion of 16 July. (It is uncertain when Collier's first opinion reached British authorities.) Much later, probably late evening, the undersecretary for foreign affairs, Austin H. Layard, sent his second batch of documents. These included two additional affidavits supplied by Dudley, plus Collier's all-important opinion of 23 July. This material went to the law officers with Russell's approval.

*   *   *   *   *

At this point, one encounters mystery multiplied and confusion compounded. From 23 July to 28 July, the *Alabama* case remained in suspended animation, in a kind of legal limbo. As best one can determine, those papers were sent to the chief law officer, Sir John Harding, who unfortunately had been incapacitated by a nervous breakdown. It is not known when he became unable to work, though his last official opinion had been delivered in late June. (He did *not* sign the 30 June opinion on the *Alabama*.) In any case, for five days after the delivery of the dossier, his wife neglected to inform his superiors about his inability to work. Finally, another law officer, William Atherton, retrieved the papers late on the evening of 28 July, consulted his remaining colleague, Roundell Palmer, and on the next day, early in the afternoon, sent to Russell their joint recommendation for an order to prevent the *Alabama*'s departure. The foreign secretary immediately authorized a detention order against that ship, but it was not sent to Liverpool until late on 31 July.

Candor compels me to confess that my own 1970 account of the escape of that vessel did not properly convey this chronology of events. It is now certain that the *Alabama* left Liverpool more than what I described as a few "whiskers" ahead of the detention order. Indeed, it is equally certain that the vessel left her Merseyside berth several hours *before* the law officers had even advised her seizure. By the time that order was authorized by the foreign secretary, it was fairly common knowledge in official circles that the bird had, indeed, flown the coop. Moreover, it was soon recognized in and out of governmental offices that the Confederates had carried out a daring coup and had done so with some delicacy — and against nearly insurmountable odds.

Consider for a moment the implications of what had happened on the morning of 29 July 1862. An underfinanced Confederate naval agent had outwitted all the forces of his Union adversaries, while eluding a tightening noose of British counter-

measures to keep him from going to sea. He did so with panache, with finesse, with virtuosity. So cleverly was the deed
done that it set in motion two sets of consequences. On the one
hand, the Americans said, or at least their minister hinted, that
the escape could not have been carried out without British assistance. Furthermore, they said that help would have had to come
from high up. In no time at all, they found an obscure clerk in
the Foreign Office who allegedly leaked a warning to Bulloch to
get his ship out of Liverpool. Tenuous as the evidence for that
charge was, it satisfied a need to believe that only a plot in high
places could explain the *Alabama*'s escape. In time that flimsy
evidence gave rise to thoughts of British complicity in the escape, then to charges of government responsibility for it, and
then — when Bulloch's ship began its wholesale destruction of
the Union's merchant marine — to demands for British compensation for that damage.

On the other hand, the British too were faced with awkward
repercussions. It seemed to many of the Queen's subjects that
the Confederates had evaded the laws of the realm, especially
the Foreign Enlistment Act, which was supposed to prevent such
incidents as Bulloch had concocted in Liverpool. Demands for
revision of that law, along with growing evidence of similar Confederate exploitation of British neutrality, coupled with growing
American ill will over the ministry's failure or unwillingness to
halt such activity, gave rise to a groundswell of domestic discontent and international criticism. In time, it became necessary to
defend the government's response to the *Alabama* affair. The
structure and content of that defense, when it reached the
House of Commons in March 1863, did much to mislead Owsley and Adams about how that ship got away, about what the
government had done to prevent the escape, and about the
chronology of those counterefforts.

Future historians may conclude that the real defect in the accounts of Adams and Owsley was their failure to come to grips
with the human dimension of the story of the escape. They failed
to recognize the true drama of the story and hence paid insufficient homage to Bulloch, who masterminded the only plot
necessary to get his ship safely to sea. And he succeeded in do-

ing so despite suspicious customs collectors and well-financed Union adversaries. To attribute that success to a leak or a wink in high places is surely too simple. Such an explanation does serious injustice to a man who, for four long years, demonstrated himself to be one of the South's most astute, resourceful, and dedicated public servants. A hint from on high may prove in time to be an essential part of a British plot to aid the Confederacy, but until evidence for that plot emerges more clearly than it has done to date, we who study such matters might be well advised to lodge our explanation of the *Alabama*'s escape where it properly belongs — in the talent, determination, skill, and virtuosity of James D. Bulloch.

The seminal works of Adams and Owsley remain classics of their genre. To this day they are cited favorably and frequently in the literature of Civil War diplomacy. Both authors still retain an aura of invincible scholarship. Their interpretations of the British response to that war have achieved a status approaching that accorded to Holy Writ. It is a rare thing to see the views of either of these masters brought into question. It sometimes seems to me that few who cite them with such reverence can have read them with much care. In the present essay my focus has been narrow, but my ongoing work has convinced me that there are many more — and more important — imperfections in their works. If the mistakes of these masters had remained within the scholarly community, then perhaps the influence of their errors might have been more restricted and less pernicious. Unfortunately, they inspired the misinterpretations that characterize popular history books read by a larger public.[6]

*   *   *   *   *

Why did a historian of the stature of E. D. Adams go astray in his account of the *Alabama*'s escape? I argue that his error derives mostly from a speech made by the solicitor general, Roundell Palmer, in the House of Commons in 27 March 1863 and reported in volume 170 of the third series of *Hansard Parliamentary Debates*.[7] This speech was the first official British account of the escape, one with what is now called spin. On the one hand, it may also be considered the opening gun in a decade-long campaign to protect Her Majesty's government against claims for the *Alabama*'s destruction of Union commerce during the war. On the other hand, it may also be considered the first published version of the escape, a sort of historical memoir. The person who provided this unique window into early British reactions to what was going on in Liverpool in June and July 1862 was himself deeply involved in the events he recounted. I argue that the gloss that he provided has led generations of historians astray.

There are a couple of things that one should immediately notice about the speech. Its primary purpose was to defend the government from charges that it had been guilty of delay in responding to American complaints against the *Alabama*. There is irony here: A speech designed to allay Union suspicions of procrastination in proceedings against Merseyside shipbuilding for the South eventually provided support for the far more serious charge of British complicity in Bulloch's success in getting his ship to sea. This unintended consequence of the speech had its roots in the way Adams and Owsley misinterpreted it. Beyond any reasonable doubt, their error on a vital point in the British response to the Civil War (and to King Cotton diplomacy) derived from an uncritical — even naïve — misreading of a piece of British propaganda about the departure of the Confederacy's most famous cruiser. Their error, in turn, permeates many subsequent accounts of the escape, even today. Students interested in the fine points of historical criticism may note that E. D. Adams read the speech in its 1863 context and then applied its slanted dating and viewpoints to the circumstances of 1862. Is it any wonder that such a reading resulted in error? Notice that his other primary sources (the British blue books) are also a form of propaganda or at least a form of special pleading. Mercifully, he did not subject his readers to the complexity of the Geneva arbitration papers.

This critique of the work of Adams (and, with less detail, of Owsley) does not depend on any startling discovery of new information, though, as earlier noted, my reexamination of the *Alabama*'s escape was triggered by such a discovery, the memoir of the English captain who took the ship out of Liverpool. But that material merely forced me to confront a problem that had been troubling me for some time. That new document may be regarded as the catalyst, not the cause, of my revisionism. So my intent here is to persuade with old material. Part of my own misunderstanding of the fine points surrounding Britain's response to the war in *Great Britain and the Confederate Navy* stemmed, I now think, from an overreliance on the authority of E. D. Adams and from a failure to read Palmer's speech in the right way. In retrospect, it seems wisest to read it as a sort of memoir. When so read, it is impossible to accept Adams's version of what happened in late July 1862. Such a reading also demonstrates the ways in which that speech lies close to the heart of his error. Perhaps this essay will clear the way for some fresh thinking on a subject that for too long has been dominated by unquestioned acceptance of views that are outdated and just plain wrong.

It is important for the reader to remember that the context of March 1863, when Palmer spoke in Parliament, was not that of July 1862, when an obscure vessel left Liverpool. In the interim, the *Alabama* affair had taken on a much different overlay of economic, emotional, and psychological responses at home and abroad. For one thing, between these two dates much ill will had been generated against John Bull's allegedly soft neutrality and his easy toleration of Confederate shipbuilding in the Queen's realm. In no time at all, the new Southern cruiser had become one of history's most deadly commerce destroyers. It is not always recalled that the *Alabama* did the bulk of her destructive work in the early months of her cruise. Soon after he began his deadly work of maritime mugging, Raphael Semmes reported "capital success" and chortled that the "little bill which the Yankees threaten to present to our Uncle John Bull is growing apace, and already reaches $3,100,000." Naturally, there was talk of British responsibility for such losses, and not all of it came from American representatives. In short, whatever the circumstances of the escape had been in July 1862, the government's policy on that occasion had come under serious and sustained attack in press and public outlets. By March 1863 Lord Palmerston's ministry had to defend itself in the House of Commons for allowing the ship to escape. The climate of opinion and the context of the case had changed in significant ways.

The principal defender of government policy in that historic debate was the solicitor general, Sir Roundell Palmer, one of the three law officers of the Crown. Of course, he was in a unique position to know the facts of the case and to gloss them with panache. If ever a man qualified as an expert witness to history, Palmer did. Parts of the story were hidden from him, but he had a special vantage point on the government's official response to American allegations of unlawful activities in Liverpool. He had signed the opinion that the law officers had sent to Russell on 30 June, a month before the ship left Liverpool. More important, he had signed the detention order of 29 July and presumably knew something of the circumstances that had delayed that order. To be sure, he was a government servant and spoke as a partisan of the Palmerston ministry. For personal and professional reasons, he spoke with great authority at some length and with much learning on the law and circumstances of the case as he understood them.

It was a government brief that he delivered. Even when one tries to take the most charitable view of what Palmer said in Parliament, suspicions linger that he did not tell the whole story as he knew it. He was in a position to shed light on one of the war's great mysteries. He did not do so. His defense of the government policy was a thicket of misinformation, half-truths, and linguistic evasions that has led generations of historians astray because the speech was cleverly crafted and seemingly authoritative.

Let me be blunt. Parts of his account are demonstrably false. And it is difficult to believe that he did not know they were false. It is nearly impossible to reconcile what he said with the record as it has now been reconstructed. On a subject where dates, timing, sequence, and chronology are all-important, he exhibits a cavalier disregard for them. He juggles these elements with such dexterity that they appear to be what they are not. At some points his account is dangerously disingenuous. It is a long speech, in some ways a brilliant one. Much of it is taken up with some of the larger dimensions of British neutrality as it was understood in the nineteenth century. Other segments explicate some of the arcane permutations of the genesis, evolution, and interpretation of the Foreign Enlistment Act. Those sections need not concern us here.

The problems of analysis of a memoir, a firsthand account by one who participated in the events being described, are compounded by Palmer's legal authority and by the peculiar records that the case of the *Alabama* generated. Much of that documentary record must be read with extreme caution, but the enormous mass of material makes that task a difficult one. Many of those pages constitute a form of special pleading, for both parties to the postwar claims controversy put their best facts forward and in the best possible light. That practice began almost as soon as the case left Liverpool — and it is still going on. Palmer's speech also requires a number of observations about the difficulty of getting at historical truth once the forces of officialdom have begun turning the records into self-protection.

How does Palmer explain the escape, and how does he defend Russell's response to American complaints against the *Alabama*? His account begins with Adams's first official remonstrance on 23 June. He asserted that Russell's answer to that complaint was "usual and proper." It was also prompt, though Palmer did not say so. When the foreign secretary referred that complaint to the local customs agents, they could find no justification for any legal action against the ship. Those officials reported on 1 July that the vessel "evidently" was a warship, that she was being built for a foreign government, and that the builders refused to identify its destination — but those things, they pointed out, did not constitute a violation of the law. When Russell sent this information to Minister Adams, he also informed him that if any "further evidence" could be procured, the government would reconsider the complaint. All of this, Palmer intimated, had been done expediently and in a spirit of friendly cooperation. The solicitor general then asked his House colleagues whether the ministry was at fault for failing to act in the absence of "any evidence whatever." Naturally, he answered that question in the negative: "The seizure of that ship would have been altogether unwarrantable by law." There was no evidence to support legal proceedings against the ship, Palmer said, and even the Americans did not think Her Majesty's government could proceed without it. This statement by Palmer appears straightforward and unequivocal.

Again one must pause to draw attention to several interesting features of this account. Perhaps one should first direct attention to what it does *not* say. In context, the omissions are curious. Nowhere in the speech is there any mention that Russell had sent that initial complaint to the law officers of the Crown, that is, to Palmer himself. Nor does the speaker tell his audience anything about the advice that he and his colleagues had given to the government on 30 June 1862. Neither does Palmer allude to Russell's decision to ignore that advice. Finally, there is the matter of the words Palmer has chosen. He carefully speaks of a "seizure" rather than a "detention." He is technically correct in what he says, though the passage is provocatively misleading.

It is difficult to square his March 1863 defense of policy with the advice the law officers had given to Russell on 30 June. They said then that *if* American allegations were correct, and *if* their charges could be confirmed by a government investigation, then "a manifest violation" of the Foreign Enlistment Act was under way in Liverpool and the government ought to take action to *prevent* the vessel from going to sea until the matter could be resolved.

Palmer's parliamentary defense centered on the question of delay. Did the ministry take too long in responding to American complaints against the ship? As might be expected, he found no validity in that charge. Such a conclusion should not surprise, but the reasoning that he offered might raise an eyebrow. My own review of the case supports Palmer's view on that point. Many American historians prefer to ignore that aspect of the *Alabama* story. As a matter of fact, it *did* take Adams and Dudley much too long to coordinate their efforts and produce the kind of evidence that would move British officials to a more serious concern about the ramifications of Confederate shipbuilding on the Merseyside. When they produced that evidence, the wheels of British officialdom moved very efficiently and reasonably fast.

Palmer properly pointed out that it took the Americans nearly three weeks to get their act together: "Eighteen days passed before he [Adams] furnished any evidence whatever." From 23 June until mid-July, little in the way of binding legal evidence had been produced or presented to British officials. From about 16 June to 23 July, the pace of events picked up in significant ways. Improved financing enabled Dudley to hire a prominent Liverpool solicitor to prepare the American case in proper form. With his new legal adviser he consulted one of Britain's leading authorities on maritime law and the meaning of the Foreign Enlistment Act. That expert, Robert P. Collier, on 16 July strongly supported American contentions about unlawful activities in Liverpool. He also provided valuable advice on how the case could best be presented to the authorities. Perhaps most important, Dudley and his solicitor began compiling affidavits in support of their contentions that the activities in Birkenhead contravened the enlistment act. Those documents were important elements in the story, and the time of their arrivals at their official destinations is a matter of critical importance in the unfolding drama of late July. They were nine in number, and they reached British officials at different times. For our purpose, only four of them need to be identified, and the time at which those were received officially needs to be specified with some precision.

First we must allow Palmer to give the official version of those events. Palmer was a wizard with words, and his legal legerdemain is a wonder to watch. He has cleverly constructed a chronology that is at variance with the facts of the documentary record.

Let us grant the accuracy of those "eighteen days without evidence." Palmer refers to the period from 4 July, when Russell replied to Adams's initial complaint, to 22 July, when the first batch, numbers 1–6, of the American affidavits arrived in the bureaucratic maze of British officialdom. Palmer performs his task better than I can, so a lengthy quotation is called for.

On the 22nd he [Adams] transmitted his first series of depositions; he did not complete his evidence till the 24th, and the
letter in which he sent the last two depositions [i.e., numbers 7
and 8] was not received at the Foreign Office till the 26th. So that
he did not place the whole evidence on which he relied in the
hands of the government till the 26th of July. In the meantime he
obtained the opinion of the hon. and learned Member for Plym-
outh [R. P. Collier], who on the 16th stated his belief that there
was a cause of suspicion that might prove enough to justify the
detention of the vessel. That first opinion was not communicated
to Her Majesty's government, and the collector of customs of
Liverpool did not think himself warranted in acting upon the
evidence . . . without higher authority. When the evidence was
completed, it was laid before the hon. and learned gentleman
[Collier], who, on the 23rd, thought there was a cause sufficient
to warrant her detention. Upon that evidence the legal advisers
of the government came to the same conclusion.

Palmer then correctly noted that this first batch of depositions contained "a great mass" of hearsay and invalid evidence
that would not justify any action against the ship. Of those initial
six depositions, only one "was good for anything at all." That
was the testimony of William Passmore, and it was sufficient "to
prove the material facts." Palmer also noted the arrival of the
two additional affidavits (numbers 7 and 8) that corroborated
Passmore's testimony. But he says these were sent on the 24th
and "were received by Russell" on the 26th. How then could
Her Majesty's government be guilty of delay? "The complete
evidence," Palmer says with some disingenuousness, "was not in
the hands of Earl Russell till the 26th, and he told Mr. Adams on
the 28th . . . that the law officers of the Crown had been consulted. He got their opinion on the 29th, the next day, and the
very same day a telegraphic message was sent down to stop the
ship."
    There the defense rested—almost. In a passage worthy
of Claude Raines in *Casablanca,* Palmer confessed himself
"shocked" at the "perversion of mind" that could entertain the
idea that Her Majesty's servants had not acted promptly and in
good faith. The *Alabama,* he explained, had escaped "only by an

evasion and a stratagem"; she slipped away by "violating the laws of the port." The Americans had nothing to complain of, he told his audience, because British actions in this instance emulated similar cases across the Atlantic. He reminded House members that much of the so-called delay was caused by the dilatory way in which Americans collected evidence against the ship and forwarded it to the proper authorities. He repeated that none of the pertinent depositions had been produced before the 21st. "They were not *all* sent in to the Foreign Office till the 26th; and the [detention] order of the government was given on the 29th" (italics added). Hearing such an account, no reasonable critic in the House could say that it was unreasonable for the government to take three days, from Saturday the 26th to Tuesday the 29th, to consult their highest legal advisers "on the *completed* state of the evidence" (italics added). Especially was it unreasonable when customs authorities, from first to last, had been adamant in their view of the insufficiency of the American case. If the present law seemed inadequate to deal with such problems, then it was "for this House to consider whether it ought to be amended."[8]

To evaluate this strange account, one has to be able to separate what is true from those things that are also true but not the whole truth. There are a few pieces of inaccurate information in the passages mentioned, and on those one must assume either that the solicitor general did not know that he misspoke or that he had been misinformed. The most egregious error was the assertion that a telegraphic order of detention for the *Alabama* went from London to Liverpool on the same day the law officers had advised Russell to issue such an order. No such order was sent on 29 July. Indeed the law officers' advice reached Russell several hours after the *Alabama* escaped.

There are strange silences in Palmer's speech. The greatest of these and the one most difficult to understand, considering who was speaking, is the absence of any mention of the illness of Sir John Harding and the resulting delay in processing the *Alabama* dossier between 23 and 29 July. Even though Palmer did not himself retrieve those papers from Harding's wife, it defies logic and credulity to think that his colleague, Atherton, who had retrieved them on the 28th, did not comment on that aspect of the case as the two of them hammered out the advice that they would give to the foreign secretary on the 29th. While a reluctance to speak in public of the misfortune of a colleague is commendable, the way that omission was covered up is difficult to excuse.

The silence about Russell's decision not to act on the advice that he received from Atherton and Palmer on 30 June may be charitably chalked up to ministerial discretion. It would have been a breach of confidentiality to reveal that the foreign secretary had had ample legal power to detain the vessel a month before she escaped. The advice of 30 June was no blank check for arbitrary legal despotism, but broadly interpreted, it would have justified a detention order until the legal technicalities of the case could be sorted out by judicial investigation. That was all the law officers had recommended at the end of June. That particular aspect of the case, incidentally, remained unknown for a long time, though if one looks hard enough it can be discovered in the papers of the Geneva arbitration tribunal, published in the early 1870s.

A brief word about Palmer's terminology in relation to Adams's initial remonstrance is needed here, though the structure of his argument and the words used in it will require extensive comment at a later point. Palmer says, not entirely truthfully it seems to me, that Adams's first complaint lacked "any evidence whatever." But on 30 June the law officers saw enough suspicious grounds in his complaint to suggest to them that "a manifest violation" of the Foreign Enlistment Act might be going on in Liverpool, and their suspicions were sufficiently aroused for them to recommend a special investigation of the circumstances surrounding the American complaint. That Russell refused to authorize that investigation was not the fault of the law officers. They do not make policy, but occasionally they must defend it as best they can.

Such was the position in which Palmer found himself in March 1863. No doubt, in a narrow legal sense, no "seizure" would have been justifiable on 30 June. But that really was not the question before the law officers. One can come much closer to the circumstances of late June and to the ambiguities in both the complaints of the Americans and in the Foreign Enlistment Act by simply inserting the word *detain* for Palmer's *seizure.* While a seizure would have been "unwarrantable," a detention to determine the truth or falsity of the American allegations might not have been. In all probability, such a detention order, had it been challenged in court, would have been overturned by British jurors. And that supposition probably would have been true if the *Alabama* had not left port on 29 July—as the law officers seem to suggest in the opinion they rendered on that day. The circumstances of the *Alabama* in June and July 1862 were analogous to those of the *Alexandra* in June 1863. The verdict in that case, as I argued in another place, was a stinging rebuff to government efforts to halt Confederate shipbuilding in the Queen's domain.[9]

One now comes to the odd way Palmer chose to refute the charge of delay. No one can reasonably believe that three days for the *Alabama* dossier to go from customs to Foreign Office to law officers and then back to Russell constituted inordinate delay. Charges to the contrary about British procrastination cannot be sustained. But I cannot accept the chronology that Palmer used to demonstrate the falsity of the accusation. In my view there was more delay than he allows, though much less than many critics of British policy have asserted. Much hinges on the matter of dates, especially one very important day, Saturday, 26 July 1862 (a day that looms large in the interpretations of Adams and Owsley and their disciples such as Dalzell).

Why is that day so important? On that day Bulloch received a mysterious telegram warning him to get the vessel out of Liverpool within forty-eight hours. Although that agent strongly denied that this tip came from any British official, many have asserted that the warning came from the prime minister or the foreign secretary or from clerks who worked for them. There can be little doubt that a warning was sent. No one knows who sent it or why it was sent on the 26th, but the source of the tip has often been identified as a Foreign Office clerk.

It becomes a matter of importance to determine what Russell and his clerks knew and when they knew it. To put the matter another way, did the office of the foreign secretary receive any vital new information on the 26th that might have triggered a warning to Bulloch? (Of course, one must assume that there was a clerk sympathetic enough to the Confederate cause to betray his trust or that Lord Russell was willing to do so.) Since no reliable evidence of that leak or ministerial tip has ever come to light, we can concentrate our attention on the flow of information to Russell and on how Palmer explicated the sequence of events by which the foreign secretary received the details of the American case against the *Alabama*.

Earlier the reader was warned about Palmer's odd way of constructing his chronology. Now we shall see why that warning was necessary. He tells us correctly that Adams's first series of depositions did not reach British officials until 22 July. That set of six affidavits included the evidence of William Passmore. For convenience, that may be designated deposition number 6. What Palmer does not say is that by that date lower-echelon London customs and treasury officials already had become concerned enough about that evidence to suggest that it be referred to the law officers. In conformity with that suggestion, depositions 1–6 were sent to the law officers early on 23 July.

Later that same day, the Americans produced two additional depositions that supported the testimony of Passmore. These may be designated as numbers 7 and 8. Later on the 23rd, these also were sent to the foreign secretary and then forwarded to the law officers, along with an opinion written by Collier on the same day. As noted, that opinion was a strong affirmation of American allegations against the *Alabama*. Let me stress — for it appears to contradict Palmer's account — that in the late evening of 23 July, British officials had received the bulk of the American evidence against that ship. By that time the law officers had received all the evidence they needed to support a detention order, as even Palmer unintentionally acknowledged (as will be seen). The key items in the American case were the deposition of Passmore, number 6, the one that Palmer said was enough "to prove the material facts"; depositions 7 and 8, which amplified and confirmed the evidence of Passmore; and — in many ways the most vital element of the American presentation — the opinion of Collier that their case was strong enough to "warrant" a seizure order. He argued that British officials had a "duty" to issue such an order. He went further and warned of possible American claims for damage if the ship destroyed Union merchant vessels.

The only element that those officials did not have — the only evidence they received on 25–26 July — was the ninth deposition. There was nothing magical about it. Henry Redden merely corroborated information the government already had. He said little that could not be gleaned from the depositions of William Passmore, Edward Roberts, and John Taylor. In short, there was little in it likely to trigger a desperate, last-minute warning to Bulloch to get his ship to sea within forty-eight hours. Two features about it, however, deserve to be noticed: It arrived at the Foreign Office on 26 July, and it was the *final* portion of the American evidence. It *completed* their case. Those two aspects of that deposition have special resonance for Palmer's version of the events of late July.

Before returning to that account, one additional piece of evidence must be introduced. It bears directly on what the solicitor general said in Parliament. At 5:30 P.M. on 23 July, George Hamilton at the treasury wrote to Austin Layard at the Foreign Office that "additional papers" had come from the Americans. These were the depositions of Roberts and Taylor plus Collier's opinion. To this document a note had been added: "This letter has attached to it a minute, written on paper stamped 'House of Commons,' in Mr. Layard's handwriting: 'I have just received this paper from the treasury. Shall I send this at once to the law-officers?' And in Lord Russell's handwriting: 'Yes, at once — J.R.' With an instruction from Mr. Layard: 'Let the covering letter be ready for my signature as soon as possible.'" Soon thereafter Layard sent "a further letter," his second of the day, to the law officers enclosing those "additional papers" and requesting a reply at their earliest convenience. The sequence of events outlined here suggests several reasons to challenge the one given by Palmer in the House of Commons.

Notice that in the lengthy extract quoted above, Palmer says that Adams "did not *complete* his evidence till the 24th, and the letter in which he sent the *last* two depositions [presumably the reference is to numbers 7 and 8] was not received at the Foreign Office till the 26th." Then he points out that the American minister "did not place the *whole* evidence on which he relied in the hands of the government till the 26th of July." A careful reader probably notices the mantralike repetition of "26 July." That recognition must be accompanied by another — the evidence that Palmer places on the words *complete, last,* and *whole* when referring to the transmission of Adams's depositions and evidence. As the reader will recognize, what Palmer says is true, except for one small mistake. It may be useful to correct the mistake first. It was the *last* deposition, number nine, which was received on the 26th. It *completed* the American evidence and provided the *final* part of the indictment against the ship. That is, it constituted the *whole* evidence upon which the Americans relied to move the government to action against the ship.

If this dossier had arrived all in one package on the 26th — as Owsley and Adams believed — it might lend credence to the story of a spy in high office or the supposition of a clerk who was sympathetic to the South and willing to warn its agents of danger by sending a telegraph to Bulloch on this date. As noted, that is not the way the case evolved. To repeat: The ninth and final deposition was in fact received at the Foreign Office on the 26th and was sent in some urgency to the law officers that same day. It may have been the trigger that finally led Atherton to retrieve all the prior *Alabama* papers from Sir John Harding's wife, who had neglected to inform her husband's superiors of his disabling illness while those important papers lay unattended on his desk from 23 July to the evening of 28 July.

Palmer's reference to materials that arrived at the Foreign Office on the 26th had a double flaw. He did not mention that two of the depositions were merely copies of documents already sent to Russell and the law officers three days earlier. These documents had traveled to their destination via the House of Commons late on the evening of 23 July. They bore the endorsements that Russell and Layard had affixed to them to expedite their passage to the law officers. These materials consisted of the depositions of Roberts and Taylor and the opinion that Collier had written for the Americans on 23 July. These documents reached their destination on the 23rd, not the 26th, although the *final* piece of evidence did reach Russell on that day.

That "last" deposition — only *one* could be so described — was that of Henry Redden. It was the only new material received on the 26th, and it did not significantly strengthen the American case. In reaching their decision of 29 July, Atherton and Palmer lumped it with the affidavits of Passmore, Roberts, and Taylor as one of the four main pieces of evidence against the *Alabama*. In a narrow, technical sense, "the *complete* evidence was not in the hands of Earl Russell till the 26th," as Palmer says. He does not say that the bulk of that evidence — all the material that the law officers needed to evaluate American allegations of unlawful activity on the Merseyside — was in the hands of Her Majesty's government on 23 July. Unfortunately, at that inconvenient time, those hands belonged to the distracted Sir John Harding and his distraught wife. That sad fact does much to explain the *Alabama*'s escape. On such unhappy accidents, history often turns. Not plots, not tips, not conspiracy. Just chance: a madman and his sad wife. Not much complicity in that.

There are two other strange aspects of Palmer's account that should be mentioned. The first appears to be a simple mistake. He says that Collier's first advice to the Americans, the opinion he wrote on 16 July, "was not communicated" to the British government. We now know that it was, but the date of that transmission remains unclear. The document became part of the voluminous records of the Geneva arbitration, and it is reprinted in a number of British collections. My reading of the case and my concern for chronology leads me to suspect that Collier's first opinion, or knowledge of it, had reached some British officials before his second one did. That would narrow the time of presentation to the period between the 16th and 22nd of July, with a great probability for the latter part of that period, say the 21st or 22nd. Moreover, there is reason to believe that the first Collier opinion triggered the chain reaction that propelled the American case from the lower rungs of Britain's bureaucracy to the higher level of the law officers of the Crown late on 22 July or early the next day. I have no documentary evidence for my supposition. All that one can say for certain is that *before* Collier's opinion of the 23rd was written, someone or something had speeded up the ponderous machinery of Her Majesty's government. The only possible catalyst for such a reaction — as I reconstruct the case — was Collier's first opinion.

A second point that requires attention revolves around Palmer's peculiar way with words. Toward the end of the lengthy passage quoted above, he says that when "the evidence was completed" it was given to Collier on the 23rd and that he concluded on the basis of it that there was sufficient reason "to warrant" a detention order for the *Alabama*. Then he says something that requires comment: "Upon that evidence the legal advisers of the government came to the same conclusion." What evidence was *that*? In this context of the passage quoted, it can only refer to the evidence upon which Collier had advised the Americans on the 23rd that they had a good case. It will be remembered that by that day, he had considered depositions 1–8. The ninth deposition did not reach British authorities until the 25th or 26th, and it is not known whether Collier said anything about it.

If, as seems clear, the Crown's highest legal advisers "came to the same conclusion" as Collier had on the 23rd, there was no need for that ninth affidavit. It means that no information critical to formulating a government response to Merseyside mysteries was needed after the 23rd. So all those references in Palmer's speech to the importance of the 26th and that *last* and *final* and *complete* American evidence arriving on that day were legal legerdemain, tricks with mirrors, an illusion created by a masterful word magician. However one might criticize that speech, its power was very great.

*   *   *   *   *

Palmer continues to mesmerize those who study the strange circumstances of the *Alabama*'s escape from Liverpool. Owsley and Adams were not the only ones to fall under its spell. Its powerful, baleful influence still resonates in much of the literature of the foreign response to the American Civil War, even among writers who have not read Palmer's speech. They have learned from it by hearing its echoes in the works of Adams, Owsley, and Dalzell.

Sadly, at the heart of their misinterpretations of the escape of the *Alabama* is a simple misreading of a key piece of evidence, one that has been available to researchers since it was published in the *Hansard Parliamentary Debates* in 1863. Surely, the time has come to banish a pernicious error of Civil War diplomacy. Palmer's emphasis on 26 July has misled historians to overvalue the telegram that Bulloch received that day and leap to the conclusion that it was a governmental leak.

The unhappy legacy of Adams and Owsley on our understanding of Civil War diplomacy is not confined to the misreading of the evidence for the escape of the *Alabama*. In their respective works other errors—and more grievous ones—have distorted the way historians have approached the international dimension of that war.[10] To that larger subject—to those distorting errors—I hope to return in another place and at another time.

FIVE | CAPTAIN BUTCHER'S MEMOIR OF THE ALABAMA'S ESCAPE

*O*N THE morning of 29 July 1862, a stately ship slipped down the river Mersey from her birthplace in Birkenhead and headed for the Irish Sea. Thus began the CSS *Alabama*'s rendezvous with history. The curious circumstances surrounding that abrupt departure have never been fully explained. That story remains obscure at many points, and it still retains elements of mystery.[1] Many of those engaged in that enterprise carefully covered their tracks. Despite several extensive searches, the papers of the plot master have never come to light. Many had reason to disclaim complicity. To get their ship away, Confederates had to forestall the countermeasures of Union adversaries and avoid arousing the suspicions of British officials. In addition, they had to circumvent the prohibitions of Queen Victoria's 1861 Proclamation of Neutrality and the ambiguities of the Foreign Enlistment Act of 1819. Southern success in surmounting those formidable obstacles has created one of the most intriguing chapters in the international history of the American Civil War.[2]

That story has a vast literature. The official records of three governments are voluminous, and many of them have never been properly examined. Many participants have left accounts of their roles in the cruiser's career. Those of her captain, Raphael Semmes, and the Confederate naval agent, James D.

Bulloch, are perhaps the best known of such works. A number of sailors who served during her cruise have also tried to tell her story; Arthur Sinclair's *Two Years on the Alabama* represents the best of that genre. Then, too, a large number of historians — the present editors among them — have tried to relate the epic saga of the South's search for sea power in Europe and the *Alabama*'s place in that drama.[3] But all of those accounts are unsatisfactory in one way or another. Until now, an important part of Civil War naval history has been missing; the testimony of a vital witness has never been heard.

The crucial role played by an unassuming English sea captain in the events of 29 July 1862 has often been noted and sometimes praised. But his own account of the "precipitous departure" from Liverpool and of her commissioning in the Azores has never before been published with explanatory scholarly apparatus. To appreciate the significance of this document, one must see it in the context in which his story unfolded. Like many other participants in the escape, Butcher does not — indeed, he cannot — tell all we would like to know. He modestly does not emphasize just how vital his role was in the escape. His pages convey almost nothing of his decision to take command. Nor does he expound on the costly consequences of the conversion of his ship into a Confederate cruiser. After all, the ship that Butcher helped unleash virtually destroyed the Union merchant marine and cost his country millions of dollars in postwar damage claims.

The *Alabama*'s escape brought the careers of two men, one English, one American, into brief but crucial juxtaposition. James D. Bulloch of Georgia had, like many of his professional colleagues, "gone South" when the War Between the States broke out. To the new cause he brought a wide array of talents and maritime experience: the genial manners of a prominent Southern seafaring family, a distinguished record of service in the Old Navy of the United States, and a long career in business and maritime enterprises in New York City (where he was related to the socially prominent Roosevelt family).[4] He possessed a wide knowledge of Atlantic and Caribbean ports and routes. In a serious diplomatic crisis in Cuba during the 1850s, he handled himself with commendable courage. He was an astute judge of men, and he possessed in full measure that trait of character best described as rectitude. Though he had extensive financial and family interests in the North, his head and heart, as he phrased it, led him to resign his commission and follow his state into the Confederacy. It was a momentous choice for the thirty-eight-year-old Bulloch.

When he presented himself to the Confederate naval secretary, Stephen Russell Mallory, he received an important mission. Mallory wanted him to go to Europe to procure a modern navy for the new nation. It was an awesome task, and we still know too little of how that decision came about. It was, however, a fortunate meeting of man and mission. Bulloch's struggle to surmount the obstacles to its successful conclusion still staggers the imagination. He came perilously close to giving Jefferson Davis a naval weapon of considerable potency. During the war he gave a virtuosic performance as a naval officer at the cutting edge of statecraft. None, save the sainted Robert E. Lee, made a greater contribution to the Confederate cause. And even though he himself left a magnificent record of his wartime exploits in Europe, that contribution still remains largely unrecognized.[5]

Bulloch arrived in Liverpool in June 1861. He came with a daring plan to redress the naval balance of power between North and South. To compensate for the South's lack of industrial resources, he planned to exploit European technology to buy and build a modern navy. His plan had three main parts: (1) to build a fleet of commerce raiders to sweep enemy trade from the world's oceans; (2) to construct a flotilla of ironclad rams to smash the Union's blockade of the Confederate coast; and (3) to procure a squadron of specially designed steam blockade-runners to supply the South with the sinews of war. And he had to do all these things without challenging British neutrality. All in all, it was an imaginative approach to the problems of Southern sea power. Bulloch had rare talents for implementing it.[6]

When he arrived in England, he immediately set to work on the cruiser component of his plan. Within weeks he had established good relations with important financial and business leaders in Liverpool and Birkenhead. Among the chief of these

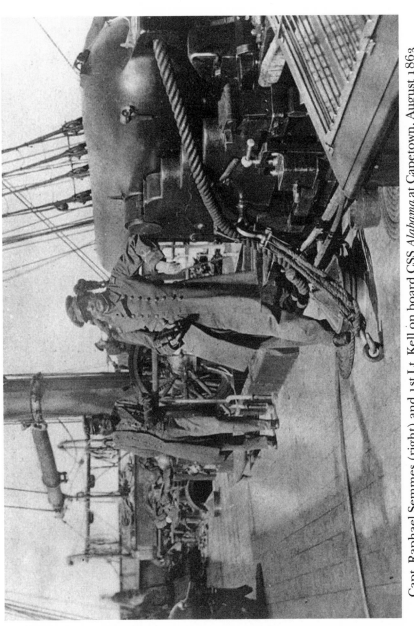

Capt. Raphael Semmes (right) and 1st Lt. Kell on board CSS *Alabama* at Capetown, August 1863 (Naval Historical Center).

contacts were the firms of Fraser, Trenholm and Laird. In August he signed a contract with the latter company for construction of the 290th ship to be built in their famous Birkenhead shipyard. That vessel, destined to become one of history's most famous ships, was designed and built with special care, perhaps because Bulloch himself expected to command her. The vessel incorporated several innovative features to fit her for the special tasks the South had in mind for her. She had a unique combination of steam and sail power to enable her to stay at sea for long periods and lessen her dependence on coal. A special condensing apparatus and cooling tanks assured the crew of adequate fresh water. In addition, her propeller could be disengaged and lifted aboard to lessen drag while under sail. The contract, which is extant, spells out in loving detail the careful planning that went into her construction.[7]

As she grew gracefully toward the Birkenhead sky, all could see that she was becoming a thing of beauty, a magnificent testimonial to the men and machines of Merseyside. Though built primarily for speed, she would acquire a potent punch. It is important to note that she acquired her armament beyond the Queen's jurisdiction. After leaving Liverpool, she was "equipped" in the Azores, and her subsequent two-year cruise made her the most successful commerce-destroyer of all times.

But it is a long, long time from contract to completion, in this case from August 1861 to July 1862. During that period Bulloch resolved a number of difficulties that threatened his ship. First, he had to determine with some precision the legal barriers to his work. These were many and ambiguous: It might be said, as the British foreign secretary did on one occasion, that no one in England *really* knew the limits of the law regarding belligerent shipbuilding in a neutral nation. Although deadly dangers lurked in the prohibitions of the Enlistment Act, Bulloch's local solicitor, Frederick S. Hull, did a superb job of guiding his client around them. For his part, Bulloch was always scrupulously careful to stay within the limits specified by Hull. Second, other responsibilities of his mission took Bulloch away from Liverpool for extended periods. At one time, November 1861–March 1862, he had to return to the Confederacy, and this absence slowed work on his cruiser, for it prevented his personal supervision of that special ship. Third, communications with superiors in Richmond were often snarled. That difficulty, in turn, led to considerable misunderstanding about who would take this ship to sea.

Beyond doubt, however, the principal obstacle was posed by Bulloch's Union adversary in Liverpool, American consul Thomas Haines Dudley. That redoubtable foe had arrived in Liverpool soon after Bulloch did. From the start they were engaged in an epic David and Goliath struggle in the bars and brothels, the docks and dives of Merseyside. Dudley was determined to thwart Bulloch's efforts to procure ships in England, and he had the North's ample financial resources to assist him in that work. Furious over his earlier failure to prevent the departure of Bulloch's first ship (the *Florida*), he began to mount a formidable array of forces in June and July 1862 to prevent the second Confederate cruiser from leaving Liverpool.[8]

Those efforts centered on what Dudley saw as his adversary's toughest English foe, the Foreign Enlistment Act. In that antiquated statute, Dudley saw a means for British officials to detain and condemn the Mersey mystery ship. In the summer of 1862, he intensified American efforts to convince Crown officials that Confederate ship construction on the Mersey contravened Her Majesty's neutrality. His superior in London regarded such activity as a threat to Anglo-American wartime relations. The legal dimensions of the struggle between Dudley and Bulloch — between Confederate naval procurement and British neutrality — are exceedingly complex. They cannot be examined here, though the reader must remember that the arcane debates on international law did much to shape the course of events in July 1862. Indeed, some say the law's delay made the *Alabama*'s escape possible. On this subject one must not be too dogmatic, however. Much depended on precise definition of the law's provisions, and these were in short supply as the crisis crested in late July. Dudley and his superior, the American minister in London, Charles Francis Adams, believed the evidence against the ship was conclusive. They were convinced that Confederate shipbuilding in Liverpool contravened the law. Moreover, in late July, they stepped up efforts to have customs officials and their superiors detain the Mersey mystery ship for legal condemnation.

Of course, such activity did not go unnoticed in the Confederate camp. There, they had, so Bulloch said, the means of knowing with some certainty what was in store for their ship. And so when he received information on 26 July from a "most reliable source" that his ship was in danger and must leave Liverpool within forty-eight hours, he was ready and speeded up his own carefully contrived countermeasures.

One man played a vital role in Bulloch's plans to thwart Union efforts to prevent the *Alabama*'s escape from Liverpool. To comply with port regulations and to provide a cloak of respectability for his mystery ship as she prepared for sea, he had put her under the command of a captain who held a British Master's Certificate. The person chosen for the post would hold the fate of the venture in his hands at its point of maximum danger for the Confederate cause. Not only would this acting captain have to have the necessary professional qualifications; he would also need to possess personal qualities of a rare and peculiar kind.

Outfitting the ship for an unspecified purpose and recruiting a crew for an unknown destination required nice discernment and delicate inventiveness. A careless word in the wrong company, an unwise order for improper equipment, a minor infraction of maritime law or customs regulations would put the vessel in grave peril. All preparations would have to be carried out under the eyes of skeptical customs agents and suspicious Union spies. It was a task to test the mettle of any man. Matthew Butcher did not disappoint. He deserves to rank as one of the great heroes of the Confederate navy in Europe. And yet he is all but unknown to students of that subject.[9]

Butcher was born on 12 December 1832 to a seafaring family in the East Anglian port of Great Yarmouth. In the 1840s the family moved to Liverpool to take advantage of that city's burgeoning economy. A key element in that prosperity was the transatlantic trade, especially in cotton. The city seemed to have an insatiable need for sailors, and before his eleventh birthday, Butcher had signed articles as a boy-seaman. Like his peers, he served his apprenticeship on sailing vessels, but again like others in that age of transition in maritime technology, he felt the lure of steam power. He joined the Liverpool-based Cunard Line, where he soon became a second officer on their Royal Mail steamers. In time he became familiar with Atlantic and Caribbean routes, especially the runs between New York, Havana, and Nassau. On one of those latter voyages, probably in 1857, he chanced to meet in Cuba a young American engaged in similar enterprises. That prewar meeting with James D. Bulloch was destined to have historic consequences for both of them.

Butcher earned his coveted Master's Certificate before he was twenty-five, an age too young for him to command one of Cunard's vessels. In 1859, to increase his professional training, he joined the Royal Naval Reserves of the merchant marine. Vigorous practice in gunnery and habits of command — as well as an affiliation with the Royal Navy — added new dimensions and luster to his maritime qualifications. Despite his credentials and experience, his superiors still had not promoted him to command a Cunarder when war broke out in America.

We can only guess at the circumstances and motives that led Butcher to cast his fortune with the Confederacy and to become a vital part of their Merseyside enterprises. Because of the patterns of prewar trade, Liverpool had close connections with Southern cotton interests. Soon after war began, it was said that Merseyside flew more Confederate flags than Richmond. As a member of the city's mercantile community, Butcher would know of the profits of blockade-running and of the participation of his peers in it. Nor was it any secret in the city's commercial community that Bulloch did business at the firm of Fraser, Trenholm or that Fraser, Trenholm had a lively interest in cotton and the Confederate cause. It was, after all, an affiliate of a prominent Southern mercantile house. There is no evidence that the editors have been able to find, however, to suggest that in the first year of the war Butcher had become an active supporter of the South.

But it does not strain credulity to suppose that his inclinations were leading him in that direction. At any rate, when the call for Southern service came, he was ready. In May 1862, a Cunard shipping agent, George Barnett, brought Butcher to Bulloch's "office" at Fraser, Trenholm. As chief of European naval procurement for the Confederacy, Bulloch had a problem. With his second cruiser nearing completion across the river in Birkenhead, he needed someone to take that ship to sea. The selection of the right man was, he tells us, a matter of "grave" concern. It was necessary to tell that man "more than what appeared on the surface." The job required "professional competence, prudence, control over the tongue, and absolute integrity." Less than an hour's conversation convinced Bulloch that he had found his man. He never regretted the "prodigious trust" he had placed in the character of M. J. Butcher.[10]

The *Alabama*'s first captain completed his mission to perfection. Against heavy odds he got the ship out of British jurisdiction just barely ahead of a Whitehall detention order that would have ended her career before it began. He took the embryonic cruiser safely to the Azores, installed much of the "equipment" that he had wisely neglected in Liverpool, and turned her over to Raphael Semmes nearly ready to begin one of the most successful commerce-destroying careers in history. He had reason to be pleased with his contribution to the Confederate cause as he returned to England with the man who had entrusted that ship to his command. What, one wonders, did Bulloch and Butcher talk about as they headed back to Liverpool after watching Semmes sail away with their ship?

There is a footnote to Butcher's involvement with the Confederacy's most famous warship. Two years after the war, he married his childhood sweetheart. And family legend tells us that fees and wages gained from wartime Confederate enterprises gave the marriage a sound financial base. They had six children, and Butcher continued a successful sea captain's career, much of it in the Far East. By 1889 he was himself a shipowner.

For most of his postwar life, Butcher practiced that reticence which had so endeared him to Bulloch. Of course, as a British citizen at the time of the postwar *Alabama* claims controversy, prudence about his role in getting that ship to sea was probably well advised. But in December 1880, on his forty-eighth birthday, in the cabin of the SS *Moray* as she lay in Hong Kong harbor, he composed his chapter of Civil War history. What prompted him to break his silence and revisit one of the most dramatic incidents in that war's naval history must remain a mystery, as must the identity of the person or persons who led him to record his version of that momentous adventure. It may be that he yearned to relive that grand and glorious moment of his youth. Or he may have sought a way to lay to rest those ghosts of a lost cause in which he had played such a memorable part. In all probability, we shall never know the real contours of his Confederate connections.

Still, all students of Confederate naval affairs must be grateful for this fragment of history. To be sure, his account, like so many postwar recollections, contains some distortions, some inaccuracies, even some effort at self-glorification. But, for all its imperfections, it adds one important element to the mosaic of Civil War history and brings students of that subject a little closer to understanding how Bulloch, against all odds, got the *Alabama* safely to sea. Her first captain speaks from a perspective no one else can match.

BUTCHER'S MEMOIR

I have much pleasure in complying with your request to give you in writing as circumstantial an account as my memory will allow me to do of the escape of the Confederate cruiser *Alabama,* or "290," as she was called at the time, her intended name not having been made public. I must premise my relation by asking you to excuse the absence of dates, as my journal of that period is at home and I cannot trust my memory to give them accurately.[11] It was in the month of May that while occupying the position of chief officer of one of the Cunard Company's steamers, then laying in Liverpool, I was sent for by a friend, who said that he wished to see me on business of a special nature.[12] On going to his office he told me that a steamer which might be adapted to war purposes was being built for a foreign government and that the agents of that government were desirous of obtaining the services of an English officer, who might be relied upon for prudence and good faith, to take command, and having fitted her out according to instructions, which would be given by the accredited agents of the government for whom she was intended, to procure a crew and proceed to whatever place he might be ordered to; that a very liberal remuneration would be given and a commission in their navy also, if desired. I at once felt quite sure that the government alluded to was the Confederate, and I said that I would gladly take charge of the vessel, but that I should not think of serving under a foreign flag. After some further conversation my friend said that if I would call on the following morning he would introduce me to those who had full authority in the matter and then a final decision could be arrived at. I accordingly went the next day and was introduced to the Confederate agent who had contracted for the building of the ship, and after some half hour's conversation with him we went to the builder's yard and there I saw the "290," which had just been launched and was introduced to the builder as the commander. I at once took charge and hastened the outfit as much as possible, for even at that time we were aware that danger might arise from delay and a careful watch was kept on the course of events. It was some six weeks after first taking charge that I had just reached home, on a Saturday afternoon, that a note was brought to me from the builder requesting my immediate attendance at the office. I lost no time in getting there, as I felt sure that some intimation must have been received from London of intended action on the part of the government, and on arriving found the Confederate commissioner and the superintending engineer of the builders and the builder.[13]

Mr. L—— then told us that he had just received a telegram from London warning us that no time should be lost in getting the vessel away from Liverpool, as the American Minister, Mr. Adams, had laid such evidence of the ships being intended for war purposes before the officials of our government as had decided them upon taking immediate steps to prevent her departure.[14] A consultation then took place, and it was determined to work night and day, by which means everything essential could be finished in forty-eight hours. Accordingly, on the Monday evening following we steamed out of the Birkenhead dock and anchored in the river, no one having yet molested us. On Tuesday morning we were to go outside the river for a trial of the engines and return during the afternoon to complete our outfit. After receiving a small party of ladies and gentlemen on board, and with a steam tug in attendance, we left the Mersey about 10 A.M., and spent a very pleasant day in the bay, the trials of the engines being very satisfactory and the speed of the vessel also.[15] It was during this time and when some of the party were suggesting that it was getting time to turn homewards that it occurred to me that as the machinery was in good working order, and the work still remaining to be done was not absolutely essential, and as there was increasing danger in every hour of delay, that it would be the wisest to keep her out of port and remain at one of the numerous anchorages along the Welsh coast between the river Dee and Holyhead, and as I had now become as anxious as any one for the success of the enterprise, I made this suggestion to the Confederate Commissioner, who was on board, viz.; That under the advice of the pilot we should fix upon an anchorage as unfrequented as possible, and that having done so we should induce the ladies and gentlemen on board to proceed home by the tug, by telling them that we wished further trials of the engines, which would delay our return until 8 or 9 P.M.; that I would give him a list of all I required to complete the outfit of stores and also the address of a man whom I had employed to pick up a crew, and that he could engage the tug steamer to bring them, not telling the master of the tug where he was going until he was out of the river and it was quite out of his power to communicate with anyone.[16] The commissioner fell in with the idea at once, thought it would be decidedly the best thing if it could be done, if the pilot were reliable. I assured him he need not fear on that account, and then calling the pilot we settled that Moelfra Bay, about thirty miles from the entrance to the Mersey, would be the best place. It was then intimated to the visitors that the ship would not return until late, and that they had better take advantage of the tug, which was going back at once, which they all did, and I at once steamed away with the "290" for Moelfra, where we came to an anchor at about 8 P.M.

Now having placed the "290" in safety I must relate to you what happened to the tug, and how the commissioner prospered.[17] On arriving in the river they found a man-of-war's boat awaiting the return of the "290," with a warrant for her seizure, and as the ship did not return the tug was closely watched, and when the next morning, in obedience to instructions received from the Confederate commissioner, she came to the landing stage and proceeded to take in a small cargo of barrels, cases, bags, etc., and also a number of sailors the officer in charge of the man-of-war's boat went on board and asked the master of the tug what it all meant and where he was going to. He replied that he neither knew nor cared where he was going to, that he was engaged by the hour and he knew he should be paid, and that was all that he concerned himself about. Finding that no information could be got from the people connected with the tug, he made his boat fast to the stern of the tug, resolving to go wherever she went. Shortly afterwards the commissioner came on board, and seeing that all the things ordered were on board, gave orders to proceed out of the river. When the tug master told the commissioner of the inquiries made by the officer in charge of the man-of-war's boat and of his having made his boat fast to the stern, the commissioner suggested to him that he might oblige them to let go by setting on full speed, which he did, and those in the boat were glad enough to let go before they got as far as the mouth of the river to save themselves from sinking. After getting outside the commissioner told the tug master to proceed as rapidly as he could to Moelfra Bay, where they arrived and came alongside about 10 P.M. and we at once commenced transferring her cargo to the "290."

Not having been able to engage a crew in the legitimate manner we then had to draw up a written agreement, giving it as much of the legal form as we could and then assembling the whole crew read it over to them in which the voyage was described as going to "Havana," and offering the usual advance wages and allotments to wives and mothers, and then called upon them to come forward and sign.[18] Most of them did join, but some twenty or thirty refused; however, I managed to get a crew of ninety-seven all told; seventeen of them had never been to sea before, and many of those who had were a decidedly "bad lot." We did not get this matter finally settled until 2 A.M., left Moelfra Bay, and as we knew that the American frigate *Tuscarora* had been cruising in the southern entrance of the channel for the last three days with the special intention of intercepting us if we succeeded in getting out of Liverpool we went north.[19] Again we had a very narrow escape, for six hours afterwards, at 8 A.M., the *Tuscarora* came into Moelfra Bay looking for us, having received information through a spy who had escaped on shore the previous day and sent a telegram to Mr. Adams at once.[20] Although the weather was bad we made rapid progress through the night, steaming thirteen knots per hour, and the following morning the weather changed and became very fine, and you may be sure we felt much pleased with having got away so successfully. At 5 P.M. we hailed a fishing boat off the entrance to the port of Londonderry, into which we put the pilot and Confederate commissioner, who had accompanied us so far, and then steamed out into the Atlantic bound for Praya Bay, in the island of Terceira, one of the Azores.[21] On the second day after leaving the Irish coast the weather became very bad, but the "290" proved herself an excellent sea boat and very comfortable. During our nine days' passage we were employed in getting things into their proper places and finding out the character and capabilities of our crew. Although we had amongst our large number many that were almost worthless, yet we had many good men, and soon succeeded in getting something like order and discipline on board. Among the best and most reliable of the men were eight Savannah pilots, who had formed part of the crew of a bark that had run the blockade of Savannah and arrived safely in Liverpool.[22]

I must now tell you that the armament, with ammunition and about 300 tons of coal, had been dispatched about a month previously from London, in a bark which had been purchased for the purpose, the master having orders to proceed as quickly as he could to Praya Bay, and cruise about in the neighbourhood, if he found that the steamer had not arrived, and also having a code of private signals previously arranged, in order that each might recognize the other.[23] As it happened I got there first, and during the week that elapsed before the bark came in we were fully occupied in getting everything on board into good working order.[24] Praya Bay is on the east side of the island, and as may be supposed a quite unfrequented locality, the settlement being nothing more than a fishing village, having about a thousand inhabitants.[25] Of course, a Portuguese official boarded us immediately after anchoring, and desired to know who we were and why we came there, instead of proceeding to the proper port on the other side of the island. I asked him into the cabin, and after setting wine and cigars before him told him that she was a gunboat built in England for the Spaniards and that we were taking her to Havana for delivery. He evidently did not believe much of what I told him, excepting that she was a gunboat, and quietly remarked that we had a larger crew than seemed necessary just to navigate the vessel to Havana; to this I replied that the vessel had to be delivered within a certain time and that most of the men he saw were tradesmen, who were there to complete work that was unfinished when we left. He then told me that he hoped I would not allow any of my men to go on shore, as they had no soldiers in the town, and I assured him that I did not intend to allow such a thing; that I had only anchored there because the machinery was a little out of order and after the engineers had made everything right we should proceed on our voyage. I also told him that I would be very much pleased if he would arrange with the townspeople to sell me fresh meat, vegetables, fruit and fish, for which I would pay him or them in English gold as they were brought on board each day. This at once put him into good humour, and seeing a stroke of profitable business to be done he became quite friendly, and before leaving assured me that we should not be molested and asked me if he might bring a few of his friends on board in the afternoon to look at the vessel. I at once assented to this, and accordingly in the afternoon entertained about a dozen of the inhabitants with champagne, cakes, etc., and sent them all on shore in a high good humour. Of course, we were very anxious, as we did not know what military force was on the island or what men-of-war were in the harbour, and as we had no papers of any kind, not even a port clearance or register, we could have been seized by men-of-war of any nation, and consequently a good lookout was kept night and day and steam always ready, and also always prepared to slip the cable and be off, for I had determined that if any attempt was made to seize us, and especially by a Federal cruiser, I would do my best to run into Lisbon and give the ship up to the senior English officer there. Happily, however, we were not disturbed, and the only demonstration made against us was by the Portuguese authorities, who, we observed on the second day, mounted three guns (about eighteen pounds) on a small and partly ruinous fort close to the town and within a quarter of a mile of where we lay, and for the rest of the time we observed that a soldier was always stationed there.

After being at anchor six days the next morning at daylight a sailing vessel was observed in the offing, and you may be sure she was anxiously watched and every preparation made for running away if anything looked suspicious. At last we could see that it was a bark steering in for the bay and having a signal flying. This, of course, raised our expectations greatly, for not only was I extremely anxious with regard to the final success of the enterprise, but many of my crew were showing symptoms of discontent, and some among them I knew were ready for any treachery, having been heard to wish that a Yankee man-of-war might come and capture us, and so I was greatly pleased to see at last that the signal was the one hoped for, and that if the weather kept fine another important step towards success would be made by having arms, ammunition and coals on board.[26] As soon as the bark came in I went on board and arranged with the master to haul alongside at once and commence taking on board the guns. The Portuguese officials, seeing the bark come in and communication taking place between us, became very excited and came off and warned us that we were acting illegally and that they would lose no time in sending a messenger to the Governor to represent our illegal practices. This, of course, only made me more anxious than ever to complete the work, and now also the weather became unsettled, and the wind, which had been westerly ever since our arrival, showed signs of veering round to the eastward, which would make it impossible to keep the bark alongside; so we worked with a will. The first gun we got on board was the heaviest, weighing five tons, and while it was suspended in the tackles both ships began to roll a little and, as luck would have it, in opposite ways, which, as the gun at this time was between the two ships and held by tackles from both vessels, was a very severe strain upon the gear, and at one moment I thought certainly we should lose it. However, we managed to land it safely on our decks, and the rest came on board with comparative ease. Each gun, carriage and implements were in a separate case, marked and numbered according to a list that I possessed, consequently I knew the contents of each case as it came on board, and as we took them on board we broke up the cases and throwing the pieces overboard put the contents of each in its proper place. As soon as the Portuguese, who were closely watching us from the shore, observed the broken cases thrown overboard they sent out boats to gather them up, and they took a careful note of all marks and numbers found on them.

As the vessels lay very uneasily together it was well into the second day before we got the whole on board, and then the coal remained. I was now getting very anxious to see a steamer with Captain Semmes and his staff of officers to take her over and commission her as a Confederate man-of-war. We had just commenced coaling when the lookout reported a steamer's smoke on the horizon, and you will understand how anxious and excited we felt, for there were very many on board who were deeply interested and extremely anxious for success[,] and to be captured now, with guns mounted, ammunition on board, and a fair stock of coals already in the bunkers, would have been doubly disappointing. At last, to my intense joy, I could make out the well-known signal, to which, in answer, I hoisted the new Confederate ensign, with which we had supplied ourselves in Liverpool, and I went out in the boat and met the steamship *Bahama* as she came into the anchorage, and you can judge how pleased Captain Semmes and his officers all were when I told them how successful we had been in getting everything ready for them.[27] Captain Semmes returned with me to the "290" and inspected the vessel and armament, which I may as well say here consisted of a ninety-five hundredweight or solid sixty-eight pounds shot gun aft, a Blakely one hundred [110] pounds shot gun amidships, and three thirty-two pounders on each side as broadside guns, making eight in all. The wind had now come in from the east, and though light caused sufficient swell in the bay to make it hardly possible for the vessels to lay any longer side by side and Captain Semmes proposed going round to the other side of the island to get smoother water. I should tell you that on asking Captain Semmes if he would take charge at once he said he would rather that I should keep charge until I had completed the transfer of coal, and then, when all was on board, he would relieve me of my responsibility. We took the bark in tow and proceeded about 6 P.M. for the lee side of the island, with the view of going into Horta Bay, the proper port, for by this time I had found out that there was not even a Portuguese gunboat in the port, but there was a rumor that an American ship-of-war was coming shortly. We were steaming slowly into the bay about 8 P.M., with the bark in tow, when, without any previous warning, a shotted gun was fired at us, the shot passing close to the foremast.

Captain Semmes was standing not far from me on the bridge, and I asked him if he would advise me to continue going into the port, and he replied that he thought I might as well do so, at all events, until they showed further hostility. As soon as the gun was fired at us the bark let go his ropes and sailed out; the steamship *Bahama,* which was following us, also turned round and went outside, but we went in and came to anchor. One more gun was fired, but we were not struck, and afterwards all remained quiet. At daylight the bark came in and anchored close to us and the harbourmaster came off to ask what our business was, and when we told him that we had purchased the bark's cargo of coal and only wanted to transfer the remaining part of it, he told us that it was against the regulations of the port and could not be done. As there was no object in setting the authorities at defiance, we made up our minds to tow the bark out of the harbour and finish our work under the lee of the island in the smoothest water we could find. Before getting away, however, a boat came off with three official-looking envelopes, bearing the inscription "On Her Majesty's service," and addressed to the masters of the three vessels flying the British ensign, and calling upon us to bring our ship's papers to the British Consulate, and there to explain our conduct in Praya Bay. I thought it would be as well to call and see the Consul, even though I could not offer any (to him) satisfactory explanation. This I did, and had a very pleasant interview, for, as it was out of his power to detain us, he accepted the situation pleasantly. I then called upon the Portuguese Governor and complained that on the previous evening a shotted gun had been fired from the fort at a peaceful merchant ship under my command when entering Horta Bay. The Governor was a very pleasant young man; he was profuse in his apologies, declaring that the commander of the fort could not have been aware that the gun was loaded, or he would never have ordered it to be fired, and that it was only intended to remind us that we should not enter the port after sunset. Of course I thanked him and said that I was quite sure it was a mistake, and then left and came on board.

We then hove up our anchors, and taking the bark again in tow went outside and took in the rest of the coal, and when all was completed and the decks washed down, the hands were piped aft and Captain Semmes and his officers appeared in the Confederate naval uniform; then, mounting on the breech of one of the broadside guns Captain Semmes made a very stirring speech, telling the men of the purpose for which the ship was fitted out and how well adapted she was for that purpose, and that he now took her over and commissioned her by the authority of his government as a Confederate man-of-war. At this time the Confederate ensign was hoisted and after three ringing cheers for the ship and the cause, Captain Semmes invited the men to come forward and enter the service by signing the articles which were laid out for that purpose by the paymaster's clerk, at the same time telling them that those who did not wish to join would be paid for the time they had served and sent home to Liverpool in the steamship *Bahama*. A very lively scene took place and several of the officers went among the men painting the nature of the service in glowing colours and recommending them to join, but in no case was there the least approach to compulsion or intimidation. At length a total crew of

The *Alabama* drawn from a description given by Captain Hagar of the *Brilliant* (*Harper's Weekly*, 1 November 1862, Bulloch, *Secret Service*). The original caption in *Harper's Weekly* is less friendly to the *Alabama*; it is "The pirate *Alabama* alias 290, certified to be correct by Captain Hagar of the *Brilliant* whose ship is burning in the background."

eighty-four were entered on the articles, and as several of these had wives or mothers in Liverpool allotments of half-pay had to be given them and these enclosed in letters from the men for transmission by the *Bahama.* All this occupied some time, and it was quite dark when we bade Captain Semmes and his officers good-bye and heartily wished them success.[28]

I should have said ere this that the Confederate commissioner met the *Bahama* on her arrival in the Mersey and accompanied Captain Semmes to Terceira. When all finished, the mail bag made up and all our good-byes said, the commissioner and myself left the then called *Alabama* and took passage back to Liverpool by the steamship *Bahama,* where we arrived in all safety after an uneventful passage of seven days.[29] Thus began and ended my connection with the now celebrated *Alabama.*[30] I think I have succeeded in telling you the whole of the proceedings, and I am only sorry that the absence of my note-books renders it impossible to give you the dates.

Hongkong, December 12th 1880.

SIX | RAPHAEL SEMMES AND THE CHALLENGE AT CHERBOURG

*M*UCH about the challenge at Cherbourg remains obscure. In part, this lack of clarity is simply the result of a general neglect of Confederate naval history. Until recently it has remained about where it was left by James Soley and Thomas Scharf late in the nineteenth century.[1] Fortunately, this has begun to change. For instance, the discovery of the wreckage of the *Alabama* by French divers in the 1980s has stimulated research on that ship.

The other source of the problem is more surprising. Many of the circumstances at Cherbourg are murky because the *Alabama*'s captain, Raphael Semmes, wished them to be so. When they put their life's work before the public, heroes rarely hurry through their most dramatic moment. But that is just what Semmes did in 1868 — his massive 800-page tome, *Memoirs of Service Afloat during the War between the States,* describes the 19 June 1864 battle in four pages — and no one has ever been able to explain why.[2]

Why did Semmes elect to fight at Cherbourg on that famous Sunday? Was the captain's decision prudent, that is, based on a realistic appreciation of risk, or was it quixotic? Did it serve Confederate national interests? Or was it the result of personal pique and hunger for glory? How should one assess the motives of a man who hid them behind some of the most difficult prose in all of nineteenth-century naval history?

In all probability, history will not remember the details of the many kills that Semmes scored against Yankee commerce between 1862 and 1864 (by one calculation, sixty-six ships) and certainly will pay scant attention to his justification of secession and his tedious excursions into arcane areas of oceanography and meteorology. In contrast, what happened off Cherbourg coast retains a timeless interest. Although the Confederate captain achieved apotheosis through his historic encounter with the *Kearsarge,* readers of *Service Afloat* are expected to believe that he did not notice.

In some respects, Semmes was not a typical Confederate officer. His birth state of Maryland never seceded, he was a practicing Roman Catholic, his wife's Ohio family was Unionist, and he already was in his fifties when the war broke out. But in other respects, he was the stereotypical Southern cavalier for whom honor, vanity, and the proper judgment of posterity were ruling passions.

His preface to his postwar account of his wartime career stands as one of the strangest statements of the historian's craft that the nineteenth century produced. Semmes explained his intentions in writing his 1868 memoir, but he did so ambiguously, in ways more likely to confuse than to clarify. He asserted that his career was a "sealed book" to all but himself, and in an intriguing phrase he said that the "fetters of a mere writer of history" did not suit his style. To tell his story properly, he needed more freedom than the historian has. He adopted the method of the "memoir writing" to obtain more "latitude" in describing men and events.

I have three objectives in this essay: to direct attention to the curious conception of history that animated Semmes in the composition of his own story; to measure it against a perceptive British telling of the tale that has mostly escaped notice since it was published shortly after the battle (written in part by the novelist and poet George Meredith); and to compare Semmes with one of the finest firsthand accounts that we have for Cherbourg (the letters of a young Confederate naval officer, George T. Sinclair).

To penetrate the disguises of Semmes, it is necessary to peel away from his account large bunches of sour grapes and to never take at face value his carefully contrived romantic tale.[3] The clever captain often conceals where he seems to reveal. But who has challenged his account of what went on at Cherbourg (or elsewhere on his cruise) or has examined his sources? One of Semmes's recent biographers, Jack Taylor, has noted that the enigmatic captain did nothing to aid posterity's assessment of his life. He suggests that Semmes possibly erased all vestiges of a paper trail to his life and work that might have contradicted his 1868 memoir.[4]

The retrospective musings of the memoir are so surrounded by self-justification that they constitute an apologia for his career, rather than a factual account of it. (Taylor calls the memoir a legal brief for the Confederacy.[5]) All who have hefted the original edition will attest that it is at least twice as long as it needed to be. But Semmes does not lend himself to summary, nor does he give up his secrets easily. Fortunately, there are a number of ways to tease truth from his pages, but to do so requires knowledge of what really took place at Cherbourg.

When my study of Civil War diplomacy began in the early 1960s, the abridged Van Doren Stern edition of Semmes's memoir was my constant companion, and much of my knowledge of the *Alabama*'s cruise came from its pages.[6] My mentor, Robert H. Ferrell, always advised me to go to the original. So when my financial circumstances improved, I purchased a copy of the 1868 Baltimore edition of Semmes's *Memoirs of Service Afloat*. It is necessary to direct attention to a small but important alteration that Stern made in Semmes. For many years those useful and dangerous four dots that Stern used to condense the preface concealed from me and from many readers a vital clue to what went on at Cherbourg. In the deleted passage Semmes had complained that earlier treatments of his career had not done him justice and he wanted to set the record straight. Fair enough. No student of history could possibly object to that purpose.

Semmes then launched an ugly, mean-spirited, peevish, and most ungallant attack on a fellow memorialist of the *Alabama*'s career. In a few vicious strokes of character assassination, Semmes sought to discredit an attempt by a true friend of the South to pay homage to him, his ship, and his cause. That friend was trying to rally public support in Europe for the South. Why, this reader wondered, was Semmes so anxious to bite a feeding hand? For many years that ungracious tirade puzzled me, for it seemed completely out of character.

Soon after the contretemps came to my attention, I acquired an unexpurgated version of the anonymous book that had so displeased Semmes, *The Cruise of the Alabama and Sumter: From the Private Journals and Other Papers of Commander R. Semmes, C.S.N., and Other Officers*, published in 1864 by the London firm of Saunders, Otley and Company. Despite several careful readings of that work, I was unable to discover any substantial reason for the scorn that Semmes had heaped on it.

Then I got lucky. As a result of advice obtained in a London pub, I discovered that Meredith had written the introductory and concluding sections of *The Cruise of the Alabama and Sumter.*[7] Meredith was a committed friend of the South. After the battle at Cherbourg, he told a friend: "The *Alabama* sunk and my heart's down with her."[8]

According to a letter Meredith wrote to a friend in July 1864, C. Warren Adams, owner of the London publishing firm Saunders, Otley, had been present at Cherbourg. According to Meredith, when Adams arrived on the eve of the battle "Semmes hailed him with joy: he wanted some one to whom to confide his papers, and was despairing of finding one; gave the papers (Journals, etc., Log) to Adams to do as he pleased with them." Adams arranged to publish an account of the battle. Meredith explained: "I have done the 1st and last chapter — offered to do the whole, but Adams could only wait five days to get the book out so I declined this fiery proximity to the printers' devil."[9]

Aside from newspaper reports, *The Cruise of the Alabama and Sumter* was the first published account of the Confederate cruiser at Cherbourg. Semmes dismissed it as a "meagre and barren" record of his career, but it was much more than the pennya-pager work of an ambitious hack. No well-informed reader would deny that it depended on and received the full cooperation of the Confederate community at Cherbourg.

Semmes's account is well known, that of his ghostwriter far less so. Here, then, is the 1864 Saunders, Otley description of that all-important prelude to the challenges of Cherbourg:

> It has been denied that the captain of the *Kearsarge* sent a challenge to the *Alabama*. Captain Semmes . . . says nothing of it himself. [What the Union vessel did] was . . . to enter the breakwater at the east end, and she "*passed through the west end without anchoring.*" Few will deny that among brave men this would be considered something equivalent to a challenge — it was defiance! [According to a French naval officer] anyone could then see her outside protection. It is easy to see everything after the event. It is distinctly averred by the officers of the *Alabama* that from their vessel the armour of the *Kearsarge* could not be distinguished. There were many reports abroad that she was protected on her sides in some peculiar way; but all were various and indistinct, and to a practical judgment untrustworthy. Semmes believed that reports of her plating and armour were so much harbour gossip, of which during his cruises he had experienced enough.

The Cherbourg chronicler then tried to capture something of the crew's enthusiasm as they prepared for a showdown with the enemy. "At last, our day of action has come!" He then directed attention to an important point little noticed in the literature: a duel was not an unpopular thing in France; a beau geste just off their coast by "equally matched" foes would have "melted" the scruples of any French officials at the port. They were "only too happy to assist . . . an engagement between Federals and Confederates."

This account also confirms that Semmes was "anxious" to convince himself that in a duel with a hated foe the odds were nearly equal, although he did acknowledge some *small* Union advantage in "ship, battery, and crew." In this work, the most contemporary history of what went on at Cherbourg, Semmes insisted he "did not know" of his adversary's "ironclad" protection. The Saunders, Otley author also sheds light on one of the most troubling problems of what took place in the French harbor as the celebrated Confederate captain contemplated his rendezvous with destiny. As Semmes evaluated odds that ought to have counseled or even compelled caution, he still "desired" a confrontation. "The instigations of an enthusiastic crew, unanimous for action, as also of friendly foreign officers, are to be taken into account." Indeed so.

But how much weight should be allotted to external factors in assessing the mind of one who was largely impervious to them? It may be that Semmes did not fully comprehend the magnitude of his decision, but to accept such a simplistic view only diminishes the stature of a superb commander. Semmes knew exactly what he was doing and why.

Other standard sources do little to show how Semmes arrived at his fateful decision to challenge the *Kearsarge*. The journal of the ship's boarding officer, George T. Fullam, stops some days *before* the most famous event in the *Alabama*'s career. For a key piece of the puzzle that is the mind of Semmes, students had to wait nearly four decades. Only then, in a memoir published in 1900, did the executive officer of the *Alabama*, John McIntosh Kell, reveal a conversation in which Semmes had informed him of the decision to challenge the Yankee cruiser. Semmes told Kell that he was tired of running from the Yankees. Although Kell reminded his captain that only one shell in three had fired properly in a recent target practice, Semmes already had made up his mind to fight.[10]

There is little firsthand source material from which to construct an accurate account of the Confederates at Cherbourg. There are, however, two letters written by George T. Sinclair which offer a rare perspective on the preliminaries of the battle. Although these letters were published over twenty-five years ago, they have rarely received the attention they deserve.[11] A Confederate naval officer who once had served on the *Alabama*, Sinclair volunteered to rejoin the crew of his old ship. Hearing that a battle was likely, he had hurried to Cherbourg from Paris to offer his services. Sinclair was not permitted to participate in the historic battle, but he talked with Semmes on board the

The U.S. Sloop of War *Kearsarge*, 7 Guns, Sinking the Pirate *Alabama*, 8 Guns.
Lithograph published by Currier & Ives, New York City, 1864.
Collection of President Franklin D. Roosevelt, 1936 (Naval Historical Center).

Alabama and witnessed the preparations there before watching the fighting from the shore.

Sinclair's account of the battle possesses a quality rare in Civil War sources. His tone is difficult to convey with precision, but it might be described as an unusual blend of emotional involvement and intellectual detachment, as different from Semmes as night is from day. To be sure, the passion of a partisan leaps from his pages, but those same pages possess another quality — one which might be described as a search for objectivity, a desire to get the story straight, whatever the cost. Witnesses rarely capture with fidelity the immediacy of historical events, and seldom do they provide new insights into old events or furnish fresh opportunities to look at history in the making. Sinclair's letters are an exception. His ability to encapsulate a sense of time, place, and circumstance (and to convey these with the perfect pitch of truth) still strike me as extraordinary, even though it has been many years since I prepared those letters for publication in the *Mariner's Mirror.* It now seems to me that in my youth I may have underestimated their potential for illuminating larger issues of the war.

Certainly, I failed to notice their utility for shedding light on the special circumstances of Cherbourg and the Semmesian mind-set on the eve of one of the epic naval battles of the war. In the early years of my postgraduate career, my interest in the international dimension of the Civil War centered on its diplomacy, the Whitehall-Washington-Richmond nexus. Only when my attention shifted to naval affairs, as the cutting edge of diplomacy, did I begin to appreciate what a valuable source Sinclair's letters were.

No witness likes to be caught in error, but perfection is usually suspect. It may be reassuring that Sinclair began with a mistake. He misdated the first of his two letters, but otherwise he makes a superb witness to one of the most important naval events of the Civil War, one that took place before the eyes of all Europe. In a note to his naval superior in Paris, Sinclair announced the death of the *Alabama.* He reported to Samuel Barron (who was in charge of Confederate naval procurement in France) that he had arrived at the harbor at about 8:00 A.M. on the day of the battle and had immediately visited the Confederate cruiser, where "all were astonished" to see their former shipmate. He offered his services to the captain, but, as a result of an understanding with the French port admiral, Semmes was "honor bound" not to augment his crew by "any addition" whatever. Consequently, the Saunders, Otley report of French complicity in the battle at Cherbourg seems inaccurate. Sinclair stayed on board the *Alabama* until the last possible moment, and he recorded his impression of the crew's enthusiasm for conflict. They "flew round the capstan bars" to get the ship under way. It was a "grand sight," Sinclair says.

Before he left the ship, Sinclair had a "long calm talk" with Semmes, the gist of which is that if Sinclair had been in command of the cruiser, he, too, would have found Yankee "brags and taunts" beyond bearing. In context, that conversation allows a rare glimpse *inside* Semmes, but it is one from the outside in, as it were. Among other things, the Sinclair-Semmes colloquy confirms that the captain of the Confederacy's most famous cruiser had a well-developed sense of amour propre. In the present context, it is only necessary to note that Sinclair's letters confirm that Semmes was very much a victim of his time and place. Above all, he shared the deadly ethos of the South that naively took it for granted that bravery mattered more than firepower.

In a revealing aside, Sinclair points out that he had advised Semmes to stay away from the enemy's greater firepower. He hinted that the 11-inch guns of John Winslow, captain of the *Kearsarge*, might give him an advantage that Southern seamanship would not be able to overcome. Two facets of that exchange ought to be mentioned. First, Sinclair tells us that Semmes said, "I shall feel him first [with my 110 lb. gun], and it will all depend on that." The comment suggests that before he left the harbor for international waters Semmes had decided to fight at long range. As we now know, he did so to deny his adversary the advantage of superior technology. And, as every student of that battle knows, the decision was sound. It might have altered the outcome — *if* one of the Southern shells had done its proper work in the sternpost of the *Kearsarge*. As things turned out, so

The Sinking of the *Alabama* (*Harper's Weekly*, 23 July 1864, Bulloch, *Secret Service*).

tiny a technological or human error did much to determine the outcome of the duel off Cherbourg.

Sinclair unintentionally cast considerable doubt on Semmes's notion that a *ruse de guerre* — a "cheat" — determined the battle's outcome. In retrospect, it seems clear that superior firepower from the *Kearsarge*, not its protective chain armor, decided the outcome of its duel with the *Alabama*. A day after the engagement, Sinclair informed Barron that "Shells from the XI guns" of the enemy had done "all the mischief" to Semmes's ship. Honest witness that he was, he felt compelled to confess (based on the reports of Confederate gunners that he had interviewed) that at the range selected by Semmes their cruiser's shot and shells had "no power to penetrate" the sides of the Yankee. In a slugging match with the North's firepower, the result for the South could only be disaster, as even Robert E. Lee eventually had to admit.

Despite Semmes's assertion that he did not act "rashly" in challenging the Yankee cruiser, modern students of that battle see starker disparities in the throw weight of the two vessels than he admitted. It is still difficult to comprehend how starkly ineffective the firepower of the *Alabama* was. Sinclair captured a part of that disparity, and the account that Kell wrote many years after the war resonates with a truth that Semmes could not force himself to tell two days after he lost his ship. That honest salt, Kell, says that the 11-inch guns of the Union cruiser did "severe execution" to his beloved ship; he acknowledges that Winslow's heavy guns demolished the pride of the Confederacy, "plank by plank," as another author described the outcome of the challenge off Cherbourg. Kell, of course, understood that no ship could long survive such a pounding.

Battles at sea are usually decided by how much punishment ships can sustain and how much damage they can inflict on the enemy while sustaining it. In this context the circumstances of Cherbourg are instructive. After detailed analysis, one contemporary authority has concluded that of some three hundred salvos fired from the guns of the *Alabama,* only twenty-eight reached the enemy. Of these, the same expert estimates, only two or three did what they were intended to do.[12] Many of those salvos were aimed too high to do any significant damage to the Yankee vessel. All in all, it was not an impressive performance in naval gunnery, even when one makes the requisite allowances for a worn-out ship, for gun crews with limited experience, for defective powder and fuses, and for a captain who had asked for sick leave after having just about reached the limits of human endurance.

As a result of the detailed researches of a generation of scholars, it is now possible to assert that the death of the *Alabama* resulted from the superior firepower of its Yankee adversary. The challenge at Cherbourg confirmed on a small scale what had been happening on a large scale in America since 1861. The South had overmatched itself. At Cherbourg, in ways that Semmes could not bring himself to understand, even in 1868, the long shot of the South had failed.

But before the mundane, unromantic forces of technology and material advantage could administer the coup de grace to a noble cruiser, it had been necessary for Semmes to put himself and his ship in harm's way. He had three choices: flee, fight, or de facto surrender.

The last and perhaps the most sensible option was also the least desirable. To abandon his vessel to port authorities would have replicated his experience with the *Sumter* at Gibraltar, a loss that still rankled. By odd coincidence, when his first command had been bottled up at that British colony in early 1862, the *Kearsarge* was the cork that kept it in port. Students of the wartime career of Semmes tend to pay insufficient attention to his time as commander of the *Sumter.* Finally, to surrender to the hated Yankees — and to do so before the eyes of all Europe — would have made him and his ship a symbol of defeat, not an honorable prospect for a proud warrior who identified heart and soul with his cause and country.

And if Semmes had fled, as he had twice done in giving his heels to Yankee pursuers in the Caribbean, where would he have gone and how long would the worn-out cruiser have been able to sustain itself, assuming it could run an augmented Union blockade of Cherbourg?

In composing his memoir Semmes did not fully escape the "fetters" of history. Not even the flexibility of the memorialist could free him from the burden of Southern history. No son of the South was more in thrall to what Mark Twain called "Sir Walter's disease" and what Jack Taylor calls romanticism. No cavalier had a more highly developed sense of honor than Semmes. Indeed, Taylor quotes him on that point and uses those words as the theme of his study of Semmes. It should follow, therefore, that a sense of history was central to the cap-

USS *Kearsage*, CSS *Alabama*, and English Yacht *Deerhound*. Painting by John R. Johnston, courtesy of Doug Robertson, Book Guild, Portsmouth, N.H.

tain's worldview. He certainly had a nice appreciation of the *Alabama*'s reputation and of his role in creating it. No reader of the memoir can fail to notice the emphasis Semmes put on his position as a legally commissioned naval officer of the Confederacy. He had a deep loathing for the Union press because of its constant charges of piracy. One does no violence to the record by suggesting that the Semmesian conception of history lay close to the heart of his decision to challenge his foe at Cherbourg. That inner imperative dictated that he would fight on that fateful Sunday.

Such a conclusion can only be derived from a careful and critical reading of the memoir, for in its artful camouflage of its pages, though not in his account of the battle itself, Semmes tells us why he fought, but he does so indirectly, almost inadvertently. Readers of his memoir, however, must test the validity of my conclusion for themselves. It is, of course, worth noting that his course of action in June 1864 ensured that he and his ship would receive an honored place in naval history, an outcome unachievable by any other means. Semmes accepted his fate by conscious choice, by a deliberate act of will to defy the God of Battles, to vindicate a dying cause, and to procure a place for himself in history's pantheon of Confederate heroes. (He also seems to have had another, more mundane motive, but this is not the place to mention it.[13]) Of course, no one knows whether Semmes actually had such thoughts as the *Alabama* steamed out of Cherbourg on 19 June 1864 to meet his nemesis. But everybody knows that his encounter with the *Kearsarge* ensured those results.

The mystery of what went on inside Semmes at Cherbourg becomes even more complex when one considers his postwar reaction to the Saunders, Otley treatment of his career. George Meredith wrote about two chapters in a two-volume work, its beginning and final sections. In other places, editors mostly paraphrased Semmes or other Confederate sources. The firm worked at fever pitch to ensure timely publication, and the project was designed as homage to Semmes and his ship.

On one point there should be no controversy whatsoever.

Meredith was a strong partisan of the South. In my mind, there is no doubt at all about the sincerity of his dedication to the Confederate cause. His private correspondence for the war years is filled with expressions of sympathy for the South, and at times Meredith's letters glow with his passionate attachment to the new nation. Some of the most moving sentiment in support of that cause that I have seen in a lifetime of research came from his pen. No one — not even Semmes — ever better captured the heart-wrenching poignancy that the loss of the *Alabama* brought to European friends of the Confederacy.

How did Semmes react when he sat down to compose his own history? What testimony did he leave about a gifted Englishman's effort to exalt the Confederate cause? What was his verdict on a fellow memorialist's attempt to galvanize goodwill for the South when the duel in the Channel generated much favorable sentiment in England for the captain and crew of the *Alabama*?

The most generous thing that Semmes could bring himself to say about George Meredith (or perhaps his publisher, C. Warren Adams) was to call him a "cormorant." It is a revealing word choice. Bird-watchers describe that ugly shoreline scavenger as large, rapacious, and *black.* Some see it as a seaside cousin of the buzzard; others see it as a maritime garbage scow. Some even see it as a symbol of evil incarnate. In any event, its use in context does not represent praise. In the Semmesian lexicon there is no opprobrium that matches the sting of *black,* unless it is *Yankee, Puritan, New Englander,* or *Republican.* In most instances of usage, the adjective of color usually preceded the above nouns. But in the memoir even the evocation of blackness was not sufficient to vent the full splenetic wrath of Semmes. He next accused his fellow memorialist of being a mere speculator, one who had espoused the Confederate cause for profit. In his view the Saunders, Otley work was nothing more than incompetent hackwork.

Why such scorn? It is difficult to say. One does not wish to read too much into what may have been nothing more than pique at homage insufficiently generous, though in an objective mind there can be little doubt that his critique of the Saunders,

Otley book is unbalanced. It is, of course, a scathing indictment—but it is a fiction and false on its face.

There is another, symbolic dimension to the story, one that
will perhaps appeal to diplomatists more than to navalists. One
does not distort history to say that Semmes's contempt for a
foreign friend mirrors many elements of a fatal weakness in
Confederate diplomacy. From the beginning of the war until its
end, foreign representatives of Jefferson Davis demonstrated a
near pathological inability to recognize their friends in Europe.
With distressing frequency they failed to sell themselves or the
South where it mattered most. Again and again, they missed opportunities to mine sympathy for their cause and to tap strong
currents of support for their underdog status. In wooing transatlantic support, they were truly cavalier.

The case of Semmes encapsulates fatal defects in the South's
search for international recognition. In his assault on the Saunders, Otley book, Semmes aped his superiors. He repeats on a
small scale many of the defects inherent in Judah P. Benjamin's
shameful dismissal of James Spence, another friend and publicist of the Southern question in Britain. The failure of Confederate statesmen to exploit international support in their search
for independence had tragic consequences for their dream.
Apparently, no one in the upper echelons of Richmond's foreign policy elite had any sophisticated understanding of the
nineteenth-century world of *Realpolitik*. Jefferson Davis, Judah P.
Benjamin, James Mason, John Slidell, and Raphael Semmes all
suffered from misunderstandings and misperceptions about the
world of Lord Palmerston, Lord Russell, and Louis Napoleon.

It is not always properly appreciated just how detrimental that
defect was. The leaders of the new nation and their diplomatic
and naval agents were victims of a warped worldview. Those
illusions cost the South dearly. Its inept diplomacy did much to
abort the birth of a new nation. Of all the variables that went
into that result, manipulation of the foreign response to the war
might have done the most to alter its outcome. In retrospect,
there was probably little that the South could have done to
redress the domestic balance of power with its adversary. But in
the international arena the situation was far different. There

conditions were more in flux; there the South was presented with marvelous opportunities for maneuver. The European capitals offered possibilities for imaginative initiatives in diplomacy. In the transatlantic world, the Confederate States of America might truly have transcended the fetters of history. But those chances went with the wind.

SEVEN | THE CONFEDERACY'S CHINESE FLEET, 1861-1867

*T*HE AMERICAN Civil War presented the government of Great Britain with many intricate problems in international relations. One of the most important of them, the proper limits of neutrality, has not yet received the attention it deserves from historians. Of course, several scholars, myself included, have wrestled with that problem, but those accounts have a number of serious defects. For one thing, no one has yet attempted a general history of neutrality in the nineteenth century, and the absence of such a work limits appreciation of the special circumstances confronting Her Majesty's ministers as they sought to cope with the challenges posed by Confederate efforts to procure naval craft in British shipyards. For another, all treatments of Civil War diplomacy have failed to treat an important part of the story: no one, it seems, has yet directed attention to a curious connection between affairs in China and the objectives of Southern sea strategy. Few people are aware of the strange way in which the two great civil wars of the nineteenth century briefly came together in the corridors of Whitehall.[1]

That missing chapter — "The Confederacy's Chinese Fleet" — provides unique opportunities for reassessing misunderstood aspects of the foreign response to the American Civil War. The story of the Lay-Osborn Flotilla (as the fleet is known to students of Asian history) reveals hidden meanings in the British Foreign Enlistment Act of 1819, the antiquated statute that had a crucial role in ministerial efforts to define the limits of proper neutral conduct. While the general outline of those limitations have been known for some time, the special circumstances of the Chinese fleet add unsuspected nuances to neutrality. British efforts to prevent the Confederacy from acquiring eight "fully armed and equipped warships" have some unusual features, and the reading of the Enlistment Act given by the law officers of the Crown in relation to those ships differs significantly from other interpretations of that statute during the war. That reading exposes new facets of neutrality and gives to that protean concept meanings not hitherto discerned. The intricacies of "recruiting, procuring, arming, and equipping" take on suggestive overtones when viewed from the perspective of the East, rather than from that of the South. That reading also suggests that the story of British moves to counter the naval program of James D. Bulloch is far more complex than even the most detailed researches on that subject have so far disclosed.

In addition, this material widens the international context of the American Civil War by giving it an Asian dimension. At the same time, it provides an altered perspective on the national interests and foreign policies of the prime minister, Lord Palmerston, and the foreign secretary, Lord Russell.[2] The contretemps surrounding those ships allowed Palmerston and his colleagues to take another dispassionate look at the perplexing issues thrown up by Southern efforts to buy and build naval craft in the United Kingdom. More important, that review was conducted away from the tumult of press and parliamentary criticism; it was also carried out undisturbed by "superfluous" notes from an irate American minister. British leaders could therefore evaluate the consequences of their decisions free from outside distractions. Indeed, their assessments of national interests in this case have an air of clinical detachment about them. They offer a unique window on the workings of Victorian diplomacy in general and on Anglo-American relations in particular; they furnish a useful means of comparing British responses to rebellions in Asia and in America; and they provide insights into the ambiguous status in the relations of governments and revolutionaries.

The British decision to sanction and supply a joint Anglo-Chinese paranaval force contains elements of paradox. The willingness of the government to probe the limits of neutrality at a time when Confederate challenges to those limits were becoming a major headache for the Foreign Office and an increasing source of friction in transatlantic affairs must strike an impartial observer as odd. At the very least, the tale of the "Bombay boats," as Bulloch once called them, affords a rare opportunity for rethinking some of the problems connected with the diplomacy of the Civil War. One might almost wish, in the manner of Sherlock Holmes, to write a small monograph on the subject.[3]

In the nineteenth century, the neutral's lot was not a happy one. By the early 1860s, just as the Confederate States of America sought international recognition of its independence, the British search for a proper neutral stance in China encountered grave problems. The revolt of the Taipings, one of the world's bloodiest and most costly uprisings, was creating a power vacuum of awesome proportions and threatening to destabilize foreign arrangements in the region. The decline of central power in China also eroded the efforts of European states to maintain their interests and to avoid unacceptable challenges to the status quo. And a more ominous threat loomed. Growing chaos there might impede Western desires to implement a larger objective: "reorganizing China so that it could assume a suitable position in the modern world." While that goal might be layered over with a patina of lofty idealism, its bedrock of self-interest, its emphasis on "security, economic advantage, or elevation of status" stood out in bold relief, especially to the Chinese — and was the more deeply resented for that reason.[4] Circumstances in China clearly required new initiatives in British policy.

Pressure for a reconsideration of responses no longer adequate came from many sources. John L. Rawlinson has attributed the reorientation of 1862 to fundamental shifts in British perceptions of Chinese affairs. He notes a number of "important considerations" confronting Her Majesty's government: (1) the growing rapacity and impudence of pirates and their serious threat to trade; (2) the lessening ability of Peking to police its waterways and a corresponding increase in the responsibility of the Royal Navy to take up that task (with a concomitant risk of increasing embroilment in Chinese domestic affairs); (3) alterations in the military balance between the rebels and the central government that posed a serious threat to existing arrangements and raised the possibility that the insurgents might be emboldened to violate the thirty-mile neutral zone around Shanghai and bring the rebellion into the treaty ports; and (4) the Palmerstonian perspective that saw foreign maneuvers to augment power and prestige in the region as inimical to British interests.[5] The prime minister knew all too well that international rivalries and cross purposes would permit Peking to play its age-old game of setting foreigners off against each other.

Her Majesty's government needed a policy that would do many things. It needed a course of action that would maintain British prestige at minimum cost, forestall foreign interventions, and protect the Queen's reputation for honest and impartial friendship for China. Conditions in that country also called for a way around the restrictive features of a neutrality growing increasingly irksome. Some way had to be found to shore up Chinese authorities and help them protect British trade against pirates while at the same time keeping Her Majesty's subjects from a too-deep embroilment in an Asian quagmire—by any standard, a nice set of problems in statecraft. Nor did they occur in isolation. Domestic political constraints and a confused international scene, in Europe as well as in America, narrowed the options of a ministry much disposed toward delay. Still, something had to be done. But what could be done in circumstances in which all choices looked equally unappealing? Could the government find a mechanism to achieve its purpose and avoid dangerous commitments? Was there a way to project British power into so turbulent an area without assuming unacceptable risks and taking up intolerable burdens?

The origins of the flotilla project remain shrouded in mystery, and though there are many claimants for the title, its progenitor cannot be precisely identified. The plan for China to acquire a modern steam fleet may have originated in the minds of obscure Chinese provincial officials who realized more quickly than their colleagues the profound implications that Western technology would have for their country. Possibly the inspector general of customs, Horatio Nelson Lay, a prime mover of the project, planted the seeds of the idea in the mid-1850s when he urged the Chinese to upgrade their naval forces. He claimed that the article stipulating "joint action for the repression of piracy" had been inserted in the Treaty of Tientsin to give him "a handle" for inducing the Chinese to buy vessels for that purpose.[6] It may be, also, that the plan had its inception in conversations between the resident British minister, Sir Frederick Bruce, and Prince Kung, the emperor's brother and the official designated by that "deity" to handle relations with the treaty powers. Or the scheme may have originated in the fertile brain of Robert Hart, who, in the absence of Lay, was acting inspector-general of Maritime Customs and who, some say, had designs on his superior's job. But even if, as Lay put it in a letter to his lieutenant, "the idea of a Chinese naval force *had* entered other minds besides your own," the plan matured and took final shape in conversations between Hart and Kung in the summer of 1861, long after Lay had returned to England on leave. A version of that plan received a sort of quasi, semiofficial endorsement from Bruce, who, for obvious reasons, wished to keep the still neutral Victoria a discreet distance from any complicity in the convolutions of Chinese court intrigues.[7]

If the origins of the Lay-Osborn flotilla can best be described as obscure, the purposes of the participants pose problems of an entirely different order. A scheme, which on the surface seemed so simple and straightforward, soon revealed that it contained an infinite variety of ways to cause trouble and thwart the objectives of its adherents, Oriental as well as Occidental. A paranaval force, a squadron of some six or eight ships of a class that contemporary terminology might designate coastguard cutters (or what one historian has cleverly called a "mosquito fleet"), had much to recommend it.[8] That plan opened opportunities for plunder and profit. It also posed some intricate problems in finance, politics, diplomacy, and international law.

No sooner had the outline of the plan emerged than bureaucratic inertia, petty jealousies, cross purposes, and power plays followed. Some of these problems were, of course, built into the situation. Time lag between China and England and the dead-weight of inefficiency at both ends of the communication chain troubled the enterprise from its inception in 1861 and be-deviled it until all accounts were settled and the books closed in 1867. There was also the problem of cost and finance, the va-garies of international currency and exchange rates, and the not insubstantial matter of how the Chinese were to raise the money and guarantee its availability in England in the amounts and at the times it would be needed. Such things, endemic to all similar enterprises in the mid-nineteenth century, caused no surprise and in themselves posed no insurmountable obstacles. Indeed, to anyone who had read a representative sample of Confederate complaints about the difficulties of securing ships, the lamentations of Lay on that subject lead only to a sense of déjà vu.[9]

Failure of the flotilla program must be sought in another category of problem, and, unfortunately, the documentation does not permit a firm assessment of responsibility for its de-mise. One student of the affair has assigned the major blame to Lay's "overambitiousness" and calls the scheme "unfortu-nate."[10] In a more detailed analysis, another historian cites a number of other interrelated reasons and stresses the ambigu-ities of the interests and motives of the participants. While ab-solving Hart of inordinate ambition, Jack Gerson notes a ten-dency for his "enthusiasm and energy" to warp judgment and prevent careful consideration of the consequences of "pre-cipitous commitments." A lack of priorities caused Hart to over-extend himself. By mid-1862, he appeared as one who promised all things to all men. Nor does Minister Bruce emerge from the affair unscathed. Gerson sees him as aloof, reluctant to commit himself, given to procrastination, and adverse to decisive ac-tion. Noting that the participants were "deeply committed" to China's need for expanded naval power, he hints that the objec-tives of the plan were so important that such incidental disagree-ments as arose among them might have been worked out in a spirit of common purpose. But then Gerson pinpoints the fatal flaw in the venture: "In London, Lay proceeded as though he were accountable to no one but himself."[11]

A number of circumstances contributed to Lay's independent action, some of which were beyond his control. An unusual kink in the chain of command perhaps exacerbated latent antagonisms or professional rivalries between him and Hart. By historical accident, the superior, Lay, appeared to become the agent of his subordinate, Hart: "Without meaning to do so, I fully believe you reversed our positions. You made yourself Inspector-General and me your agent."[12] This arrangement caused much trouble for their joint enterprise. It meant that Lay, a man entrusted with vast power for the supervision of China's customs service (and, presumably, of its ships as well), could not know the emperor's wishes about those ships except through Hart. Whether Hart understood those wishes and relayed them accurately to Lay, or whether the Chinese themselves were clear about the functions of the flotilla, cannot now be precisely determined. It is clear, however, that either the instructions of the government were not properly conveyed to Lay or that he chose to ignore or "misinterpret" an essential provision of them. A case can be made that he violated the spirit, if not the letter, of his instructions.

Admittedly, Lay bears a large portion of blame for failure of the project, but before one places all responsibility for that failure on him, it is necessary to note one further defect in the negotiations to equip China with a modern fleet. Part of the trouble stemmed from that information gap, the 15- or 20-week cycle of communication from China to England and back.[13] With the best of luck and the most unambiguous wording, instructions from Peking might be out of date and no longer applicable when they arrived in London. Such circumstances precluded detailed discussions between principal and agent; they made last-minute adjustments impossible; and they required a large measure of flexibility and mutual confidence at both ends of the chain of command. Dispatches had to be worded so that much could be read into them, and many things had to be left to Lay's discretion. He, of course, was a past master of reading between the lines and finding there whatever justification he needed for making his "full powers" somewhat fuller than perhaps the Chinese court envisioned.

Crossed signals, garbled communications, personal antipathies, vanity—all these played a part in frustrating the flotilla scheme. But deeper down, at the center of the circumstances leading to failure, lurked the perennial problem of power: Who would control the fleet and for what purpose? Here Lay saw or created opportunity. For a man of his temperament, the lure of power and the goad of ambition proved irresistible. They led him to see himself as the patron of China's modernization, the savior of the West's "large" policy there. His "real master" was the chimera of progress and his conception of himself as its advance agent. He began to think that *his* ideas about the fleet's function were the only correct ones. He wanted his vessels to be the finest and best equipped; he wanted his ships to carry the blessings of Western civilization eastward. He wanted to open China with technology, not with treaties. He wished to play a prominent part in leading that country into a new era of Asian history, and he wanted his work to endure. Motive enough, surely, to take an expansive view of his instructions.[14] Ample reason, then, for him to put the broadest possible interpretation on the operative clause in them that allowed him to appoint an assistant and to make "whatever arrangements" seemed necessary to carry out the emperor's wishes.

So, in his arrangements with Captain Sherard Osborn, the man who would command the fleet and take it to China, Lay carefully structured the contract so that the commander would owe his primary allegiance not to the government which had authorized the flotilla but to him, the agent who had purchased it. Then, at some point (the record is ambiguous and parts are missing), Lay interpreted his commission from Prince Kung (those "full powers" he had so adamantly demanded) to allow him to insert a curious clause in his contract with Osborn. That clause would allow *him*—Lay—to decide whether or not the emperor's orders would be carried out! In effect he sought to give himself ultimate authority over the way the fleet could be used and to arrogate to himself a veto power over all Chinese orders. Lay arranged that Osborn would command, in the words of Rawlinson, "all foreign-built ships purchased by China, and that this imperial steam fleet would be subject only to the orders of the emperor — save that Lay alone would transmit the imperial orders, *if he held them to be reasonable.*"[15]

Whether that arrangement was motivated by lust for power, or by overweening ambition, or by hubris, it led to the demise of the flotilla, to Lay's dismissal from his post as inspector-general of customs, and to the ultimate ruin of his career. The Chinese did not envisage Lay as a sort of Lord High Admiral of the Imperial Navy — and most definitely not one with a veto over the emperor's orders. When the fleet arrived in China and when the exact nature of the arrangement between Lay and Osborn became known at court, the Chinese naturally refused to accept it. Osborn, in turn, loyal to Lay and perhaps sharing some of his ideas about the proper purpose of the fleet, refused to alter his commission or accept a substitute. Consequently, eight fully armed and equipped ships, a small fleet, came on the market in late 1863, just as Her Majesty's government was attempting to confront the problems posed by the Confederate Laird rams and Union complaints about them.

The Chinese refusal to accept their fleet posed a nice dilemma for the Queen's government and the international community in China. The ships belonged to the Chinese, who had a heavy investment in them and in the cost of bringing them halfway around the world. The obvious solution, a public sale in China, raised tricky economic and political problems there. It would not do for the ships to fall into the wrong Oriental hands. It soon transpired, however, that other hands had, or were supposed to have, designs on the fleet. A public sale might allow the Chinese fleet to become a Confederate one. Suddenly and quite unexpectedly Her Majesty's government confronted an awkward problem in a new guise. That problem had been causing serious concern in Whitehall for a long time, ever since another foreign agent with a discerning eye for the products of British shipyards had arrived in Liverpool in June 1861.

The chief naval agent of the Confederate States of America, James D. Bulloch, reached England in the same month as Horatio Nelson Lay, and his purposes were not too dissimilar from those of the agent of the Chinese government. They encountered many of the same problems and experienced many of the same frustrations in matters of finance, communication, and command structure. Each in his own way sought to benefit from the transformations being wrought by the new naval technology of the mid-nineteenth century. Lay, especially, hoped to exploit the opportunities for ship purchases as the Royal Navy switched from wood to iron construction, when, in the words of one historian of the evolution of the modern navy, wooden ships could be bought in England "in batches at the price of firewood."[16] Both Lay and Bulloch sought to take advantage of innovations in steam engineering and to acquire ships suited to the peculiar requirements of their rivers and coasts. They may even have competed for some of the same ships. Lairds of Liverpool, a major supplier of ships to the Confederacy, built two of the vessels in the Anglo-Chinese flotilla. It is even possible that if Captain Osborn had had his way, he and Captain Bulloch might have found themselves competing for ironclads on the Mersey and the Clyde.

In both cases successful procurement of ships ultimately depended upon how well each agent surmounted the restrictions placed on such activity by the Foreign Enlistment Act and by the Queen's announced neutrality in their respective civil wars. Both agents recognized the broad governmental powers inherent in an Order in Council (even if each saw a different aspect of that power). Both of them sensed room for maneuver within the law. But there is a fundamental difference in the way each of them approached the obstacles inherent in the law, as well as significant differences in the way British officials responded to their missions. On that point there can be no disagreement, and that fact remains a central feature of the story.

Lay assumed — his absolute assurance on this point astounds me — that the restrictive features of the law would be swept aside as a matter of course so his work might proceed without hindrance. Throughout the initial stages of his mission he acted as if official approval of his plan would be "a foregone conclusion."[17] And while it would be going too far to say that the Royal

Navy gave preferential treatment to one of its own, it does seem as if Captain S. Osborn, RN (on temporary leave), had doors opened and facilities provided that were denied to Confederate captains, even before the Queen officially sanctioned his activity on behalf of the Chinese government. It is another odd feature of this story that three of the six vessels comprising the main unit of the flotilla had been purchased from Her Majesty's dockyards. And it is also true that the secretary of the Admiralty "smartly supported" the flotilla scheme, as did, apparently, a number of other high officials.[18]

Despite official neutrality, Her Majesty's ministers had few qualms about cooperating with Lay and found little difficulty in taking those fatal first steps "along the road to less-than-neutrality."[19] Lord Russell himself, long before he had been formally approached to support the scheme, gave one of the clearest, most dispassionate statements of British reactions to conditions in China and of their implications for the course of government policy. In a dispatch of 26 April 1862 he expressed a fear that half of China might be devastated before the "wretched Taipings" could be brought under control, and with chilling candor he revealed his thoughts on an intricate and delicate problem of international affairs: "I do not care much about our observance of neutrality," he told Bruce; "the difficulty is one of policy not of right."[20] (Students of the British response to Confederate naval procurement might ponder the implications of that statement.) Bismarck himself could hardly have put the essence of *Realpolitik* in smaller compass.

Nor was the foreign secretary unaware of the economic underpinnings of his policy. In a later letter to Bruce he emphasized that the China trade was "too important" to be quietly surrendered, and in a rare acknowledgment of the interconnection between Confederate and Chinese conditions he noted, "Our trade with China is now of vast importance — all the more as the U.S. by their quarrel have deprived us of so much of our most valuable importations."[21] Neither should it occasion much surprise to find the British minister in China displaying keen interest in the statistics of rapidly expanding cotton exports from there to England. For Chinese agents the way might be made smooth — if smoothing the way advanced British interests.

Confederate naval agents, it seems safe to say, never enjoyed a similar Foreign Office predisposition to waive the "observance" of neutrality. Sooner and more clearly than many of his co-workers, Bulloch realized that a favorable reception for his work could not be taken for granted. In this, as in so many other things, he showed a keener appreciation of the realities of international politics than many of his countrymen. From first to last many Confederates, especially those operating in Europe, deluded themselves with unreasonable expectations of a sympathetic foreign response to their cause. They expected preferential treatment from Her Majesty's government and relied on the coercive power of cotton diplomacy to nudge the Queen's ministers into a compliant frame of mind. By and large Bulloch was free of such illusions, especially about the obstacles posed by the laws of neutrality. He saw the law not as a petty annoyance to be brushed aside but as a major obstacle to be surmounted or circumvented. As he began his task, one of his first steps was to seek out the best legal advice he could find to guide him through the restrictive features of the Foreign Enlistment Act and to determine its relationship to the work that had been entrusted to him. He never underestimated the difficulties confronting him, nor did he expect that those obstacles would be swept away by a pro-South prime minister or foreign secretary.

Although Bulloch and Lay arrived in England at about the same time, their respective naval projects had reached entirely different stages of development. It is almost impossible to determine how much serious thinking Lay had devoted to the flotilla plan before his arrival, and, as noted, that project took form only after he had left China. Bulloch, on the other hand, came to England with a clear conception of what the Confederacy expected of him and with few illusions about what his task entailed. He was obliged to confront the problems of his mission almost from the day he arrived on English soil. Lay took a more leisurely approach and did not officially employ Osborn for the emperor until 29 May 1862, and even then their agreement provided for a "fresh engagement" some six or seven months later. It was not until mid-June 1862 that Lay forwarded his first official request "to obtain the sanction" of the British government for his plans.[22] For some time neutrality remained official policy, but, as Gerson puts it, the unofficial "cooperation" being extended to the plan amounted to driving "a rather large wedge into a rather large crack."[23]

The ways in which various units of Her Majesty's government responded to Lay's overtures, and the language they used in so doing, strongly suggested that he had prepared the way carefully before initiating formal contacts. Indeed, many of the rationalizations used by royal officials to support the scheme seem to have had their origins in material that Lay fed into the network of offices concerned with various subdivisions of the plan. For example, Secretary of the Admiralty Somerset's memo to Russell in support of the project was dated a day *before* the plan had been submitted to the Foreign Office, and it parrots arguments appearing in Lay's official submission to the foreign secretary. That initial approach to Russell, as mentioned, "was phrased as though government approval for the project was a foregone conclusion."[24] Almost as a matter of right, it assumed repeal of the neutrality ordinance of 1854 and a grant of permission to recruit men and equip ships for service in China.

Beyond doubt, Lay had divined which way the political winds were blowing at Whitehall, and his reading of the signals was astute. It should be noted, however, that the logic of events and the calculus of national interests, not the arguments of Lay, led Palmerston and Russell to sanction the flotilla project. Many of the influences that generated the predisposition for approval were beyond Lay's power to control. Reasons of state transmuted vague yearnings of support in London into specific commitments to China. Lay expected, and received, a sympathetic hearing and a measure of government assistance that would have been the envy of every Confederate agent in Europe.

The nuances of neutrality impinged more directly upon Bulloch than they did on Lay, and at one point their missions reached an odd juxtaposition. On 4 April 1863, the day the first units of the Chinese fleet left England, the law officers — the same men who had devised the instrument of dispensation for China — advised Russell to take action against an unarmed ship suspected of having Confederate connections. It seems strange that as one fleet sailed to China with royal approval, Her Majesty's government instituted legal proceedings designed to halt the departure of similar ships for the South.[25] That encounter in the law courts remains a central incident in the history of the Confederate navy in Europe.

But in discussing the proper meaning of the Enlistment Act as it applied to Bulloch's work, it should be noted that in nearly every instance in which legal advice was sought on the limits of neutrality, the opinions of the best legal minds in Great Britain did not vary significantly from the advice Bulloch received from his legal adviser in the summer of 1861. It may also be useful to recall that in the only cases in which such questions came before British courts during the war, the decisions of those courts confirmed the essential correctness of that adviser's reading of the law. The outcome of the *Alexandra* trial hinged on the "true construction" of Section Seven of the Act of 1819, and arriving at the proper meaning of that section proved far more difficult than anyone had anticipated.[26]

As he grappled with the problem of cutting off Southern ship procurement, Russell found that if the law did not quite tie his hands, neither did it give him a free hand to interfere with such activity. Many instances could be cited to show that by late 1863 the Enlistment Act had proved to be an inadequate barrier to Bulloch's work. Right up to the end of the war, as will be seen, the law officers could discover no legal means to impede the sale of ships to the Confederates — especially ones that had been equipped for the Chinese.

When China rejected its fleet, Russell and his colleagues were engaged in an extensive reevaluation of their neutral responsibilities, and at that point they encountered that problem in a variant form. They had to contend with the unexpected appearance on the world market of a virtual war fleet-in-being, one built, armed, and equipped in Britain with the express approval of the Queen.[27]

Because of the communication lag between China and Britain, news of the events of October and November 1863 did not reach London until mid-January 1864. The dispatches that informed Whitehall of Bruce's activities in connection with the decision to reject the fleet and send it back to India and England for sale contained in their voluminous pages a few casual words expressing a fear that the vessels might fall into unfriendly hands. They also alerted Russell to the possibility that if the ships went on the market in China, they might become "Confederate cruisers in these seas."[28] For these and other reasons Bruce thought it expedient that the vessels leave China as quickly as possible, and he took the necessary steps to achieve that end. Russell, in turn, casually informed the minister of the Queen's "entire approval" of the actions taken in withdrawing the flotilla from China.[29] The dozen or so words that Russell used to express that approbation proved very costly. Moreover, by his approval of Bruce's action, he set in motion a long and expensive process to keep those ships out of the naval service of a belligerent power.

Like all other efforts to impede the transfer of ships to the Confederacy, the one centering on the Chinese fleet set off political, economic, and legal debates. That decision also opened vistas on the law that few officials could have foreseen when they took their first casual steps toward a policy of "less-than-neutrality" in the summer of 1862 when Lay first broached his plans for an Anglo-Chinese fleet.

In May 1866 the Foreign Office prepared a most unusual review of all the circumstances surrounding the flotilla project and circulated it under the title "A memorandum showing on what grounds the flotilla was first purchased, why it failed, why we took it over, and on what terms as between Prince Kung and Sir F. Bruce."[30] That handwritten memo (and its marginal commentary) offers a fascinating exercise in the proper reading of diplomatic documents. Detailed analysis of that paper is not possible here, but it is necessary to draw attention to some of its salient features and more *outré* statements. The reader is warned that the document should be treated with more than the usual skepticism one reserves for official pronouncements on sensitive subjects. The words do not always mean what they purport to mean. The impression they seek to convey is not perhaps the one a dispassionate commentator might extract from them. By calculated omission, misplaced emphasis, slanted argument, selective quotation, and a host of other devices that a charitable critic might describe as duplicitous, the government set out its version of events.

At one point Russell inserted a comment that Lay had been asked to produce his authorization to purchase the flotilla, and he noted that Lay "assured the Foreign Office that he was fully authorized to do so." The foreign secretary did not mention, perhaps did not know, that this request to Lay was made *after* the Order in Council had made it lawful for him to purchase and equip ships for China and that whatever "authority" Lay produced for the Foreign Office, it could not have been those "full Powers" he had insisted were a necessary precondition for him to start his mission. It would appear that Her Majesty's principal secretary of state for foreign affairs — a man much and rightly admired in government circles for his awesome mastery of detail — authorized suspension of the Foreign Enlistment Act and the sale of fully equipped warships to a foreign power without bothering to ascertain whether its agent possessed adequate authority to carry out his commission! In fairness to Russell, however, it should be noted that he once admitted that he was "too much occupied with the affairs of Europe and America to think much of Asia."[31] Still, his lapse, if that is the correct word, his premature endorsement of Lay's scheme and his subsequent offhanded (dare one say "absentminded"?) approval of Bruce's decision to keep the ships away from China exposed the government to a potential financial liability of nearly £400,000; actually it cost about £150,000.[32]

The memo contains another Russell observation: "It is not intended to deny that this office and still more the Admiralty were privy to what was going on. There is no doubt the government gave their countenance and support to Lay and to give him importance with the Chinese he was made a C.B., but we incurred neither responsibility nor liability." The context in which this observation was made does not permit one to pinpoint the time referred to, but as the remark occurs near the beginning of the draft, Russell presumably meant to imply that, in a narrow, technical sense, the government had incurred no responsibility or liability when the ships left England. Fair enough. At some point in the proceedings of this strange affair, however, the government assumed a considerable responsibility for a large liability. The foreign secretary made that decision.

Several pages later, another hand (not Russell's) noted that "Lord Russell objected to the sale of the vessels in China lest they should fall into the hands of the Confederate States." The government, in effect, refused to allow China to keep its ships or to sell them. As a consequence, this unidentified commentator argued, Britain, by its "politically expedient" interference with their sale, had made itself responsible for "the value of the vessels." Further on in the memo yet another hand acknowledged governmental liability for their value because Bruce kept them away from the Chinese and Russell kept them away from the Confederates. Government restrictions had "made their sale almost impossible."[33]

Examination of this memo has carried the reader backward and forward between the years 1862 and 1866. But before one can fully appreciate the awkward position into which Russell had led the government, one must subject another piece of documentary evidence to detailed scrutiny. That document, a Law Office opinion of 21 May 1864, though more restricted in scope than the memo examined above, casts a different kind of light on the dilemma confronting the British as they sought to cope with the unforeseen complexities created by their effort to thwart Confederate access to the Chinese fleet.[34]

This opinion probed the specific legal problems posed by the fleet. Roundell Palmer, Robert Collier, and Robert Phillimore told Russell that proper consideration of the issues raised by Osborn's request to be relieved of responsibility for the Anglo-Chinese fleet required a clear understanding of the position in which the government had been placed by the course it had taken, as well as of the consequences of any decision that might be adopted. They absolved the government of "original responsibility" for arrangements between Osborn and his Chinese principals, but they stressed that when Russell approved Bruce's disposition of the flotilla, Her Majesty's government was no longer "equally free" from the obligation to carry out those responsibilities that the minister had assumed in the Queen's name. They called attention to Bruce's admission on 29 October 1863 that his government had taken "an active part" in equipping the vessels and alluded to the minister's assurances to the Chinese that London authorities would assist in disposing of the vessels on the best terms possible.

The law officers told the foreign secretary that these arrangements had resulted in a situation in which the Queen's minister, deeming it "inexpedient" that ships bought and paid for by China should be sold in that country, had devised a plan whereby Osborn would sell those ships elsewhere, and Her Majesty's government would help facilitate that sale. When Osborn arrived at Bombay, however, local officials, warned by Whitehall, thought that if the ships went on the market they "might be purchased by agents for the Confederate States of America." They therefore prohibited their sale and took them into custody. After many months of restrictions on his efforts to dispose of the ships according to Bruce's instructions, Osborn quite naturally wished to divest himself of any further connection with the Chinese fleet. In April 1864, he asked the Foreign Office for permission to surrender custody of the inconvenient vessels, "conceiving," as the law officers put it, that it would be "illegal" for him to sell those armed warships.

At this point the law offices made a number of surprising statements about the limits of the law of neutrality. "We conceive Capt. Osborn to be in error," they wrote, "when he supposes that the sale, within Her Majesty's dominions, even to a belligerent power, of armed ships of war, already lawfully equipped . . . under Her Majesty's license, would be illegal. The Foreign Enlistment Acts does not . . . prohibit such a sale." This error, this misapprehension of the law, had led Bombay authorities into an incorrect course of action and into unwarranted interference with the sale of those ships. They pointed out that the Admiralty instructions of 11 January 1864 suffered from a similar misunderstanding of the law, though they politely refrained from mentioning that those instructions had been sent out by Russell's express order.

Then they shifted the argument to new ground and introduced the troublesome element of expediency: "Viewing this as a question, not of law, but of policy, we presume that it may still be the policy of Her Majesty's government to prevent, if possible, the sale of these ships to the Confederate States. But we see no means of securing that object . . . unless Her Majesty's government themselves choose to purchase the ships or can find purchasers for them."

The law officers then arrived at the "practical conclusion" of their argument. In words that to a layman's ear sound suspiciously like Baron Pollack's charge to the jury at the *Alexandra* trial, Palmer, Collier, and Phillimore told Russell that *unless* the government was prepared to allow Osborn "full liberty to sell these ships in the best market which he can find for them . . . at his own time, and under his own arrangements, to any customer who may be willing to purchase," the government would be "morally" bound to assume responsibility for the vessels.

If, however, the government was prepared to give Osborn "full liberty" — to allow him *carte blanche* to sell the ships — it was not obligated to accept the responsibility which he desired to transfer. But if, after careful consideration of the probable consequence of such a decision (sale of the ships to the South), the government still wished to decline the agency which Osborn wanted to surrender, then the Queen must no longer "interpose" any restrictions on the sale of those vessels. Osborn would then be free to sell them *as they were* to anybody or in any way he thought best. Such a sale, the law officers emphasized, was "in no way contrary to law."[35]

So, in the spring of 1864, the law officers gave Her Majesty's government substantially the same interpretation of the Enlistment Act that Hull had given Bulloch in the summer of 1861 and which Pollack and his jury had confirmed in the summer of 1863: There was little that the government legally could do to keep ships away from the South. In this instance, however, the law officers seemed to be saying that there was nothing that the government could do to keep *armed* ships away from the Confederates. Such a reading of the law would indeed stretch the limits of neutrality. Such an interpretation would be a long step toward deciding that the Foreign Enlistment Act of 1819 was a "dead letter."[36]

No student of Chinese or Confederate history would argue that conditions in America and Asia were analogous during the 1860s. But the civil wars in those regions forced the government of Lord Palmerston to confront again one of the most intractable problems of nineteenth-century diplomacy: the many faces of neutrality. One wonders why Her Majesty's government favored China's efforts to procure naval craft and frowned on those of the Confederacy. As Lay began his work, officials had no difficulty in deciding that support for China constituted an interest of the first magnitude, but when Bulloch took up his task, those same officials could not decide whether the Confederacy deserved similar support.

The 1860s, as Brian Jenkins has again reminded us, were not a golden age in British diplomacy. Domestic and international constraints counseled caution in foreign relations. In Asia there was no hostage for circumspect behavior, as Canada was in North America. India, of course, performed something of the same function: Russell told Bruce that foreign troops probably could not put down the Taipings "without taking China out of the hands of its government, a change much to the benefit of China but likely to ruin England. India with its 130 millions is quite as much as we can manage."[37] Prevailing ideas of cultural superiority (racism, if one wishes) allowed an approach to Asian affairs that would have been totally inappropriate in Anglo-Saxon America.

In China, neither side possessed a navy capable of any threat to British commerce, as Union *Alabama*s might become. Each region possessed enormous economic resources that had to be taken into account. Russell and his colleagues knew the value of their China market and appreciated that country's utility as a source of imports. They were equally aware of the profits of neutrality in transatlantic trade and of the demand for Confederate cotton in the hungry mills of Lancashire.[38] That is not to say, however, that only the ledgers of profit and loss determined Palmerstonian policy. Although he himself was something of an apostle for free trade, Russell recognized the dangers of unbridled capitalism in Chinese and Confederate trade: "The grasping at mercantile advantage" was, he told Bruce on 10 February 1863, "a fine part of the national character, but it is one which may get us in trouble, if not checked by government."[39] In this instance he was fulminating against the rapacity of British merchants in China, but he could be just as critical of the enthusiasm of some of his countrymen for Confederate enterprises. He long held a "grudge" against Liverpudlians who carried such ventures to new heights of audacity and profit. As the war went on, he grew increasingly irritated with Confederate efforts to "flout" the Enlistment Act.[40]

The China fleet forced Palmerston and Russell to take one more look at an old problem. The cynic, of course, will say that the outcome of that review could only have been dictated by the handwriting on the wall foretelling Southern military defeat. But the matter is not so simple as that. It took time, too much time, many critics said, for British officials to clarify their thinking on the issues of the American Civil War and on the challenges it presented to the Queen's neutrality. Naturally, their responses were conditioned by the context in which they worked, and the military situation in America was only one of the many things they had to consider.

One of the "givens" of Civil War diplomacy, as much a reality as economic pressures or military assessments, was the mind-set of the Queen's ministers. Russell and Palmerston had to contend with their own ideas on domestic law, international affairs, and the proper implementation of neutrality. On such matters they had firm views and little inclination to change them. But change they did!

The Palmerston who defended government policy toward the *Alabama* in the House of Commons in March 1863, the man who had sneered to the American minister, "Catch her if you can," when news of that cruiser's deadly efficiency against Union commerce began filtering back to Britain, surely had moved toward a more circumspect view of the meaning of neutrality when he advised Russell in February 1865 that no matter what difficulties might arise in consequence, they must "take no chance" of allowing the Chinese fleet to fall into Confederate hands.[41]

The Russell who told that same American minister in March 1862 that there was "nothing" Her Majesty's government could do to prevent the departure of the *Florida* had surely modified his views in January 1864 when he approved, however casually, Bruce's initiatives to ensure that enemies of the North did not get the ships of the Anglo-Chinese fleet.

It is probably impossible to date with precision the point at which this "tightening of neutrality" occurred. In his recent study of Britain and the war for the Union, Jenkins suggests that a new hard line toward the South predates Vicksburg and Gettysburg.[42] But the circumstances of the Chinese fleet may permit one to assign a somewhat later date to the final decision to cut off the supply of ships to the South. The outcome of the *Alexandra* trial in June 1863 exposed the imperfections of the Enlistment Act as a barrier to Bulloch's work. The Laird ram crisis in September of that year set off a comprehensive review of the implications of that work. At some point in the ensuing debates, Russell decided that the law was inadequate. Reluctantly, but surely, he and his colleagues concluded that, since it appeared politically impossible to amend the law by parliamentary action, other means must be employed to do what was necessary. The problems of Southern naval procurement had passed from the realm of law into regions of policy and into areas where reasons of state allowed a certain flexibility that the law did not permit.

To ensure that a Chinese fleet did not join the South's assault on the North's merchant marine, Russell went beyond the legal and constitutional forms he revered. During the American Civil War he could find no proper answer to the "question of neutrality" posed by Southern efforts to acquire naval craft in Her Majesty's dominions.[43] Some years later, however, Parliament painted a new face on neutrality by giving the Foreign Enlistment Act additional powers to cope with fleets, Chinese or Confederate. But that is another story.

APPENDIX: FOREIGN OFFICE MEMO

MAY 1866
Reprise of memo: FO 17/493, ff. 63–74

1. The scheme both in its conception and its development was entirely Chinese, and considerable progress had been made in the purchase and equipment of the vessels before we heard a word about it. [This would have been illegal, to say the least.]

2. Our being mixed up with it at all, however slightly, was apparently a mere casual circumstance. [Not quite the whole truth.]

3. Lay discovered that he could not engage the services of Osborn and his men unless the Enlistment Act were suspended — Lay came therefore to the Foreign Office for assistance and partially developed his plans.

4. Those plans were, in general terms, to organize a navy which should first capture Nankin and put down the rebellion and secondly put a stop to piracy.

5. The objects were so excellent and the advantage to ourselves so evident both in the interests of trade and in enabling us to reduce our own squadron in the China seas that two successive Orders in Council were issued giving Mr. Lay the facilities he asked for.

6. This done, our communications with Lay and Osborn ceased; in no other way, directly or indirectly, were we parties to his arrangements.

7. It is enough to say that Sir F. Bruce kept entirely aloof from subsequent negotiations between Lay and the Chinese government. [Entirely? Well, perhaps not quite entirely!]

8. What the Chinese had wanted were revenue vessels rather than ships of war, but the extraordinary conditions insisted on by Lay were the real stumbling block in the way.

9. The stipulation that Osborn should receive his instructions from Pekin and through Lay was opposed to their whole system of government under which the flotilla would necessarily be dependent upon the provincial government within the area in which it was destined to operate.

10. Osborn wrote to Bruce to ascertain whether the minister saw any objection to surrendering the ships to Prince Kung, observing that they were imperial property and that he had no right to detain them.

11. Bruce replied that he had told Kung that the British government would not have consented to the organization of that powerful squadron had it not been on the understanding that it was to be placed under the orders of an officer in whose prudence and high character they had full confidence. Bruce would not consent to the ships being handed over to the Chinese government without instructions to that effect from Her Majesty's government.

12. Bruce had instructed Osborn to dispose of the vessels on the most advantageous terms and to remit the balance, after expenses, to the Chinese.

13. Endeavors were made to dispose of the vessels, but so anxious was the government to prevent the possibility of their becoming Confederate property that no sale was effected.

14. On 1 June 1864, the matter having been settled in the Cabinet, Bruce was informed that the government could not allow the flotilla to be sold lest the vessels fall into the hands of a belligerent power and, by reason of these being

sold in a British port, in some degree compromise Her Majesty's neutral position.

15. The British government would assume the responsibility of detaining unsold the vessels in question until further notice, but would take care that the Chinese should not ultimately lose the value of the vessels.

16. After being informed of this decision, Kung asked whether it would be possible for the British to retain the flotilla for their own use, thereby fulfilling Bruce's engagement of the previous year, sparing China any further loss, and leaving the neutrality of Great Britain uncompromised.

17. It may admit of question whether Bruce, by the steps he took when the Chinese refused to satisfy Lay's conditions in 1863, did not relieve the Chinese government of what might not unlikely have proved to be overpowering embarrassment for them. [NB: So far as I know, no such question had arisen earlier, and this comment seems to slide by the "entire approval" that Russell accorded Bruce's action.]

*   *   *   *   *

In "The Chinese Context," the opening chapter in Merli's book-length version of the story of the Confederacy's Chinese fleet, he was dependent on English-language printed materials. For instance, he added a few secondary works such as Alexander Michie, *The Englishman in China during the Victorian Era, as Illustrated in the Career of Sir Rutherford Alcock* (2 vols.; Edinburgh: William Blackwood and Sons, 1900), and S. Y. Teng, *The Taiping Rebellion and the Western Powers* (Oxford: Clarendon Press, 1971), to those that he had used for his 1988 article. Merli's most important new primary sources were the journals of Robert Hart. The relevant volumes are Katherine F. Bruner, John K. Fairbank, and Richard J. Smith, eds., *Entering China's Service: Robert Hart's Journals, 1854–1863* (Cambridge: Council on East Asian Studies, Harvard University, 1986), and Richard J. Smith, John K. Fairbank, and Katherine F. Bruner, eds., *Robert Hart and China's Early Modernization: His Journals, 1863–1866* (Cambridge: Council on East Asian Studies, Harvard University, 1991). Some of the documents that Merli had consulted at the Public Record Office became available in Kenneth Bourne, Donald Cameron Watt, and Ian Hill Nish, eds., *British Documents on Foreign Affairs—Reports and Papers from the Foreign Office Confidential Print*, Part 1: *From the Mid-Nineteenth Century to the First World War*, Series E. Asia, 1860–1914, vol. 19, *Lord Elgin's Missions, Taiping Rebellion, and Proposed Naval Force for China, 1858–1865* (Frederick, Md.: University Publications of America, 1994).

Here are a few paragraphs excerpted and edited from Merli's unpublished chapter:

When China's great civil war erupted in the 1850s, Great Britain adopted a policy of neutrality. Then, a decade later, when the Confederate States of America launched their bid for independence, Her Majesty's government responded in a similar fashion. Those intervening years, however, had taught the Queen's ministers some hard lessons about the nature of neutrality. In the chaos of China, they had learned that pious proclamations did not, of themselves, protect the nation's interests. They also discovered that a mask of neutrality could cover a wide assortment of activities perhaps best described as Machiavellian. Sometimes alone, sometimes in concert with other Western powers, including the United States, Britain exploited conditions in China to advance its drive for commercial concessions, even at the expense of that nation's sovereignty. Britain sought a wide spectrum of specific rewards in China, and, to put the matter bluntly, it was not too scrupulous about the methods used to achieve them.

Professions of neutrality were one thing, practice another. One authority (S. Y. Teng) has described the Western response to conditions in China as "watchful opportunism." Jackal diplomacy might be a more apt characterization, for truth to tell, neutrality in the context of China's Taiping Rebellion had many strange guises. Queen Victoria's ministers of this period were practitioners par excellence of *Realpolitik*. When they confronted the problems churned up by the two great civil wars of this time, they did not suffer from illusions. Pragmatic reasons of state set the foundations of their policies, both toward China and toward the Confederacy. And they could be remarkably ingenious in coping with conditions in either of these regions, especially when it came down to defining the limits of proper neutral conduct.

In all probability the succession of foreign secretaries who directed British diplomacy at the midcentury had no inkling that the civil wars in China and in the Confederacy would converge in London and Liverpool, in Birkenhead and Bombay, and force them to rethink and revise the limits of that amorphous concept. Many problems stemmed from built-in ambiguities of the policy itself. By its very nature, neutrality could never be evenhanded. Whether a neutral took an active or a passive role in its response to war, its policy would have grave consequences for itself and for the belligerents. Nor could a neutral always foretell what the results of that policy might be. Noninterference — official indifference — would, ipso facto, favor one or the other of the contending factions in a civil war. So, at least, it proved to be for China and for the Confederate States.

In the early 1860s, when the war in America broke out and when the one in Asia reached a critical stage, the governments of China and of the Confederacy required one thing that Britain was well equipped to supply: The president of the Confederacy and the emperor of China needed ships to redress the naval balance of power in their respective wars. Those two widely different searches for sea power were destined to change the nature of neutrality in nineteenth-century Britain. Despite a long debate dating back to the Napoleonic wars and beyond, international and domestic law had not yet clarified a neutral's right to sell to a belligerent ships that might be converted to warlike purposes. Imprecision on that point caused endless troubles for the Queen's ministers; it also cost the country many millions of pounds in postwar damage claims. One aspect of that problem must therefore be kept clearly in mind. The pages that follow are primarily a study in statecraft. They seek to show the ways in which Britain used the flexibilities of neutrality in responding to the two great civil wars of that era.

China and the Confederacy were belligerents in wars in which Britain had adopted a neutral stance. That status provided endless room for maneuver, but that concept, for all its flexibility, also contained limits beyond which it was not prudent to go. At the very least, that policy carried with it a set of rules for proper conduct toward belligerents. For Britain, those were spelled out in the Foreign Enlistment Act of 1819. Both Confederate and Chinese agents had to find ways around the restrictions of that act, and the ways in which they did so have much to tell us about British statecraft in the twilight years of the age of Palmerston. The contrast in his responses to the efforts of Horatio Nelson Lay and James D. Bulloch to procure ships in the Queen's realm shows us two very different faces of Britain's neutrality in an era of worldwide civil wars. Of course, in any particular context the contours of proper conduct are usually defined by power.

Britain's effort through Lay's scheme to extricate itself from its Asian dilemma provides a unique view of the workings of Victorian statecraft. The curious decision to sanction and supply a joint Anglo-Chinese paranaval force under special license from the Queen had about it elements of paradox. The willingness of Russell and Palmerston to probe and extend the boundaries of neutrality must strike an impartial observer as uncharacteristic, perhaps even mysterious. That they tested the limits of proper conduct in wartime ship procurement for China just when Confederate challenges to neutrality were becoming a major headache for the Foreign Office and an increasing source of friction in Anglo-American affairs strikes this observer as damn-near incomprehensible. To date, no convincing explanation for this strange initiative in foreign affairs has been offered

In China, as in America, the projection of central power required control of the coast and of the major rivers of the interior. The ships of the Lay-Osborn flotilla were ideally suited for such services. Though the records show no collaboration between Confederate and Chinese agents, Lay's vessels had many of the features that Bulloch could easily have converted to his own purposes.

The failure of the Lay-Osborn scheme had wide-ranging ramifications: (1) It added a new dimension to the legal and diplomatic history of Britain's response to Confederate naval affairs; (2) it gave rise to a novel and entirely unexpected interpretation of the Foreign Enlistment Act of 1819; (3) it undermined the traditional meaning of nineteenth-century neutrality; and (4) it ushered in a search for new definitions of that amorphous concept.

Several disparate pieces of evidence attest to a Confederate presence in Far Eastern waters and in China itself. The sometime commander of China's Ever Victorious Army, Henry A. Burgevine, was a son of the South and was thought to be sympathetic to its cause. In his 1968 dissertation about Burgevine, Robert H. Detrick, citing Foreign Office correspondence in London's Public Record Office, asserts that the British minister "believed" that the American adventurer might "cooperate" with the Confederate cruiser *Alabama*, "which was then in Asian waters." Suspicions of Confederate sympathies even extended to the commander of the American Far Eastern Squadron. Raphael Semmes, commander of the *Alabama*, tells us in his memoir of the warm reception he and his cruiser received in East Asian ports. Then, too, there is an entry in Robert Hart's journal for July 1863 telling us that he and a young English colleague had a "long argument" over the Confederate cruiser's presence in the Far East. Another entry alludes to a discussion he had with the American minister about the pros and cons of allowing the famous commerce destroyer to use China's ports.

A further testimony to the efficacy of that cruiser's deadly work was furnished by the American consul at Hong Kong. Horace N. Conger wrote to his counterpart in Liverpool to say that the *Alabama*'s presence in the Far East made it virtually impossible for American ships to secure cargoes. An unusual testament of the Confederate presence in China comes from still another Northern source. When Franklin D. Roosevelt's mother and her family traveled to China in this period, they feared an encounter with the Confederate cruisers known to be operating in the South China Sea.

For present purposes, there is yet another piece of evidence — one that must be given pride of place in any assessment of a link between Confederate and Chinese naval affairs. This evidence furnishes a graphic illustration of such a conjunction. Several years ago, after I had tried out a preliminary version of this story in a public lecture, a fellow student of Civil War naval history brought an unusual picture to my attention. The visual proof that Kevin Foster sent to me provides an important link in the chain of evidence connecting the Chinese fleet to the Confederacy.

In April 1864, the *London Illustrated News* published a remarkable picture, a sketch made the previous Christmas Eve by Commander Allen Young of the Royal Navy. That officer had captured for posterity an important slice of history. In his sketch the famous CSS *Alabama* is shown destroying yet another vessel in her unrelenting war on Northern commerce. The victim on this occasion was the *Texan Star,* also known as the *Martaban*. The incident occurred in the Malacca straits near Singapore. That act of destruction symbolized the end of the corsair's cruise in the South China Sea, and there was nothing unusual in reporting that the "infamous pirate Semmes" had engaged in yet another maritime mugging of his hated Yankee enemy. Such reports had become commonplace in the months since J. D. Bulloch had spirited his famous cruiser out of Liverpool on 29 July 1862.

But it is something else that provides this picture with special resonance for my study. What gives Young's sketch its prominent place in the story of Lay's fleet has not yet been mentioned: it is the third ship depicted in it, perhaps the one from which the commander made his drawing. The *Alabama*'s destruction of the *Texan Star* took place in full view of a ship identified in the picture's caption as the "*Kwan-Tung,* a Chinese war-steamer." Moreover, the wording of the captain suggests that the artist may have received the encounter from yet another ship — a distinct possibility, for we know from other sources that at the time of the action the *Kwantung* and several other ships of Lay's flotilla were en route to Bombay and England for sale. Coincidence? Perhaps.

Surely, the date, the place, and the confluence of these ships supports a supposition that the Confederates did indeed have some small interest in those Chinese ships. The newspaper, of course, did not mention that both the *Alabama* and the *Kwantung* had been built in the same Merseyside shipyard. Nor is it probable that many of its readers would have associated a "Chinese war-steamer" with the ill-fated Lay-Osborn venture. It is also unlikely that anyone who contemplated Commander Young's sketch would have pondered the curious twists of fate that had brought a Chinese and a Confederate cruiser together in the Malacca straits for a decidedly unpeaceful celebration of the birth of the prince of peace on Christmas Eve 1863. Certainly, it strains credulity to believe that such an encounter was a mere coincidence and nothing more.

Our skeptical age might be inclined to assume — as the British and Ameri-

"The *Alabama* destroying the *Texan Star*, or the *Martaban* in the Malacca Straits; the *Kwan-Tung*, Chinese War Steamer in the Distance," from a sketch by Commander Allen Young, RN, *Illustrated London News*, 2 April 1864.

can ministers in China did—that friends of the South had designs on Lay's ships. Still, even now, as one might expect, evidence for that supposition is hard to come by. It is equally difficult to find evidence of any official Confederate interest in those ships. Even Bulloch's famous reference to his "Bombay boats" is ambiguous. The lack of hard evidence, however, should not surprise us overmuch. The South had a distressing tendency to assign ship procurement to a host of informal, ad hoc agents, an arrangement about which Bulloch frequently complained. In these circumstances it may be wiser to approach the problem the way Minister Bruce did—on the basis of a perception about the fleet's destination. At the time Lay's scheme was wrecked on the rack of his own intransigence, Bruce had to act fast and decisively to keep a bad situation from becoming a worse one. An important element in his response was the possibility, the perception if you will, that the Chinese fleet might become a Confederate one, a conclusion that may well have been influenced by his strong friendship with the American minister, Anson Burlingame, the architect of the "cooperative policy" for the Western powers in China. Given all this, one may conclude that Bruce acted on perception rather than on proof. But, as any reader of *Othello* knows, that which is merely perceived can be a powerful motive indeed. The presence or absence of proof of a Confederate connection to Lay's ships should not distract students from the central feature of the curious case. Of course, it would be useful to have positive proof of that connection, but in its absence there is still enough circumstantial evidence to strongly suggest a Southern interest in those ships.[44]

A part of this story, however, must engage the attention of all who study the British response to the American Civil War or who have an interest in the nature of nineteenth-century neutrality. It is this: Beyond any doubt the Queen's minister in China, Sir Frederick Bruce, concluded that such a connection existed and that a transfer of the Chinese ships to the Confederacy was a distinct possibility. Moreover, he took steps to assure that it did not happen. More important, the action he took to keep the Chinese fleet away from the Confederacy led his superiors in London to adopt the same policy. Bruce also set off a search for a legal justification for that interference with free trade on the China coast.

Almost by inadvertence Bruce had set in motion powerful forces; he also triggered a thoroughgoing reexamination of the procedures and limits of wartime ship procurement in the Queen's realm. And so, with virtually no preparation for the shifting of diplomatic gears, Her Majesty's government confronted an old, awkward problem in a new guise. But that problem—the proper limits of neutrality and the Queen's responsibilities for keeping ships away from the Confederates—had been causing serious concern in the upper echelons of Whitehall for a long time, ever since another foreign agent with a discerning eye for the products of British shipyards had arrived in Liverpool in June 1861.

Appendix: Publications of Frank J. Merli

BOOK

Great Britain and the Confederate Navy, 1861–1865. Bloomington: Indiana University Press, 1970. Reprinted 2004, with a foreword by Howard Jones.

EDITED BOOKS

(edited with Theodore A. Wilson) *Makers of American Diplomacy: From Benjamin Franklin to Henry Kissinger.* New York: Charles Scribner's, 1974.

(guest editor) "Special Commemorative Naval Issue, CSS *Alabama,* 1864–1989." *Journal of Confederate History* 4 (1989).

ARTICLES AND CHAPTERS

(with Thomas W. Green) "Could the Laird Rams Have Lifted the Blockade?" *Civil War Times Illustrated* 2 (April 1963): 14–17.

"Crown versus Cruiser: The Curious Case of the *Alexandra.*" *Civil War History* 9 (June 1963): 167–77.

(with Thomas W. Green) "Great Britain and the Confederate Navy." *History Today* 14 (October 1964): 687–95.

(with Theodore A. Wilson) "Naylor's Case and the Dilemma of the Protectorate." *University of Birmingham Historical Journal* 10 (Spring 1965): 44–59.

(coedited with Peter Payne) "A Blockade-Running Charter: Spring, 1862." *American Neptune* 26 (April 1966): 134–37.

"The Navy at Newport: A British View." *Rhode Island History* 25 (October 1966): 110–16.

(edited with Richard Basoco and William E. Geoghegan) "A British View of the Union Navy, 1864." *American Neptune* 27 (January 1967): 30–45.

(with William E. Geoghegan, Thomas W. Green, and R. Steen Steensen) "The South's Scottish Sea Monster." *American Neptune* 29 (January 1968): 5–29.

(edited with Charles S. Williams) "The *Normandie* Shows the Way: Report of a Voyage from Cherbourg to Vera Cruz, 1862." *Mariner's Mirror* 54 (Fall 1968): 153–62.

(with Theodore A. Wilson) "The British Cabinet and the Confederacy: Autumn, 1862." *Maryland Historical Society* 65 (Fall 1970): 239–62.

"Letters on the *Alabama:* June, 1864." *Mariner's Mirror* 58 (May 1972): 216–18.

"A Letter from the *Stonewall.*" *Civil War Times Illustrated* 11 (June 1972): 37–39.

"The South on the Seas." *Civil War Times Illustrated* 11 (November 1972): 5–8, 39–45.

(with Leo Hershkowitz and Jack Baer) "We Have Got a Noble Set of Fellows." *Civil War Times Illustrated* (October 1975): 12–21.

(with Robert H. Ferrell) "Blockades and Quarantines." In *Encyclopedia of American Foreign Policy*, ed. Alexander DeConde et al., 3 vols., 1:90–103. New York: Scribner's, 1978.

"The Confederate Navy, 1861–1865." In *In Peace and War: Interpretations of American Naval History, 1775–1978*, ed. Kenneth J. Hagan, pp. 126–44. Westport, Conn.: Greenwood Press, 1978. Reprinted in *In Peace and War: Interpretations of American Naval History, 1775–1984*, ed. Kenneth J. Hagan, pp. 126–44. Westport, Conn.: Greenwood Press, 1984.

"Civil War Diplomacy." In *Guide to American Foreign Relations since 1700*, ed. Richard D. Burns et al., pp. 291–319. Santa Barbara: ABC-CLIO, 1983.

"Squadron of the South." In *Image of War, 1861–1865*, ed. William C. Davis, 6 vols., 5:99–152. Garden City, N.Y.: Doubleday, 1981–83.

"Alternative to Appomattox: A Virginian's Vision of an Anglo-Confederate Colony on the Amazon, May 1865." *Virginia Magazine of History and Biography* 94 (April 1986): 210–19.

"A Missing Chapter in American Civil War Diplomacy: The Confederacy's Chinese Fleet, 1861–1867." In *Global Crossroads and the American Seas: Essays from the International Commission for Maritime History and the North American Society for Oceanic History*, ed. Clark G. Reynolds, pp. 181–96. Missoula, Mont.: Pictorial Histories Publishing Company, 1988.

"Caribbean Confrontation: Letters on the *Alabama*, November 1862." *Journal of Confederate History* 6 (Summer 1991): 161–74.

"The American Way with Blockades: Reflections on the Union Blockade of the South." In *New Interpretations in Naval History: Selected Papers from the Tenth Naval History Symposium*, ed. Jack Sweetman et al., pp. 44–64. Annapolis: Naval Institute Press, 1993.

Entries on *Alexandra*, on James D. Bulloch, and (with Kevin J. Foster) on the Laird rams. In *Encyclopedia of the Confederacy*, ed. Richard N. Current et al., 4 vols., pp. 1:25–26, 1:239–40, 2:903–904. New York: Simon and Schuster, 1993.

(with Robert H. Ferrell) "Blockades." In *Encyclopedia of American Foreign Policy*, ed. Alexander DeConde et al., 2d ed., 3 vols., 1:171–84. New York: Scribner's, 2001.

BOOK REVIEWS (LISTED CHRONOLOGICALLY)

Robin Winks, *Canada and the United States: The Civil War Years*, in *Indiana Maga-*

zine of History 57 (June 1961): 166.

W. Stanley Hoole, *Four Years in the Confederate Navy*, in *Civil War History* 11 (March 1965): 102–104.

James A. Rawley, ed., *The American Civil War: An English View*, by Viscount Wolsey, in *Journal of American History* 52 (September 1965): 398–99.

Robert L. Beisner, *Twelve against Empire: The Anti-Imperialists, 1898–1900*, in *Review of Politics* 30 (October 1968): 508–509.

Warren I. Cohen, *American Revisionists: The Lessons of Intervention in World War I*, in *Review of Politics* 31 (January 1969): 140–41.

Stuart Bernath, *Squall across the Atlantic: American Civil War Prize Cases and Diplomacy*, in *Journal of American History* 57 (September 1970): 446–47.

Charles Cullop, *Confederate Propaganda in Europe*, in *Maryland Historical Magazine* 66 (Summer 1971): 208–10.

Daniel B. Carroll, *Henri Mercier and the American Civil War*, in *Journal of American History* 59 (Summer 1972): 151–52.

Mary Louise Ellison, *Support for Secession: Lancashire and the American Civil War*, in *Civil War Times Illustrated* 13 (February 1975): 49–59.

John Niven, *Gideon Welles: Lincoln's Secretary of the Navy*, in *Civil War Times Illustrated* 14 (January 1976): 48.

Charles S. Campbell, *From Revolution to Rapprochement: The United States and Great Britain, 1783–1900*, in *Journal of American History* 62 (March 1976): 977–79.

Ronald Hoffman and Peter J. Albert, eds., *Peace and the Peacemakers: The Treaty of 1783*, in *History: Reviews of New Books* 16 (Winter 1988): 54–55.

Martin Crawford, *The Anglo-American Crisis of the Mid-Nineteenth Century: The Times and America, 1850–1862*, in *Journal of American History* 75 (September 1988): 619–20.

Stephen Wise, *Lifeline of the Confederacy: Blockade Running during the American Civil War*, in *Virginia Magazine of History and Biography* 98 (April 1990): 324–26.

David Werlich, *Admiral of the Amazon: John Randolph Tucker, His Confederate Colleagues, and Peru*, in *Virginia Magazine of History and Biography* 99 (Fall 1991): 539–40.

R. Thomas Campbell, *Gray Thunder: Exploits of the Confederate Navy*, in *Journal of Southern History* 63 (1997) 678–79.

Notes

FRANK J. MERLI (1929–2000)

1. He was writing four overlapping books that bore these titles: (1) "A Question of Neutrality": Naval and Diplomatic Essays on the International Dimension of the American Civil War, (2) A Small Study in Statecraft: The Confederacy's Chinese Fleet and the Two Faces of British Neutrality in the Era of the American Civil War, 1861–1867, (3) A Fair Neutrality: The Law Officers of the Crown and the American Civil War, 1861–1872, (4) CSS *Alabama:* Birth and Death of a Confederate Cruiser.

2. The 24-volume *American National Biography,* published in 1999, did not find room for an entry on Bulloch.

3. The first quotation comes from a draft of a paper on Raphael Semmes, the second from a self-study included in materials submitted to Merli's Queens College department.

4. Merli never was on holiday when a manuscript collection was available. For instance, while visiting me at Miami University in Ohio, he explored the papers of Robert C. Schenck, a Miami alumnus who had served as ambassador to the United Kingdom during the *Alabama* claims era.

5. Merli to Norman C. Delaney, 25 September 1991.

6. Taken from Merli's "The Chinese Context," written in 2000 and intended as the opening chapter for a book on the Confederacy's Chinese fleet.

1. THE INTERNATIONAL DIMENSION OF
THE AMERICAN CIVIL WAR

This essay combines early drafts of two general chapters on the topic, different in title and structure, interspersed with excerpts from other drafts, including those on Judah P. Benjamin, counterfactual history, and slavery.

1. Stephen R. Wise, *Lifeline of the Confederacy: Blockade Running during the Civil War* (Columbia: University of South Carolina Press, 1988).

2. Roy Jenkins, *Gladstone* (London: Macmillan, 1995; New York: Random House, 1997).

3. Frank Lawrence Owsley, *King Cotton Diplomacy: Foreign Relations of the Confederate States of America,* revised by Harriet Chappell Owsley (Chicago: Uni-

versity of Chicago Press, 1959), 51. Owsley referred to William Lowndes Yancey, Pierre A. Rost, and Ambrose Dudley Mann.

4. See Robert W. Young, *Senator James Murray Mason: Defender of the Old South* (Knoxville: University of Tennessee Press, 1998).

5. Eli N. Evans, *Judah P. Benjamin, the Jewish Confederate* (New York: Free Press, 1988).

6. A recent misconception about the origins of the *Trent* imbroglio must be rejected. There is no convincing documentary proof in Europe or America to lend credence to the far-fetched supposition that the confrontation between Britain and America was part of a Confederate plot to advance the South's expectations of recognition.

7. Gordon Warren and James Rawley, among others, have traced the repercussions of the *Trent* crisis in admirable detail. See Gordon H. Warren, *Fountain of Discontent: The Trent Affair and the Freedom of the Seas* (Boston: Northeastern University Press, 1981), and James Rawley, *Turning Points of the Civil War* (Lincoln: University of Nebraska Press, 1966).

8. See Peter J. Parish, *The American Civil War* (New York: Holmes and Meier, 1975).

9. See a book published after Merli's death: James M. McPherson, *Crossroads of Freedom: Antietam, the Battle That Changed the Course of the Civil War* (New York: Oxford University Press, 2002).

10. Howard Jones, *Union in Peril: The Crisis over British Intervention in the Civil War* (Chapel Hill: University of North Carolina Press, 1992; repr., Lincoln: University of Nebraska Press, 1997).

11. David Paul Crook, *The North, the South, and the Powers, 1861–1865* (New York: Wiley, 1974).

12. David F. Krein, "Russell's Decision to Detain the Laird Rams," *Civil War History* 22 (June 1976): 158–63. The standard work is Wilbur Devereux Jones, *The Confederate Rams at Birkenhead: A Chapter in Anglo-American Relations* (1961; repr., Wilmington, N.C.: Broadfoot, 2000).

13. William C. Davis, *Jefferson Davis: The Man and His Hour* (New York: HarperCollins, 1991).

14. Jenkins, *Gladstone*, 241.

15. Merli compiled chap. 11, "Civil War Diplomacy," in *Guide to American Foreign Relations since 1700*, ed. Richard Dean Burns (Santa Barbara, Calif.: ABC–CLIO, 1983), pp. 292–319. A revised version by Howard Jones and Donald A. Rakestraw, "The Diplomacy of the Civil War," is available in Robert L. Beisner, ed., *American Foreign Relations since 1600: A Guide to the Literature,* 2d ed., 2 vols. (Santa Barbara, Calif.: ABC–CLIO, 2003), 1:353–406.

Recent publications not mentioned by Jones and Rakestraw include Pia G. Celozzi Baldelli, *Power Politics, Diplomacy, and the Avoidance of Hostilities between England and the United States in the Wake of the Civil War,* translated from the Italian (Lewiston, N.Y.: Edwin Mellen Press, 1998); Kevin Foster, "The Diplomats Who Sank a Fleet: The Confederacy's Undelivered European Fleet and the Union Consular Service," *Prologue: Quarterly of the National Archives and Records Administration* 33, no. 3 (Fall 2001): 181–93; and Gregory Louis Mattson, "Pariah Diplomacy: The Slavery Issue in Confederate Foreign Relations" (Ph.D. diss., University of Southern Mississippi, 1999).

2. TOWARD THE CSS *ALABAMA*

This memoir was written as an introduction to a book on the *Alabama* that Merli never completed.

1. The standard works are Celozzi Baldelli, *Power Politics,* and Adrian Cook, *The Alabama Claims: American Politics and Anglo-American Relations, 1865–1872* (Ithaca, N.Y.: Cornell University Press, 1975).

2. In another manuscript, Merli described his book as "an old-fashioned, rock-solid study, firmly grounded in the traditional sources of diplomatic history."

3. See Merli's acknowledgments and introduction to the special issue of *Journal of Confederate History* 4 (1989): xi–xxii. Elsewhere, in an unpublished manuscript, Merli said that the French discovery of the wreckage "sparked what might almost be called a cottage industry of *Alabama* studies."

Merli's special commemorative naval issue for *Journal of Confederate History* 4 (1989) included Christen M. Gober, "The C.S.S. *Alabama:* An Introductory Bibliography," 153–68. Since that time, relevant publications include Peter Barton, "The First Blockade Runner and 'Another *Alabama*': Some Tees and Hartlepools Ships That Worried the Union," *Mariner's Mirror* 81 (1995): 45–64; Andrew Bowcock, *CSS Alabama: Anatomy of a Confederate Raider* (Annapolis: Naval Institute Press, 2002); *Civil War and the Confederacy: The Business Records of Fraser, Trenholm and Company of Liverpool and Charleston, South Carolina, 1860–1877, from the Merseyside Maritime Museum, Liverpool: A Listing and Guide to the Microfilm Edition* (Marlborough, Wiltshire: Adam Matthew, 2000); James T. De Kay, *The Rebel Raiders: The Astonishing History of the Confederacy's Secret Navy* (New York: Ballantine, 2002); Norman C. Delaney, *Ghost Ship: The Confederate Raider Alabama* (Middletown, Conn.: Southfarm Press, 1989); Jean-Pierre Deloux, *Le corsaire Alabama: La Guerre de Sécession au large de Cherbourg* (Paris: E-dite, 2001); Chester G. Hearn, *Gray Raiders of the Sea: How Eight Confederate Warships Destroyed the Union's High Seas Commerce* (Camden, Maine: International Marine, 1992); Raimondo Luraghi, *A History of the Confederate Navy* (Annapolis: Naval Institute Press, 1996); William Marvel, *The Alabama and the Kearsarge: The Sailor's Civil War* (Chapel Hill: University of North Carolina Press, 1996); David Hepburn Milton, *Lincoln's Spymaster: Thomas Haines Dudley and the Liverpool Network* (Mechanicsburg, Pa.: Stackpole, 2002); Ethel Trenholm Seabrook Nepveux, *George A. Trenholm, Financial Genius of the Confederacy: His Associates and His Ships That Ran the Blockade* (Charleston, S.C.: privately printed, 1999); Serge Noirsain and Gerard Hawkins, *La flotte européene de la confédération sudiste* (Brussels: Confederate Historical Association of Belgium, 2000); Charles M. Robinson III, *Shark of the Confederacy: The Story of the CSS Alabama* (Annapolis: Naval Institute Press, 1996); Warren F. Spencer, *Raphael Semmes, the Philosophical Mariner* (Tuscaloosa: University of Alabama Press, 1997); William N. Still and William S. Dudley, eds., *The Confederate Navy: The Ships, Men, and Organization, 1861–65* (Annapolis: Naval Institute Press, 1997); William N. Still, John M. Taylor, and Norman C. Delaney, *Raiders and Blockaders: The American Civil War Afloat* (Washington, D.C.: Brassey's, 1998); John M. Taylor, *Confederate Raider: Raphael Semmes of the Alabama* (Washington, D.C.: Brassey's, 1994); John M. Taylor, *Semmes: Rebel Raider* (Washington, D.C.: Brassey's, 2003); and Spencer C. Tucker, *Raphael Semmes and the Alabama* (Abilene: McWhiney Foundation Press, 1996).

4. Among other problems, for reasons of space, Merli had to omit his own intended contributions. At a late stage in the journal's production, the editor for whom Merli prepared the special issue omitted or at least postponed many articles and illustrations that Merli described in his "Acknowledgments" and "Introduction." Looking at the volume as published, "it is difficult to know whether congratulations or commiserations are the proper response." Merli to Fahey, 29 March 1990.

5. Apparently Merli was a consultant and on-screen commentator for a French-American TV program on the archaeology of the *Alabama* in August 1995 and for a British TV program on the career of the *Alabama* in February 1996.

6. Merli often tantalized his readers (and friends) with hints about stories that he declined to tell. In fact, he never told Renata Eley Long how he obtained his "nugget of information," an undated newspaper fragment that mentioned that Captain Butcher lived in Edinburgh.

7. Miss M. J. Butcher, Captain Butcher's granddaughter, had a typescript copy of the memoir in her possession.

8. Our concern for the proper presentation of this material proved to be a blessing in disguise. In the early months of our preparation for publication, we had worked on the assumption that we were the first to find this document, an assumption that its owner shared. Such was not the case, however. For just as we were putting the finishing touches on our version, our ongoing research discovered that the English maritime journal, *Sea Breezes,* had published an unannotated copy of Butcher's account in November 1988 (62: 782–88). Our failure to locate that earlier appearance in print points up the perils of historical research, even for those who have practiced it for a long time. (Both editors have friends who are interested in *Alabama* affairs living in Liverpool, where *Sea Breezes* is published.) The discovery of two separate copies of the same document within a decade — and by two entirely separate routes — highlights the vagaries by which vital records of the past are accumulated. In the long perspective of history, the true importance of that document may lie in the reconsideration of the *Alabama* story it is certain to engender. Renata Eley Long and I were pleased to provide an opening gun in that debate. My book is another broadside in the battle over that cruiser's proper place in the naval and diplomatic history of the American Civil War.

9. It may be mere coincidence, or it may be symptomatic of a more serious flaw in methodology, but at two other points in his study Adams misdates a document. And, again, as in the *Alabama* case, a wrong date and an incorrect chronology distort the story and warp his conclusions — and those of generations of historians who have so blindly followed him. Those other incidents of defective scholarship, however, revolve around matters of greater importance than the departure of one Confederate cruiser. In both cases, his timing is seriously askew and those small errors strike at the heart of his reading of the British response to the war. [Presumably Merli refers to the Laird rams controversy in 1863 for which Adams, as a result of misreading an abbreviation, misdated the American "this is war" dispatch as April 5 instead of the correct date, September 5.]

10. Bradford Perkins, *The Creation of a Republican Empire, 1776–1865* (New York: Cambridge University Press, 1993), p. 242.

11. Bulloch's history has been reprinted as recently as the opening years of the twenty-first century: *The Secret Service of the Confederate States in Europe; or, How the Confederate Cruisers Were Equipped* (1883; repr., New York: Modern Library, 2001).

12. Inspired by the quotation from Seneca that concluded Philip Van Doren Stern's introduction to the Thomas Yoseloff 1959 reprint of Bulloch's *Secret Service,* 1:xvii.

3. THE LAW OF THE *ALABAMA*

1. One convenient compilation of printed documents is *The Case of Great Britain as Laid before the Tribunal of Arbitration, Convened at Geneva under the Provisions of the Treaty between the United States of America and Her Majesty the Queen of Great Britain, Concluded at Washington May 8, 1871,* 3 vols. (Washington: Government Printing Office, 1872).

2. Rupert C. Jarvis, "The *Alabama* and the Law," *Transactions of the Historic Society of Lancashire and Cheshire* 111 (1959): 181–98.

3. Douglas H. Maynard, "Union Efforts to Prevent the Escape of the *Alabama,*" *Mississippi Valley Historical Review* 41 (June 1954): 41–60.

4. Ibid., 46.

5. Ibid., 48.

6. Collier reappears later as one of the signatories of the Law Office opinion, 21 May 1864, in regard to the Confederacy's Chinese fleet.

7. Maynard, "Union Efforts," 50.

8. Ibid., 52.

9. Ibid., 54.

10. Bradford Perkins indulged in colorful hyperbole when he claimed: "The Queen's Advocate carried key documents off to an insane asylum when he suffered a breakdown," *The Creation of a Republican Empire, 1776–1865* p. 227. See also Brunson MacChesney, "The *Alabama* and the Queen's Advocate: A Mystery of History," *Northwestern University Law Review* 62 (1967): 568–85.

11. Palmer to Russell, 10 August 1869, Lambeth Palace Library, Selborne Papers, MS 1863. Palmer recollected that the treasury solicitor or other official was present at his meeting with the attorney general, Atherton. (In 1872, when he was made lord chancellor, Palmer received a peerage as earl of Selborne.) Discussing plans for a visit by his eldest son, Merli mentioned to me (13 November 1999) how he happened upon his notes for this document: "While clearing my desk for [the] visit I came across one of my Spiral Note Books from London Research, circa Summer of 1970. Would you believe that I found yet another note for my 'massive scholarly apparatus' on the *Alabama*'s escape? And it is Roundell Palmer (from Lambeth Place [Library]) 'recollecting' his impressions of that ship's dossier as it wended its way up and down the British bureaucratic maze 16–19 July 1862, and he gives a couple of useful time checks."

12. Collier's second opinion noted that "if not enforced on this occasion, [the Foreign Enlistment Act] is little better than a dead letter."

13. Merli's manuscript ended at this point.

14. A member of the Laird family later denied in a speech in the House of

Commons that his firm had done anything illegal in building the *Alabama*. He pointed out that agents of the North also had made use of British firms to arm the Union forces. *Hansard Parliamentary Debates*, 3d series, vol. 170, 27 March 1863, cols. 68–72.

15. Merli, "Crown versus Cruiser: The Curious Case of the *Alexandra*," *Civil War History* 9 (June 1963): 173.

16. Ibid., 177.

4. E. D. ADAMS, ROUNDELL PALMER, AND THE ESCAPE OF THE *ALABAMA*

Combining two of Merli's manuscript articles, this chapter omits his detailed critique of selected historians from 1940 until the mid-1990s.

1. See chapter 5 of this volume.

2. Ephraim D. Adams, *Great Britain and the American Civil War* (New York: Longmans, Green, 1925; repr., Gloucester, Mass.: Peter Smith, 1957, and New York: Russell and Russell, 1958), 2:118–21.

3. Ibid., 118–20 (italics added).

4. Owsley, *King Cotton Diplomacy*, p. 398.

5. Ibid.

6. Merli went on to critique several subsequent books: George W. Dalzell's *Flight from the Flag: The Continuing Effect of the Civil War upon the American Carrying Trade* (Chapel Hill: University of North Carolina Press, 1940), W. Stanley Hoole's *Four Years in the Confederate Navy* (Athens: University of Georgia Press, 1964), John M. Taylor's *Confederate Raider*, and Charles M. Robinson's *Shark of the Confederacy*. Merli argued that they accepted E. D. Adams's error and made it much worse and, as a result of their assumption about British governmental complicity in the *Alabama*'s escape, diverted attention from Bulloch's genius.

7. Palmer's speech is reported in columns 43–59, with columns 51–56 the most relevant.

8. In fact, the Americans had suggested the need for such revision, but those talks had foundered when Britain's lord chancellor affirmed to the cabinet that the law in its present form was fully adequate. Palmer's reference, I suspect, was a clever appeal to anti-American sentiment in the House and to its reluctance to yield to pressure from a foreign power.

9. Merli, "Crown versus Cruiser."

10. In a letter to Norman Delaney (25 September 1991), Merli complained about "a secondary source for the Russell-Mason note of February 1863" that E. D. Adams used, a source that "is just a tad tainted."

5. CAPTAIN BUTCHER'S MEMOIR OF THE *ALABAMA*'S ESCAPE

This memoir was coedited by Frank J. Merli and Renata Eley Long. The editors thank Miss M. J. Butcher, granddaughter of Captain M. J. Butcher, for permission to publish his narrative, a typescript copy of which is in her possession. In addition, we are indebted to her for sharing anecdotal family information with us. As we were putting the finishing touches on our version of this document, we learned that a copy of it had appeared in the British nautical journal *Sea Breezes* 62 (November 1988): 782–88, under the title "The Delivery Voyage of the *Alabama.*" The texts are identical and appear to be derived from a common source. We surmise that the printed Liverpool copy may have originated from another branch of Butcher's family. The *Sea Breezes* copy contains no commentary on the text, a defect our version seeks to remedy. The editors also wish to thank Norman C. Delaney and David M. Fahey for readings of early drafts of this manuscript.

 1. The literature on the subject of the *Alabama* is extensive and frequently littered with error. The overall story of Confederate naval affairs in England is concisely told in Merli, *Great Britain and the Confederate Navy, 1861–1865* (Bloomington: Indiana University Press, 1970). A most valuable contribution to the subject has been made by Luraghi, *A History of the Confederate Navy.* Our present purposes require that we cite several of the accounts by those who participated in the venture. The most valuable of these is James D. Bulloch, *The Secret Service of the Confederate States in Europe.* All citations are to the 1959 edition. A more recent work includes a contemporary source, William Stanley Hoole, *Four Years in the Confederate Navy.* The original draft of John Low's diary and log—the backbone of Hoole's book—is in the University of Alabama, W. Stanley Hoole Special Collections Library, Tuscaloosa. We are grateful to Clark Center, of that institution, for furnishing us a copy of Low's log from his archive.

 It is necessary to note, however, that Hoole's dating of the escape on p. 48 of his book is incorrect. The *Alabama* left Liverpool between 9 and 10 A.M. on 29 July, not on the 28th, as Hoole asserts. His error, we suspect, stems from misreading Low's handwritten entry for Monday, 28 July 1862, which, in turn, is itself mistaken! In *our* reading of that entry it says: "This day got the decks all clear ready for going out of dock and coming to anchor in the river[.] 9 P.M. hauled down to the dock gates and was taken in tow by steamer and came to anchor in the river[.] 10 A.M. got steam up and proceeded down channel with light breeze and fine weather with a party of visitors on Board—5 P.M. tugboat left us with visitors, and we proceeded to Molfero Bay [*sic*] where we came to anchor waiting news from Lpool." Low's entry for 29 July begins, "At 2:30 A.M. got under weigh."

 We now know from Butcher's account and from other sources that we examined in preparing this document for publication that Bulloch received a tip on Saturday, 26 July, that he must get his ship to sea in forty-eight hours; we know that the ship left her builder's dock late on Monday, the 28th, anchored overnight in the river Mersey, took on a party of visitors for a "trial trip" the next morning, and then slipped out to sea. On the basis of internal evidence alone, the events that Low includes for the 28th took place on that day *and* the next. On p. 49 Hoole quotes Low's entry but mistakes the time the ship was towed into the river. He reads "9 A.M." Low's log clearly reads "9 P.M." More seriously, Hoole fails to note that the *Alabama* did not reach Moelfra Bay until (as Butcher and others tell us) "about 8 P.M." on 29 July. And, of course, Low's entry for the 29th makes no sense, unless we assume that it refers to events *after* Bulloch took his "guests" back to Liverpool on the evening of 29 July: made a rendezvous of *Hercules* and *Alabama* at Moelfra late on the 30th, transshipped supplies from the tug to the cruiser "about 10 P.M." on the 30th, and then, with Bulloch aboard, the *Alabama* "at 2:30 A.M. got under weigh" from Moelfra Bay en route to Northern Ireland, its last landfall within British jurisdiction before setting out into the Atlantic for the Azores. The correct date for Low's second entry would then have to be 31 July, not the 29th. Such are the difficulties of establishing an accurate chronology for a much-studied incident. Naturally, Hoole was neither the first nor the last to get the sequence of events garbled. Part of the difficulty stems, we think, from Low's habit of marking his days from noon to noon.

To take but a few random examples of how historians, even in the 1990s, continue to mislead readers, one may cite Warren F. Spencer, *Raphael Semmes, the Philosophical Mariner,* p. 139, where the escape is assigned to 3 August; p. 140, where Bulloch and Semmes are put on board the wrong supply ship; and p. 150, where Captain Butcher is incorrectly put in command of the *Agrippina,* a mistake repeated in the index on p. 244. This work, incidentally, contains a surprisingly large number of errors on other aspects of Semmes's career. Even the date of his funeral is wrong (p. 212).

Robinson, *Shark of the Confederacy,* also gets the time wrong for the ship's move into the river on the 28th [at 9:00 A.M.], but correctly notes her departure from Liverpool "on the next morning" (p. 24). This error, though minor, suggests a more serious flaw in this author's approach: uncritical reliance on secondary sources, many of which are outdated and unreliable. In the example cited here, Robinson relies on Hoole, but there are other mistakes and misrepresentations as well. The author's assertions (on pp. 23–24) about the attitude and policy of Russell and Palmerston as the *Alabama* crisis reached its apex in late July cannot be substantiated on the basis of archival evidence. See also note 26 below.

2. Readers of Butcher's account of the escape may get a "feel" for the complexity of the circumstances surrounding it by consulting two other first-hand sources. The first, an unusual one, is the deposition given to the British government in April 1863 by the turncoat paymaster of the *Alabama,* Clarence R. Yonge. It may be found in Kenneth Bourne and Donald Cameron Watt, gen. eds., *British Documents on Foreign Affairs . . . : Series C. North America, 1837–1914,* 15 vols., vol. 6, *The Civil War Years, 1862–1865* (Bethesda, Md.: University Press of America, 1986), pp. 150–54, doc. 203. As Bulloch's secretary, Yonge was in a position to know the inner workings of Confederate naval affairs, but his testimony must be used with caution. He attributes the ship's hasty departure, "some three or four days sooner than we expected to sail," to received reports that "proceedings were being commenced to stop the vessel from sailing" (p. 152). He confirms Butcher's presence at the conference that precipitated the early departure, he puts that departure at "about half-past 10 o'clock," and he notes that the vessel left port with no intention of returning and that "the ladies and passengers were taken on board as a blind" (p. 152). He also asserts that the future work of the cruiser was known in advance by the builders. The possibility that Yonge's "esteemed friend" in Liverpool, the one to whom he promised to write of the *Alabama*'s adventures, might have been the American consul appears in Marvel, *The Alabama and the Kearsarge,* pp. 60 and 297n19.

Another vital piece of the story appears in Charles C. Summersell, ed., *The Journal of George Townley Fullam: Boarding Officer of the Confederate Sea Raider Alabama* (University: University of Alabama Press, 1973). This source gives the time of departure with some precision, "At 9:15 A.M. of the 29th July 1862"

(p. 5), but Fullam is mistaken in his assertion that the "guests" of the "trial trip" were aboard when the vessel anchored in Moelfra Bay. He omits mention of Bulloch's return to Liverpool with those guests and his subsequent return to the *Alabama*'s anchorage at Moelfra with additional hands and supplies for that vessel on the 30th. He does, however, confirm Bulloch's departure from the ship at the Giant's Causeway in Northern Ireland.

A part of the story virtually unknown to American students of the war has been illuminated in K. F. Sirett and K. J. Williams, "Liverpool and the American Civil War," *Journal of Confederate History* 4 (1989): 113–29.

Of course, all accounts of the escape must be read with extreme care. None are fully trustworthy, all contain errors of greater or lesser import, and until now it was impossible to use Butcher's account as a cross-reference and double check on dubious accounts. Since the French discovery of the remains of the *Alabama* off Cherbourg in 1985, there has been a virtual renaissance of interest in her career, her captain, and her place in the naval history of the Civil War. Butcher's unwritten chapter should fuel that revival. Our commentary on it seeks to establish a proper context for new perspectives on a fascinating subject.

3. Raphael Semmes, *Memoirs of Service Afloat during the War between the States* (Baltimore: Kelly, Piet, 1868). John M. Taylor edited a new edition of this work with an introduction and notes (Baton Rouge: Louisiana State University Press, 1996). Taylor also wrote a biography of the Confederate captain: *Confederate Raider.* Bulloch's postwar memoir, *Secret Service,* remains the single most valuable firsthand account of Confederate naval activities in Europe. Renata Eley Long is preparing a biography of Bulloch. See also Arthur Sinclair, *Two Years on the Alabama* (Boston: Lee and Shepard, 1895; repr., Annapolis: Naval Institute Press, 1989). The new edition has an introduction and notes by the distinguished Civil War historian William N. Still.

For works that focus on the *Alabama* itself, the ship, its captain, and its career, see Christen M. Gober, "The C.S.S. *Alabama:* An Introductory Bibliography," prepared for the special commemorative edition of the *Journal of Confederate History* 4 (1989): 153–68.

4. Bulloch was Theodore Roosevelt's "Uncle Jimmy" and may have been responsible for that president's lifelong interest in naval history. TR's mother was Bulloch's half-sister, and Roosevelt visited his uncle in England on several occasions.

5. Bulloch himself has told his story best; see *Secret Service,* 1:225–94. For the circumstances of the ship's escape and his high regard for Butcher, see 1:229–32. It should be noted that the explanation of his foreknowledge of government intentions to detain his ship might strike some readers as a bit too disingenuous. See esp. 1:260–62. But it should also be pointed out that no one has yet advanced a better one! Mallory's role in the war has been well treated in Joseph T. Durkin, *Stephen R. Mallory: Confederate Navy Chief* (Chapel Hill: University of North Carolina Press, 1954).

6. Merli, *Great Britain and the Confederate Navy,* chap. 1: "Problems and Plans," esp. pp. 14–18, 61–69, and 86–94. This account was based on materials in the British archives and relevant Union and Confederate records. The present introduction is an update of that material, enriched by research since that work was published. Of course, all accounts of Confederate naval activity

must be based on the content of U.S. Navy Department, comp., *Official Records of the Union and Confederate Navies in the War of the Rebellion,* 30 vols., plus index (Washington, D.C.: Government Printing Office, 1894–1927). The set comprises two series, with the three volumes of the second series devoted to diplomatic affairs. See the second series for early Confederate plans in Europe. Hereafter this source will be cited as *ORN,* 2d series, 2:83–87, Bulloch to Mallory, 13 August 1861. An extensive compilation of *Alabama* materials is contained in London's Public Record Office: FO 5/1318–33. This material is used with kind permission of the Controller of Her Majesty's Stationery Office. That depository will be designated as PRO. There is another cache of *Alabama* materials in Her Majesty's Customs and Excise Library in London. Their role in the affair of the *Alabama*'s escape may be traced in Merli, *Great Britain and the Confederate Navy,* 302–303.

7. Bulloch, *Secret Service,* 1:61–62. French archaeological investigations of the ship have provided new insights into some details of her construction and armaments, but the final reports of those investigations have not yet been published. For an interim report, see Max Guérout, "Last Remains of a Legend," *Journal of Confederate History* 4 (1989): 1–14.

8. Dudley's heroic attempts to prevent the ship's departure have been best told in the superb article by Douglas H. Maynard, "Union Efforts to Prevent the Escape of the *Alabama.*"

9. The English coeditor has compiled this character sketch of Butcher, in part after conversations with his granddaughter. His participation in blockade-running ventures was reported in the *Liverpool Telegraph,* 20 September 1864. The paper also carried news of his "death" that same day, an error that was corrected on the following day. A brief account of the escape and Butcher's part in it appears in Emma Kilkenny, "The Day They Played Dixie," *Suffolk Norfolk Life* 7, no. 46 (1996): 22–23.

10. Bulloch, *Secret Service,* 1:230–35. No account of this ship's history could be complete without a reference to an indispensable guide, Charles C. Summersell, *C.S.S. Alabama: Builder, Captain, and Plans* (University: University of Alabama Press, 1985). Christen Gober describes this book as "probably the best single work on the *Alabama.*"

11. For an account written some eighteen years after the events described took place, the author achieves a high level of accuracy. To preserve his style, we have restricted editorial changes to a minimum and have kept our commentary for the notes. These seek to amplify, correct, and compare Butcher's account to other primary and secondary sources. We hope to provide as correct a context as is now possible. Each of the editors—one in England, one in the United States—has had extensive experience in confronting problems associated with affairs of the *Alabama.* For the record we should mention that there are no note numbers in the original. The present ones are the creations of the editors.

That ship, as many will recall, had several names: (1) During construction she was referred to as number 290, an appellation that derives from her place in the builder's order book; i.e., she was the 290th vessel built in the Birkenhead yard of the Laird Brothers. (2) At her launch in May 1862 she received the "mellifluous" name of *Enrica,* after the lady "who performed the official service" of christening her. (The name of the lady, whom Bulloch declined to identify in his *Secret Service,* remains a tantalizing mystery for students of the subject.) (3) En route to the Azores, Butcher identified his ship as the *Barcelona* to maintain the fiction that she had been built for the Spaniards. (4) And, of course, when he took command, Raphael Semmes gave her the name under which she became famous. During the cruise she assumed several other names as a *ruse de guerre,* but those need no mention here.

12. There is some ambiguity in the dating here and in the account of the emergency meeting that follows. Butcher assigns the date of the friend's proposal and his initial meeting with the "Confederate agent" and the builder to "the month of May," and he observes that he first saw his ship after she "had just been launched." So far, so good. The ship was launched in mid-May, and that would be about the time that Bulloch needed a captain with an English Master's Certificate to supervise preparations for sea. But then Butcher introduces a problem when he says that "some six weeks after first taking charge" he was called to a sudden Saturday conference. That meeting, we know from other sources, took place on 26 July. Counting back six weeks from that date would coincide with the *Alabama*'s trial trip, not her launch. The evidence now available does not permit us to assign a definite date to Butcher's assumption of command, for the sources are silent on that point. Probably Butcher's memory, lacking access to his "journal of that period," confused the dates of the ship's launch and her trial trip.

13. From mid-June, the time of the trial trip, until late July, the time of the emergency meeting that triggered the escape, governmental interest in the ship accelerated and intensified. Customs agents literally swarmed over the ship. The sheer volume of paper generated by these inquiries is staggering. See references in note 6 to material in London's Public Record Office and in the Customs and Excise Library. Much, but not all, of the relevant papers are reproduced in the Bourne and Watt compilation cited in note 2. Much of that same material, with a Union slant, may be found in another vital source: U.S. Department of State, comp., *Papers Relating to the Foreign Affairs of the United States,* 1861–1868, 19 vols. (Washington, D.C.: Government Printing Office, 1861–70). See esp. the volume for 1862. Another useful source for the documents it contains is Mountague Bernard, *A Historical Account of the Neutrality of Great Britain during the American Civil War* (London: Longmans, Green, Reader, and Dyer, 1870; repr., New York: Burt Franklin, 1971). Bulloch, as usual, has pertinent things to say about the official interest in his ship — and of his reaction to it. See *Secret Service,* 1:260–62. A representative sample — and it is only a sample — of the all-important British customs correspondence for the period June–September 1862 may be found in *ORN,* 2d series, 2:373–93. A full dossier of all relevant material on the escape of the *Alabama* has never been compiled. Or if it has, it has escaped our notice.

14. The "Mr. L" is, of course, one of the Laird brothers. But none of the sources specifically identifies which one attended this meeting. Yonge, in his deposition cited in note 2, speaks of the "Messrs. Laird" but notes that he met one of the brothers at the office of Fraser, Trenholm; he gives neither name nor date (p. 151). He then goes on to say: "I have not the slightest doubt that they perfectly well knew that such a steamer was being built for the Southern Confederacy, and that she was to be used in war against the government of the United States" (p. 152). Bulloch, Butcher, and Yonge agree that it was not

difficult to pick up intimations that government action against the ship could be expected. Butcher's account, incidentally, confirms the arrival of a telegram from London, just before the 26 July emergency meeting. The editors, however, are inclined to think that it was sent to Bulloch, not Laird. But, again, the sources do not permit a definitive answer. And, of course, no reliable identification of the sender has been established.

That mystery deepens when one considers the larger dimensions of the *Alabama* chronology. The government could make no decision about the vessel's fate until it had taken the advice of the law officers of the Crown. Those advisers did not receive the pertinent papers until 23 July. They did not advise the Foreign Office to take action until 29 July, and their advice did not reach Russell until *after* the *Alabama* had left. From 23 July until 28 July the papers were in the possession of Sir John Harding, chief law officer of the Crown — and he was at that time incapacitated by a nervous breakdown. In all probability, no one in government service knew on 26 July what the government decision would be, though it would not have been difficult for those in the know to guess that a detention order might be in the works. In passing, it should be noted that American evidence against the ship was not much stronger in late July than it had been since the middle of the month. And, for the record, the present editors are aware that the law officers had issued an earlier opinion on this vessel in late June.

15. Compare Butcher's correct account of the events of Monday and Tuesday, 28–29 July to those of Hoole and Low cited in note 1 above and to the account of Bulloch, *Secret Service,* 1:229, 260–82.

16. Here the editors must insert a caveat. Our reading of the relevant documents and secondary accounts leads us to believe that at this point Butcher is guilty of a serious faux pas. We are convinced that Bulloch, not Butcher, was the mastermind behind all arrangements concerning the escape. The tug's attendance during the "trial trip" was no providential occurrence; the early return of the guests was no sudden inspiration; the easy availability of some thirty or forty sailors for the ship on the following morning was no accident; and the coordination of the various other parts of the plot testify to a good bit of planning. See Bulloch, *Secret Service,* 1:239; Summersell, ed., *Journal of Fullam,* p. 5.

17. Another caveat is needed here. In the first place, it is necessary to note that for Butcher this is hearsay evidence. He did not return to Liverpool when Bulloch did on the 29th. Nor was he present at the events he recounts. It may be, of course, that he is repeating what he heard from Bulloch or others who joined the ship from the tug *Hercules* on the 30th. Much of the tale seems pure embellishment, trying to make a good story better. It should be noted that these alleged events took place on 30 July, when customs officers (not an officer from a man-of-war) did inspect the *Hercules* and its cargo. They left without hitching themselves to the tug. And they did *not* have "a warrant" for seizure of the *Alabama.*

Moreover, it is necessary to correct much misrepresentation on a point of prime importance: The *Alabama* left Liverpool *before* the advice of the law officers reached the foreign secretary, no order of detention was sent to that city on the day of departure, and the famous detention order that in my 1970 book I said had arrived just "whiskers" too late was not sent until 31 July. Even John Bull did not grow whiskers that thick.

18. Here the document alludes to a key problem of American charges against the vessel, that of illegal recruitment of crew members. Insofar as we have been able to ascertain, *no* crew members were recruited within Her Majesty's realm. The number of sailors who signed articles at various points of the voyage is subject to wide variations in the sources. For this point in the voyage, that is, while still at Moelfra Bay, Butcher's estimate of total crew members is too high, as is his figure for the number who refused to sign. When Semmes took command at the commencement of her cruise on 24 August, he estimated that about sixty had come out from Liverpool with Butcher and that an additional thirty had come out in the *Bahama* with him and Bulloch. He felt himself "much relieved" at his effective recruitment of about eighty of these. Bernard, *A Historical Account*, p. 348, citing Semmes, *Memoirs of Service Afloat*. Bernard also quotes another documentary account of the *Alabama*'s voyage to the Azores. It is the affidavit of Henry Redden, boatswain mate, who left the vessel and returned to Liverpool on the *Bahama*. When he got back he reported his adventures to customs authorities. His account confirms what Butcher relates about the signing of articles at Moelfra Bay. Bernard, *A Historical Account*, pp. 247–48. The full deposition may be found in *Papers Relating to the Treaty of Washington*, 8 vols. (Washington, D.C.: Government Printing Office, 1872), "Case of Great Britain," 1:333–34. The document includes a receipt for Redden's service signed by Butcher. Readers might bear in mind that materials in this compilation are parts of the British and American presentations at the postwar Geneva arbitration of the *Alabama* claims. The editorial comments that accompany the documents should be read with some skepticism.

19. Another mild correction is called for at this point. The USS *Tuscarora* had been summoned from Gibraltar, where she was blockading the defunct CSS *Sumter*, to Southampton in early July by the American minister. She remained at that English port until 29 July. On that date Minister Adams sent her to Queenstown, Ireland, to cut off the *Alabama*'s expected escape route. Captain Craven's first Union pursuit of the rebel raider did not impress Adams. His report of that unsuccessful venture is outlined in his report to the secretary of state on 7 August 1862. It appears in the *Papers Relating to the Treaty of Washington*, 1:330.

Since the *Tuscarora* was still at Queenstown at 10:00 P.M. on 31 July, there was little chance of an encounter. Minister Adams had specifically warned Craven to avoid any hostile actions in British waters: "I had in previous conversations explained the reasons why I should not consider it good policy to attempt her capture near the coast. In point of fact this proceeding [Craven's cruise north towards Moelfra Bay] put an end to every chance of success" (1:330). Bulloch reported receipt of a telegram from a "friend" in Southampton on 30 July warning of the *Tuscarora*'s departure for Ireland. Bulloch, *Secret Service*, 1:241–42.

20. It is unlikely that a "spy" who had sailed aboard the *Alabama* was the one who alerted Adams to the escape. He had news of it from Dudley soon after it happened. Moreover, Butcher had strict orders to avoid contact with land and

other ships. A British search of the area in early August turned up information that the *Alabama,* while at Moelfra, had remained some three or four miles offshore, that is, outside British territorial waters.

21. All accounts agree on the major details of the voyage north around Ireland, though there are minor variations: Was there a "pelting rain" when Bulloch and the pilot left the ship off Londonderry? Fullam's account on p. 5 of his journal of the hasty departure from Moelfra cannot be correct, for no detention order had yet been issued. It may be that an expected visit by the U.S. cruiser weighed heavily on the minds of those who struggled to get the ship safely to sea and beyond Union countermeasures.

22. The most recent detailed study of the ship's crew lists ten Georgians. It is unlikely that all of them were "Savannah pilots." Liverpool, of course, was a major crossroad and depot for Confederate naval personnel. See Marvel, *The Alabama and the Kearsarge,* pp. 280–88, appendix 2, Ships' Rosters, CSS *Alabama.*

23. In preparation for her cruise and in part because of her hasty departure, the *Alabama* had a confusing number of supply ships: The tug *Hercules* took supplies and men to Moelfra Bay; the *Agrippina,* purchased in London about two months before the escape, had been loaded with the bulk of the "equipment" for the cruiser and had been dispatched from that port at the time the *Alabama* sailed. The *Bahama* brought Bulloch and Semmes from Liverpool to the Azores. She also brought two of the cruiser's six broadside guns and other vital supplies.

24. At this point, Butcher's account permits us to correct a small error in one of the most frequently cited accounts of the *Alabama*'s work: George W. Dalzell, *The Flight from the Flag,* p. 135. As Butcher's account now confirms beyond doubt, the *Alabama,* not the *Agrippina,* arrived first at the rendezvous in the Azores. More important, the reader should be aware that the number of mistakes and misassertions in Dalzell's account of the escape is distressingly large and that important parts of his chronology are dangerously askew. But perhaps his most long-lasting and lamentable contribution to the literature was the undocumented and unsubstantiated charge that Bulloch's cue to get his ship away "came straight from Downing Street" (p. 131). Dalzell was by no means the first to give credence to rumors of a high-level leak in governmental circles, though he did much to popularize the story and to give it wide circulation.

In the 1990s it still turns up—with no more proof than Dalzell provided. The most recent example of which we are aware occurs in Taylor's otherwise good book, *Confederate Raider,* p. 102: "Most important, he [Bulloch] recruited a spy at 10 Downing Street, the Prime Minister's Office, to provide warning of any move to impound his ship." As is so often the case, the assertion carries no source reference to substantiate it, though the citation at the end of the following paragraph is to Dalzell's book. Taylor's reliance on that work then leads to another serious error on p. 104. No decision about the *Alabama*'s fate had been made on "Friday, July 25." That decision, when it was made on 29 July, occurred after the ship had escaped. That decision, it should be stressed, was made *after* the two other law officers of the Crown — acting without Harding — had recommended detention on the 29th. That order did not reach Liverpool, however, until 31 July. And, in all probability, when that order did arrive there, the *Alabama* had not yet reached the safety of the Atlantic. In passing, it might also be noted that the spy—if such there was—is most often located in the Foreign Office, not the Prime Minister's Office. Although the origins of this rumor remain obscure, we have traced a part of its root system back to the early 1900s. We suspect that its seed was planted during the war or soon after it ended.

25. In Low's manuscript log, the arrival at Praya Bay is described as a sequence of events in the entry for 9 August: landfall at 2 A.M.; start of the run into the harbor at 4 A.M.; the notation that the ship "came to anchor" in more than seven fathoms of water at 7 A.M., with the town's cathedral "bearing NW by W at a distance of two miles." Fullam's *Journal* puts the arrival on 10 August. Although this latter source is mostly silent for the days in the Azores, it does mention a strange incident—a chance encounter with a Northern vessel and the "indiscretion" of paymaster Yonge in revealing the "real character" of the *Alabama* (p. 11).

26. The arrival of the *Agrippina,* under command of Captain Alexander McQueen, on the 18th is noted by Fullam. But then the editor of the published *Journal,* Summersell, observes that Bulloch had been "less than frank" with McQueen when he sent him from London to the Azores with the raider's equipment (p. 11). Perhaps so, though one must remember that much of Bulloch's success derived from his policy of telling co-workers only as much as they needed to know to get a job done. It was a prudent procedure, for a later resupply of the *Alabama* by the *Agrippina* nearly ended the cruiser's career because of McQueen's propensity for the loose lips that sink ships. That near-disaster took place in November 1862 at the French island of Martinique. See Frank J. Merli, ed., "Caribbean Confrontation: Letters on the *Alabama,* November 1862," *Journal of Confederate History* 6 (1991): 161–74. Bulloch's orders to McQueen on 28 July are printed in *ORN,* 1st series, 1:771–72; orders for Butcher appear on 773–74, and those for Yonge on 773. These orders are reprinted in Bulloch's *Secret Service.*

27. At this point, the reader may begin comparing Butcher's account with that of Raphael Semmes, whose log of the *Alabama* commences on Wednesday, 20 August 1862, with his arrival in the Azores. The log, from that date until 4 January 1863, appears in *ORN,* 1st series, 1:783–817. Much of that same material also is treated in the postwar memoir of Semmes, a work that should be read with somewhat more caution than some of his recent biographers have accorded it. In the preface to that work, Semmes himself artfully alerts his readers to the pitfalls of his approach to the restraints that Clio imposes on her disciples. In his *ORN* log Semmes confirms and commends Butcher's efforts to prepare the cruiser for her future work. He also notes that two of the ship's guns had come out with him in the *Bahama,* that he had thirty-seven potential hands for his new ship, and that he spent his first night on the ship that he would make famous immediately after he first saw her on the 20th (p. 784). Semmes also confirms that shots were fired from the shore, but not in anger. The incident, at any rate, did not cause him to lose any sleep. The cargo of the *Bahama* is listed in *ORN,* 2d series, 2:392.

28. The accounts of the commissioning of the famous raider agree in essential details, though there is some uncertainty as to when the Confederate flag first flew.

29. Bulloch's own contemporaneous account of these events appears in *ORN*, 2d series, 2:235–39, Bulloch to Mallory, 11 August 1862. (This letter nicely captures some of the personal and professional qualities that made him a superb servant of the South.) He reported his return from the Azores in a letter to Mallory on 10 September, *ORN*, 2d series, 263–65; this report reflects a little of his disappointment at losing command of what he regarded as his ship. Another volume in this collection contains two reports that Bulloch prepared for the Confederate commissioner in London, James M. Mason, on his *Alabama* activities: *ORN*, 1st series, 1:775–76, 1 September 1862; 777–78, 30 December 1862. It might be noted here that Butcher's references in his account to the "Confederate commissioner" are incorrect. In context they clearly refer to Bulloch, who was chief naval agent, captain, or commander but never "commissioner." That was a diplomatic and not a naval title. Properly speaking it should be reserved for Mason, who had that designation in England, or for John Slidell, who was commissioner in France.

30. Semmes did not waste any time in making himself and his cruiser celebrated. Indeed, he and his ship soon became anathema in Northern circles; there, his work was seen as nothing more than piracy. He made his first capture on 5 September 1862, not far from where he had commissioned the raider. Before he met his match in the USS *Kearsarge* off Cherbourg, France, in June 1864, he had captured, burned, or ransomed more than sixty ships. (Again, figures vary, as do estimates of monetary damage that Semmes inflicted on enemy shipping.) At the time of commissioning, Semmes estimated the cost of his vessel at $250,305.44; Robinson, in *Shark of the Confederacy* (p. 172), says "the total value of the property she destroyed came to $4,613,914, or approximately eighteen times the cost of the *Alabama*'s construction." Lists of her victims appear in Taylor, *Confederate Raider,* pp. 283–85, and in Summersell, ed., *Journal of Fullam*, pp. 197–201.

On 4 January 1863 Semmes reported his early success to Mallory in *ORN*, 1st series, 1:778–83. In the account of his first four months of cruising, he listed twenty-six victims. Among them was one of his cruise's most conspicuous failures-in-success. On Sunday, 7 December 1862, he captured (and later released on bond) a New York–Aspinwall mail steamer, *Ariel*. Unfortunately for him and his cause, that vessel was headed south with mail—not north with gold. The capture of one Yankee Panama gold ship would have been worth more to the Confederacy than all of the maritime muggings of all the Confederate cruisers combined. For a Northern perspective on the capture of the *Ariel*, see *ORN*, 1st series, 1:577–80.

6. RAPHAEL SEMMES AND THE CHALLENGE AT CHERBOURG

This essay had its origins in a comparison of Semmes's memoir with his wartime reports published in the *Official Records of the Union and Confederate Navies in the War of the Rebellion,* 30 vols. plus index (Washington, D.C.: Government Printing Office, 1894–1927). Merli presented a conference paper on Semmes in 1995.

1. John Russell Soley, *The Blockade and the Cruisers* (1883), reprinted most recently at Wilmington, N.C.: Broadfoot, 1989; J. Thomas Scharf, *History of the*

Confederate States Navy from Its Organization to the Surrender of Its Last Vessel. Its Stupendous Struggle with the Great Navy of the United States; the Engagements Fought in the Rivers and Harbors of the South, and upon the High Seas; Blockade-running, First Use of Iron-Clads and Torpedoes, and Privateer History (1886), reprinted most recently at New York: Gramercy Books, 1996.

2. In 1996 Louisiana State University Press reprinted Semmes's account, *Memoirs of Service Afloat during the War between the States,* with a new introduction and notes by John M. Taylor. According to Taylor, the book first appeared at the end of 1868 and not, as is often said, in 1869.

3. Norman Delaney has provided a good account of the mind-set of Semmes on the eve of his encounter with destiny. As an experienced scholar with a lifelong interest in the *Alabama* and as the biographer of her executive officer, Delaney had access to primary and secondary sources not easily mastered. Norman C. Delaney, "Fight or Flee: Raphael Semmes's Decision to Engage the *Kearsarge,* June 1864," *Journal of Confederate History* 4 (1989): 17–28.

4. Taylor, *Confederate Raider,* p. x. Taylor also is the author of *Semmes: Rebel Raider.*

5. Taylor, *Confederate Raider,* p. 255.

6. Philip Van Doren Stern, ed., *The Confederate Raider Alabama* (Bloomington: Indiana University Press, 1962); also published by Fawcett with a slightly different title and the addition of a subtitle. *The Confederate Raider, Alabama: Selections from "Memoirs of Service Afloat during the War between the States,"* by Raphael Semmes (Greenwich, Conn.: Fawcett, 1962).

7. In Meredith's account, the battle between the Union and Confederate warships epitomized that of the entire Civil War, that is, a conflict between the "materially stronger" North and the courage and gallantry of the South. Meredith admired aristocratic values. He also identified with patriotic nation-builders, whether Italians fighting the Austrian Empire or Confederates fighting the United States government. During the Civil War, Meredith contributed articles to a couple of Tory newspapers, the *Ipswich Journal* and the *Morning Post.* Norman Kelvin, *A Troubled Eden: Nature and Society in the Works of George Meredith* (Stanford: Stanford University Press, 1961), pp. 13, 16, 37–40; Kelvin to Fahey, 27 August 2002, 29 January 2004.

8. George Meredith to Samuel Laurence, 20 June 1864, in *The Letters of George Meredith,* 3 vols., ed. Clarence Lee Cline (Oxford: Clarendon Press, 1970), 1:271.

9. Meredith to William Hardman, 13 July 1864, in *The Letters of George Meredith,* 1:274–75.

10. John McIntosh Kell, *Recollections of a Naval Life, Including the Cruises of the Confederate States Steamers Sumter and Alabama* (Washington: Neale, 1900), p. 245.

11. Frank J. Merli, "Letters on the *Alabama:* June 1864," *Mariner's Mirror* 58 (May 1972): 216–18.

12. Merli's manuscript omits the sources for the "plank by plank" quotation and the gunnery statistics.

13. What Merli had in mind when he made this characteristically cryptic aside is unclear, but he may have referred to the state of Semmes's health.

Writing to Samuel Barron (13 June 1864), Semmes reported that for health reasons he would have to relinquish command of the *Alabama*. Taylor, *Confederate Raider*, p. 196.

7. THE CONFEDERACY'S CHINESE FLEET, 1861–1867

First published as "A Missing Chapter in American Civil War Diplomacy: The Confederacy's Chinese Fleet, 1861–1867," in *Global Crossroads and the American Seas: Essays from the International Commission for Maritime History and the North American Society for Oceanic History,* ed. Clark G. Reynolds (Missoula, Mont.: Pictorial Histories, 1988), pp. 181–96. Reprinted by permission. [The editor of the present volume has adopted Indiana University Press style and occasionally has expanded titles and author names. He also has corrected obvious errors.]

The Research Foundation of the City University of New York and the Dean of Graduate Studies and Research at Queens College have funded a portion of the expenses incurred in the preparation of this paper, and I wish to express my appreciation for that support. In addition, a number of people have commented critically upon earlier versions of this essay and, without implicating them for any of its imperfections, I want to thank John Bailey of Brentwood, Essex, England; David Fahey, Miami University; Calvin Davis, Duke University; Ted Wilson, University of Kansas; and Robert H. Ferrell, Indiana University. Mark Smith, a barrister of London, discussed with me some of the problems of international maritime law. And, once again, B. J. Rahn of Hunter College–CUNY took time from her researches to help with mine. A shorter version of this paper formed the substance of my remarks at a joint session of the Pacific Coast Branch of the American Historical Association and the Society for Historians of American Foreign Relations held at Stanford University, 25–28 June 1985. At that session, chaired by Kinley M. Brauer, University of Minnesota, I benefited from the acute criticism of Jerald Coombs, San Francisco State University, and Joseph Fry, University of Nevada, Las Vegas. I wish to thank these three colleagues for alerting me to some of the imperfections in that earlier version. And I regret that limitations of space and time and temperament prevented me from heeding all their advice. For a study of the career of one Confederate on the China coast in the Civil War era, see Robert H. Detrick, "Henry Andrea Burgevine in China: A Biography" (Ph.D. thesis, Indiana University, 1968).

1. For extensive critical commentary on the literature of the international dimension of the American Civil War, see Frank J. Merli, "Civil War Diplomacy," in *Guide to American Foreign Relations since 1700,* ed. Richard Dean Burns et al. (Santa Barbara, Calif.: ABC–CLIO, 1983), pp. 291–319. For the China context of my story I have relied heavily upon the following works: Jack J. Gerson, *Horatio Nelson Lay and Sino-British Relations, 1854–1864* (Cambridge: East Asian Research Center, Harvard University; distributed by Harvard University Press, 1972); John L. Rawlinson, *China's Struggle for Naval Development, 1839–1895* (Cambridge: Harvard University Press, 1967); John L. Rawlinson, "The Lay-Osborn Flotilla: Its Development and Significance," pp. 58–93, in vol. 4, *Papers on China,* Regional Studies Seminars, Harvard University, April 1950; James Cooley, *T. F. Wade in China: Pioneer in Global Diplomacy,*

1842–1882 (Leiden: E. J. Brill, 1981); David L. Anderson, "Anson Burlingame: American Architect of the Cooperative Policy in China, 1861–1871," *Diplomatic History* 1 (Summer 1977): 239–55. See also G. M. Spence, *A Forgotten Flotilla* (Kent, 1937). This item, apparently a pamphlet reprint from the *Kentish Times,* bears the British Museum shelf-mark number 8808.14.

2. For a sample of the debates on British policy in China and on the Anglo-Chinese fleet, see *Hansard Parliamentary Debates,* 3d series, vol. 169, 19 March 1863; vol. 172, 6 July 1863; vol. 175, 31 May 1864. For a representative slice of press commentary, see *Times* (London), 4 April 1863, p. 8, cols. 3–4. This editorial nicely captures views on the purpose of the fleet, attitudes toward China, and the British mission of civilization.

3. The author has such a monograph in preparation. [He had completed one chapter, "The Chinese Context," at the time of his death.]

4. The two quoted passages appear in Gerson, *Lay,* p. 115. For the "new" direction in British policy, see *Hansard Parliamentary Debates,* 3d series, vol. 172, 6 July 1863, cols. 270–330. Lay told Austin H. Layard that one of "the main objects of our undertaking is to benefit British interests." British Museum [hereafter BM], A. H. Layard Mss., Add. Ms., 39103, Lay to Layard, 30 July 1862. In his apologia for the demise of the project, Lay told William E. Gladstone that the fleet would "gradually have forced progress and reform upon the government [of China]." BM, Gladstone Mss., 44401, Lay to Gladstone, 10 November 1863. The British minister in Peking told one of his associates that the government was supporting the Chinese authorities "from motives of interest, not from sentiment." Public Record Office, Russell Papers, 30/22/50, Bruce to Gordon, 3 March 1864. Material from the PRO is used by kind permission of the Controller of Her Majesty's Stationery Office. In another letter, Bruce wrote movingly about the impact of Western cultural attitudes on the Oriental mind: "Is it to be wondered at that a people like the Chinese . . . hate us as brutal and despise us as uncivilized barbarians and that their feeling of courtesy [toward us] is soon changed to one of hatred . . . ?" PRO, Russell Papers, 30/22/50, Bruce to Russell, 15 April 1864. For other aspects of cultural conflict, see Morrell Heald and Lawrence S. Kaplan, *Culture and Diplomacy: The American Experience* (Westport, Conn.: Greenwood Press, 1977), esp. chap. 5.

5. Rawlinson, "Lay-Osborn Flotilla," pp. 61–63.

6. Gerson, *Lay,* p. 224 for the "handle" quote and p. 229 for "the idea of a Chinese naval force " quote.

7. BM, *British Parliamentary Papers, Accounts and Papers: Session 4 February–29 July 1864,* 63, 1864, Command Paper 3271, "Correspondence Respecting the Fitting Out, Dispatching to China, and the Ultimate Withdrawal of the Anglo-Chinese Fleet under the Command of Captain Sherard Osborn; and the Dismissal of Mr. Lay from the Chief Inspectorate of Customs," presented to the House of Commons, 9 February 1864. My photocopy of this document comes from the Official Publications Room of the BM. American readers may find it more convenient to consult this collection of official correspondence in the Irish University Press Area Studies series, *British Parliamentary Papers,* 27:225–68. (There will be some variation in pagination between the IUP and the BM copies.) For an American perspective on this affair, see U.S. Department of State, *Foreign Relations of the United States,* 1864 Part III, esp. dispatches 56, 58,

65, 66, 67, under dates 7 November 1863, 23 November 1863, 17 March 1864, 21 March 1864, and 25 March 1864. See also Anderson, "Anson Burlingame," esp. 242–47, and the documents cited. To my mind, the most revealing commentary on the flotilla imbroglio is PRO, Russell Papers, 30/22/50, Wade to Russell, 6 June 1864, ff. 233–40. I hope to prepare this document for publication. [He did not.]

8. The "mosquito fleet" phrase has been borrowed from Rawlinson, "Lay-Osborn Flotilla," p. 91.

9. For Lay's lament, see Gerson, *Lay,* pp. 228–30. For a sample of Confederate complaints, see Merli, *Great Britain and the Confederate Navy,* p. 312n12. Compare Gerson, p. 230 to Merli, p. 185 on the subject of "gaslight and overtime work" for an odd example of how the problems of Chinese and Confederate agents seem to overlap. The document printed by Gerson was not available to me when I first approached the problems of ship procurement in Great Britain. The materials from various Lay family archives and from Chinese sources make the Gerson book most useful for the study of this strange affair.

10. Rawlinson, *China's Struggle for Naval Development,* pp. 34–37.

11. Gerson, *Lay,* pp. 149–50.

12. Lay to Hart, 10 October 1862, cited in ibid., p. 228.

13. Ibid., p. 307.

14. Ibid., pp. 141, 166, 194–96; Rawlinson, "Lay-Osborn Flotilla," p. 89. See BM, *British Parliamentary Papers,* Command Paper 3271, pp. 21–25 for Bruce's perhaps excessively harsh assessment of Lay's conduct. See also his further indictment in his letter to Elgin, 6 November 1863, PRO, Russell Papers, 30/22/55, ff. 124–34, and see ff. 233–40 for Wade's and ff. 156–57 for Somerset's. For Lay's official explanation of his activity, see Command Paper 3271, pp. 17–19. For a Chinese perspective, see ibid., pp. 30–32, and PRO, FO 17/493, Kung to Bruce, 1 May 1865. For the American reaction, see BM, Command Paper 3271, pp. 33–34, Burlingame to Bruce, 7 November 1863.

15. Rawlinson, *China's Struggle for Naval Development,* p. 35. Italics in the original.

16. William Hovgaard, *Modern History of Warships* (1920; repr., Greenwich, Conn.: Conway Maritime Press, 1978), p. 10. I owe this reference to Mark Smith. The components of the Chinese fleet are listed in Spence, *Forgotten Flotilla,* p. 2; Rawlinson, "Lay-Osborn Flotilla," p. 91; PRO, FO 17/492 and FO 17/493. Jerry Williams, a local historian of Birkenhead and a student of Confederate activities along the Mersey River, tells me that the Lairds' Chinese gunboats were contracts number 296 (*Tientsin*) and 297 (*Kwantung*). Williams, a former employee of the Laird company, has had access to some of the original 1860s order books of that firm. Letter to author, 27 February 1984. For Bulloch's comments on these matters, see his *Secret Service,* 2:243, 253, 265, 269; and Merli, *Britain and the Confederate Navy.* Since the appearance of the SHAFR *Guide,* Warren Spencer has published *The Confederate Navy in Europe* (University: University of Alabama Press, 1983). His evaluation of the utility of the *Victor,* one of the Royal Navy gunboats that the Chinese rejected and that found its way into the Confederate navy, differs from Merli's assessment. See Spencer, pp. 141–42, and Merli, pp. 218–20. For Bulloch's assess-

ment, see his *Secret Service,* 2:269. Rawlinson writes that one of the ships in the Chinese fleet was "unanimously pronounced by all . . . to be one of the fastest vessels afloat." *China's Struggle for Naval Development,* p. 37.

17. Gerson, *Lay,* p. 153.

18. Ibid., p. 157. See PRO, Russell Papers, 30/22/50, ff. 156–57, for Somerset's rejoinder to Bruce's account of affairs in China and for his defense of Lay's activities there. The memo is dated 19 January [1864?]. It seems clear that Lay thought—with some justification, it must be admitted—that he had the support of a number of high-ranking government officials, including Gladstone, Russell, Palmerston, and Layard. [See citations in note 4, above.] Unfortunately, much of the groundwork for the flotilla project was done in person by Lay and Osborn in London. It is therefore impossible to determine with precision just how much support the plan actually had in the upper reaches of Whitehall. A careful reading of the evidence suggests that the project got far more support than the government could prudently admit. There is good reason to believe that the Foreign Office memo of May 1866 (PRO, FO 17/493, ff. 63–74) deserves to rank as a classic case of whitewash — what our generation would call "disinformation." In addition, the order that the FO sent to the Admiralty on 11 January 1864 (printed in BM, *British Parliamentary Papers,* Command Paper 3271, p. 15) has an odd tone that simply does not ring true, especially when compared to the various commentaries on that document that appear in FO 17/492. [My photocopies of the various drafts of this note do not contain folio numbers.] See also PRO, FO 17/382.

19. Gerson, *Lay,* p. 181.

20. PRO, Russell Papers, 30/22/101, Russell to Bruce, 26 April 1862.

21. Ibid., Russell to Bruce, 26 June 1862.

22. Gerson, *Lay,* pp. 151–61. For the response of the law officers, see PRO, FO 83/2251. My evaluation of Bulloch's work and of the responses of the British government to it are, of course, derived from Merli, *Britain and the Confederate Navy.*

23. Gerson, *Lay,* p. 165.

24. Ibid., p. 153.

25. Rawlinson, *China's Struggle for Naval Development,* p. 37; *Times* (London), 4 April 1863; Merli, *Britain and the Confederate Navy,* pp. 160–65.

26. The significance of the confrontation between the Crown and Confederate cruisers in the *Alexandra* case remains a matter of dispute among historians, but that case retains its importance for determining the point at which the British "tightening of neutrality" took place. (I have borrowed the quoted phrase from Brian Jenkins.) All students of the diplomacy of the American Civil War must acknowledge the contribution that Jenkins's magisterial study has made to the literature of the subject: *Britain and the War for the Union,* 2 vols. (Montreal: McGill-Queen's University Press, 1974–80). My own dating of the hardening of British attitudes toward the work of Bulloch and toward Confederate aspirations of statehood, however, differs from that of Jenkins. See also Merli, *Britain and the Confederate Navy,* chap. 8. There are some useful reminders of the difficulty of generalizing about the British response to the American Civil War in Kinley J. Brauer, "British Mediation and the American Civil War," *Journal of Southern History* 38 (Winter 1972): 49–64.

27. PRO, FO 83/2251, LO to FO, 21 May 1864. Never before, insofar as

the record shows, had the law officers affirmed the right of a belligerent to *armed* ships of war. The ramifications of such a view are staggering.

28. BM, *British Parliamentary Papers,* Command Paper 3271, p. 24.

29. Ibid., p. 20.

30. PRO, FO 17/493, ff. 63–74.

31. PRO, Russell Papers, 30/22/101, Russell to Bruce, 10 April 1863. Russell made this remark just six days after the first units of the Chinese fleet left England and five days after he had ordered seizure of the *Alexandra* to keep it out of Confederate hands.

32. The best calculation of the cost of the fleet is in Gerson, *Lay,* pp. 196–200 and 326n71. My own estimates differ slightly from his. See also FO 17/492, esp. under dates 29 February 1864 and 1 December 1866, and FO 117/493, esp. under 31 January 1866 and 5 February 1866. For yet another set of figures, see BM, *British Parliamentary Papers, Accounts and Papers,* 47:3, "Anglo-Chinese Flotilla, Compensation," 13 February 1867. One of Russell's parliamentary critics accused him of carelessness amounting almost to "recklessness" for getting involved in "that most wild and extraordinary scheme." *Hansard Parliamentary Debates,* 3d series, vol. 175, 31 May 1864, col. 943.

33. PRO, FO 17/493, f. 74.

34. PRO, FO 83/2251, Law Office to Foreign Office, 21 May 1864.

35. Ibid. Although Gerson cites this document (*Lay,* p. 327n81), it plays a much less prominent role in his pages than it does in mine. His reference to it, however, is just about the only one I have found in my reading of the literature of American Civil War diplomacy.

36. In July 1862, on the eve of the *Alabama*'s escape, Collier told Charles Francis Adams, the American minister in London, that it would be difficult to make a "stronger case of infringement of the Foreign Enlistment Act, which if not enforced on this occasion is little better than a dead letter." This was before Collier became one of the Crown's law officers, and he was writing to Adams as a private legal adviser. Quoted passage above is from Merli, *Britain and the Confederate Navy,* pp. 91 and 302n47. Jenkins, *Britain and the War for the Union,* 2:123–24.

37. PRO, Russell Papers, 30/22/101, Russell to Bruce, 26 April 1862.

38. For a rare look at the impact of the cotton famine, see John O'Neil, *The Journals of a Lancashire Weaver, 1856–60, 1860–65, 1872–75,* ed. Mary Brigg (Record Society of Lancashire and Cheshire, 1982). I owe this reference and my copy of this book to my Accrington pal, Bill Turner of Lancashire.

39. PRO, Russell Papers, 30/22/101, Russell to Bruce, 10 February 1863.

40. Jenkins, *Britain and the War for the Union,* 2:242 and 393–400.

41. PRO, Russell Papers, 30/22/15D, Palmerston to Russell, 7 February 1865.

42. Jenkins, *Britain and the War for the Union,* 2:397–99.

43. Quoted phrase, "a question of neutrality," is from PRO, Russell Papers, 30/22/50, Wade to Russell, 6 June 1865.

44. In a letter Merli noted "the close cooperation of British Minister Bruce and American Minister Burlingame to keep these ships away from the South." He argued that it was "one of the very few times in the 19th century . . . when the Americans and British did have a special relationship." When Bruce soon afterwards became British minister to the United States, "He meets Bur-

lingame at Seward's and reports to Russell that during dinner conversation he, Bruce, delicately alluded to British 'cooperation, good faith, etc.' in the matter of the Confederacy's Chinese fleet and asked Burlingame to confirm Anglo-American good will in China," as remembering this might reduce tensions during the *Alabama* claims controversy. Merli to Robert H. Ferrell, 25 May 1984.

Works Cited

ARCHIVES

British Museum (later British Library)
Customs and Excise Library
Lambeth Palace Library
Public Record Office
W. Stanley Hoole Special Collections Library, University of Alabama, Tuscaloosa

GOVERNMENTAL PRINTED PRIMARY SOURCES

Bourne, Kenneth, and Donald Cameron Watt, gen. eds. *British Documents on Foreign Affairs — Reports and Papers from the Foreign Office Confidential Print:* Series C. North America, 1837–1914. 15 vols. Vol. 6: *The Civil War Years, 1862–1865.* Bethesda, Md.: University Press of America, 1986.

Bourne, Kenneth, Donald Cameron Watt, and Ian Hill Nish, eds. *British Documents on Foreign Affairs — Reports and Papers from the Foreign Office Confidential Print.* Part 1: *From the Mid-Nineteenth Century to the First World War.* Series E. Asia, 1860–1914. Vol. 19: *Lord Elgin's Missions, Taiping Rebellion, and Proposed Naval Force for China, 1858–1865.* Frederick, Md.: University Publications of America, 1994.

British Parliamentary Papers.

The Case of Great Britain as Laid before the Tribunal of Arbitration, Convened at Geneva under the Provisions of the Treaty between the United States of America and Her Majesty the Queen of Great Britain, Concluded at Washington May 8, 1871. 3 vols. Washington, D.C.: Government Printing Office, 1872.

Hansard Parliamentary Debates.

Irish University Press. *British Parliamentary Papers.* Vol. 27: *Dispatches, Returns and Other Papers Respecting British Military Affairs in China, 1840–69.* Shannon: Irish University Press, 1971.

U.S. Department of State, comp. *Papers Relating to the Foreign Affairs of the United States, 1861–1868.* 19 vols. Washington, D.C.: Government Printing Office, 1861–70.

U.S. Navy Department, comp. *Official Records of the Union and Confederate Navies in the War of the Rebellion.* 30 vols., plus index. Washington, D.C.: Government Printing Office, 1894–1927.

OTHER PRINTED PRIMARY SOURCES

Bulloch, James D. *The Secret Service of the Confederates States in Europe; or, How the Confederate Cruisers Were Equipped.* London: Richard Bentley and Son, 1883; New York: Putnam, 1884; repr. with an introduction by Philip Van Doren Stern, New York: Thomas Yoseloff, 1959; New York: Modern Library, 2001.

Butcher, Matthew James. "The Delivery Voyage of the *Alabama.*" *Sea Breezes* 62 (November 1988): 782–88.

Civil War and the Confederacy: The Business Records of Fraser, Trenholm and Company of Liverpool and Charleston, South Carolina, 1860–1877, from the Merseyside Maritime Museum, Liverpool: A Listing and Guide to the Microfilm Edition. Marlborough, Wiltshire: Adam Matthew, 2000.

The Cruise of the Alabama and Sumter: From the Private Journals and Other Papers of Commander R. Semmes, C.S.N., and Other Officers. London: Saunders, Otley, 1864.

Hart, Robert. *Entering China's Service: Robert Hart's Journals, 1854–1863.* Ed. Katherine F. Bruner, John K. Fairbank, and Richard J. Smith. Cambridge: Council on East Asian Studies, Harvard University, 1986.

———. *Robert Hart and China's Early Modernization: His Journals, 1863–1866.* Ed. Richard J. Smith, John K. Fairbank, and Katherine F. Bruner. Cambridge: Council on East Asian Studies, Harvard University, 1991.

Hoole, W. Stanley. *Four Years in the Confederate Navy: The Career of Captain John Low.* Athens: University of Georgia Press, 1964.

Kell, John McIntosh. *Recollections of a Naval Life, Including the Cruises of the Confederate States Steamers Sumter and Alabama.* Washington: Neale, 1900.

Meredith, George. *The Letters of George Meredith.* Edited by Clarence Lee Cline. 3 vols. Oxford: Clarendon Press, 1970.

Merli, Frank J. "Letters on the *Alabama:* June, 1864." *Mariner's Mirror* 58 (May 1972): 216–18.

———, ed. "Caribbean Confrontation: Letters on the *Alabama,* November 1862." *Journal of Confederate History* 6 (1991): 161–74.

O'Neil, John. *The Journals of a Lancashire Weaver, 1856–60, 1860–65, 1872–75.* Ed. Mary Brigg. Record Society of Lancashire and Cheshire, 1982.

Semmes, Raphael. *Memoirs of Service Afloat during the War between the States.* Baltimore: Kelly, Piet, 1868; repr. with an introduction and notes by John M. Taylor, Baton Rouge: Louisiana State University Press, 1996.

Sinclair, Arthur. *Two Years on the Alabama.* Boston: Lee and Shepard, 1895; repr. with an introduction and notes by William N. Still, Annapolis: Naval Institute Press, 1989.

Stern, Philip Van Doren, ed., *The Confederate Raider, Alabama: Selections from "Memoirs of Service Afloat during the War between the States,"* by Raphael Semmes. Greenwich, Conn.: Fawcett, 1962.

———. *The Confederate Raider Alabama,* by Raphael Semmes. Bloomington: Indiana University Press, 1962.

Summersell, Charles C., ed. *The Journal of George Townley Fullam: Boarding Officer of the Confederate Sea Raider Alabama.* University: University of Alabama Press, 1973.

SECONDARY WORKS

Adams, Ephraim Douglass. *Great Britain and the American Civil War.* 2 vols. London: Longmans, Green, 1925; repr., Gloucester, Mass.: Peter Smith, 1957; New York: Russell and Russell, 1958.

Anderson, David L. "Anson Burlingame: American Architect of the Cooperative Policy in China, 1861–1871." *Diplomatic History* 1 (Summer 1977): 239–55.

Barton, Peter. "The First Blockade Runner and 'Another *Alabama*': Some Tees and Hartlepools Ships That Worried the Union." *Mariner's Mirror* 81 (1995): 45–64.

Bernard, Mountague. *A Historical Account of the Neutrality of Great Britain during the American Civil War.* London: Longmans, Green, Reader, and Dyer, 1870; repr., New York: Burt Franklin, 1971.

Bowcock, Andrew. *CSS Alabama: Anatomy of a Confederate Raider.* Annapolis: Naval Institute Press, 2002.

Brauer, Kinley J. "British Mediation and the American Civil War." *Journal of Southern History* 38 (Winter 1972): 49–64.

Celozzi Baldelli, Pia G. *Power Politics, Diplomacy, and the Avoidance of Hostilities between England and the United States in the Wake of the Civil War.* Translated from the Italian. Lewiston, N.Y.: Edwin Mellen Press, 1998.

Cook, Adrian. *The Alabama Claims: American Politics and Anglo-American Relations, 1865–1872.* Ithaca, N.Y.: Cornell University Press, 1975.

Cooley, James. *T. F. Wade in China: Pioneer in Global Diplomacy, 1842–1882.* Leiden: E. J. Brill, 1981.

Crook, David Paul. *The North, the South, and the Powers, 1861–1865.* New York: Wiley, 1974.

Dalzell, George W. *The Flight from the Flag: The Continuing Effect of the Civil War upon the American Carrying Trade.* Chapel Hill: University of North Carolina Press, 1940.

Davis, William C. *Jefferson Davis: The Man and His Hour.* New York: Harper-Collins, 1991.

De Kay, James T. *The Rebel Raiders: The Astonishing History of the Confederacy's Secret Navy.* New York: Ballantine, 2002.

Delaney, Norman C. "Fight or Flee: Raphael Semmes's Decision to Engage the *Kearsarge*, June 1864." *Journal of Confederate History* 4 (1989): 17–28.

———. *Ghost Ship: The Confederate Raider Alabama.* Middletown, Conn.: Southfarm Press, 1989.

———. *John McIntosh Kell of the Raider Alabama.* University: University of Alabama Press, 1973.

Deloux, Jean-Pierre. *Le corsaire Alabama: La Guerre de Sécession au large de Cherbourg.* Paris: E-dite, 2001.

Detrick, Robert H. "Henry Andrea Burgevine in China: A Biography." Ph.D. thesis, Indiana University, 1968.

Durkin, Joseph T. *Stephen R. Mallory: Confederate Navy Chief.* Chapel Hill: University of North Carolina Press, 1954.

Evans, Eli N. *Judah P. Benjamin, the Jewish Confederate.* New York: Free Press, 1988.

Foster, Kevin. "The Diplomats Who Sank a Fleet: The Confederacy's Undelivered European Fleet and the Union Consular Service." *Prologue: Quarterly of the National Archives and Records Administration* 33, no. 3 (Fall 2001): 181–93.

Gerson, Jack J. *Horatio Nelson Lay and Sino-British Relations, 1854–1864.* Cambridge: East Asian Research Center, Harvard University; distributed by Harvard University Press, 1972.

Guérout, Max. "Last Remains of a Legend." *Journal of Confederate History* 4 (1989): 1–14.

Heald, Morrell, and Lawrence S. Kaplan. *Culture and Diplomacy: The American Experience.* Westport, Conn.: Greenwood Press, 1977.

Hearn, Chester G. *Gray Raiders of the Sea: How Eight Confederate Warships Destroyed the Union's High Seas Commerce.* Camden, Maine: International Marine, 1992.

Hovgaard, William. *Modern History of Warships.* 1920; repr., Greenwich, Conn.: Conway Maritime Press, 1978.

Jarvis, Rupert C. "The *Alabama* and the Law." *Transactions of the Historic Society of Lancashire and Cheshire* 111 (1959): 181–98.

Jenkins, Brian A. *Britain and the War for the Union.* 2 vols. Montreal: McGill-Queen's University Press, 1974–80.

Jenkins, Roy. *Gladstone.* London: Macmillan, 1995; New York: Random House, 1997.

Jones, Howard. *Union in Peril: The Crisis over British Intervention in the Civil War.* Chapel Hill: University of North Carolina Press, 1992; repr., Lincoln: University of Nebraska Press, 1997.

Jones, Howard, and Donald A. Rakestraw. "The Diplomacy of the Civil War." In Robert L. Beisner, ed., *American Foreign Relations since 1600: A Guide to the Literature,* 2d ed., ed. Robert L. Beisner, 1:353–406. Santa Barbara, Calif.: ABC–CLIO, 2003.

Jones, Wilbur Devereux. *The Confederate Rams at Birkenhead: A Chapter in Anglo-American Relations.* Tuscaloosa: Confederate, 1961; repr., Wilmington, N.C.: Broadfoot, 2000.

Kelvin, Norman. *A Troubled Eden: Nature and Society in the Works of George Meredith.* Stanford, Calif.: Stanford University Press, 1961.

Kilkenny, Emma. "The Day They Played Dixie." *Suffolk Norfolk Life* 7, no. 46 (1996): 22–23.

Krein, David F. "Russell's Decision to Detain the Laird Rams." *Civil War History* 22 (June 1976): 158–63.

Luraghi, Raimondo. *A History of the Confederate Navy.* Translated from the Italian. Annapolis: Naval Institute Press, 1996.

MacChesney, Brunson. "The *Alabama* and the Queen's Advocate: A Mystery of History." *Northwestern University Law Review* 62 (1967): 568–85.

Marvel, William. *The Alabama and the Kearsarge: The Sailor's Civil War.* Chapel Hill: University of North Carolina Press, 1996.

Mattson, Gregory Louis. "Pariah Diplomacy: The Slavery Issue in Confederate Foreign Relations." Ph.D. diss., University of Southern Mississippi, 1999.

Maynard, Douglas H. "Union Efforts to Prevent the Escape of the *Alabama.*" *Mississippi Valley Historical Review* 41 (June 1954): 41–60.

McPherson, James M. *Crossroads of Freedom: Antietam, the Battle That Changed the Course of the Civil War.* New York: Oxford University Press, 2002.

Merli, Frank J. "Civil War Diplomacy." In Richard Dean Burns et al., eds., *Guide to American Foreign Relations since 1700,* 291–319. Santa Barbara, Calif.: ABC–CLIO, 1983.

———. "Crown versus Cruiser: The Curious Case of the *Alexandra.*" *Civil War History* 9 (June 1963): 167–77.

———. *Great Britain and the Confederate Navy, 1861–1865.* Bloomington: Indiana University Press, 1970.

———, ed. "Special Commemorative Naval Issue, CSS *Alabama,* 1864–1989." *Journal of Confederate History* 4 (1989).

Michie, Alexander. *The Englishman in China during the Victorian Era, as Illustrated in the Career of Sir Rutherford Alcock.* 2 vols. Edinburgh: William Blackwood and Sons, 1900.

Milton, David Hepburn. *Lincoln's Spymaster: Thomas Haines Dudley and the Liverpool Network.* Mechanicsburg, Pa.: Stackpole, 2002.

Nepveux, Ethel Trenholm Seabrook. *George A. Trenholm, Financial Genius of the Confederacy: His Associates and His Ships That Ran the Blockade.* Charleston, S.C.: privately printed, 1999.

Noirsain, Serge, and Gerard Hawkins. *La flotte européene de la confédération sudiste.* Brussels: Confederate Historical Association of Belgium, 2000.

Owsley, Frank Lawrence. *King Cotton Diplomacy: Foreign Relations of the Confederate States of America.* 1931. Revised by Harriet Chappell Owsley. Chicago: University of Chicago Press, 1959.

Parish, Peter J. *The American Civil War.* New York: Holmes and Meier, 1975.

Perkins, Bradford. *The Creation of a Republican Empire, 1776–1865,* vol. 1 of the Cambridge History of American Foreign Relations, ed. Warren I. Cohen. New York: Cambridge University Press, 1993.

Rawley, James. *Turning Points of the Civil War.* Lincoln: University of Nebraska Press, 1966.

Rawlinson, John L. "The Lay–Osborn Flotilla: Its Development and Significance." *Papers on China,* Regional Studies Seminars, Harvard University, vol. 4 (April 1950): 58–93.

———. *China's Struggle for Naval Development, 1839–1895.* Cambridge: Harvard University Press, 1967.

Robinson, Charles M., III. *Shark of the Confederacy: The Story of the CSS Alabama.* Annapolis: Naval Institute Press, 1996.

Scharf, J. Thomas. *History of the Confederate States Navy from Its Organization to the Surrender of Its Last Vessel. Its Stupendous Struggle with the Great Navy of the United States; the Engagements Fought in the Rivers and Harbors of the South, and upon the High Seas; Blockade-running, First Use of Iron-Clads and Torpedoes, and Privateer History.* New York: Rogers and Sherwood, 1886; repr., New York: Gramercy Books, 1996.

Sirett, K. F., and K. J. Williams. "Liverpool and the American Civil War: A Confederate Heritage in England." *Journal of Confederate History* 4 (1989): 113–29.

Soley, James Russell. *The Blockade and the Cruisers.* New York: C. Scribner's Sons, 1883; repr., Wilmington, N.C.: Broadfoot, 1989.

Spence, G. M. *A Forgotten Flotilla.* Kent, 1937.

Works Cited

Spencer, Warren F. *The Confederate Navy in Europe*. University: University of Alabama Press, 1983.

———. *Raphael Semmes, the Philosophical Mariner*. Tuscaloosa: University of Alabama Press, 1997.

Still, William N., and William S. Dudley, eds. *The Confederate Navy: The Ships, Men, and Organization, 1861–65*. Annapolis: Naval Institute Press, 1997.

Still, William N., John M. Taylor, and Norman C. Delaney. *Raiders and Blockaders: The American Civil War Afloat*. Washington, D.C.: Brassey's, 1998.

Summersell, Charles C. *C.S.S. Alabama: Builder, Captain, and Plans*. University: University of Alabama Press, 1985.

Taylor, John M. *Confederate Raider: Raphael Semmes of the Alabama*. Washington, D.C.: Brassey's, 1994.

———. *Semmes: Rebel Raider*. Washington, D.C.: Brassey's, 2003.

Teng, S. Y. *The Taiping Rebellion and the Western Powers*. Oxford: Clarendon Press, 1971.

Tucker, Spencer C. *Raphael Semmes and the Alabama*. Abilene: McWhiney Foundation Press, 1996.

Warren, Gordon H. *Fountain of Discontent: The Trent Affair and the Freedom of the Seas*. Boston: Northeastern University Press, 1981.

Wise, Stephen R. *Lifeline of the Confederacy: Blockade Running during the Civil War*. Columbia: University of South Carolina Press, 1988.

Young, Robert W. *Senator James Murray Mason: Defender of the Old South*. Knoxville: University of Tennessee Press, 1998.

Index

Since chapters 2 through 6 reference the *Alabama* on nearly every page, there is no separate index entry for the Confederacy's most famous commerce raider. In this index the names of ships are italicized. An italicized page number indicates an illustration.

FRANK J. MERLI (1929–2000) was associate professor of history at Queens College in the City University of New York. Educated at Indiana University under the tutelage of Robert H. Ferrell, Merli published *Great Britain and the Confederate Navy, 1861–1865* (Indiana University Press, 1970). At the time of his death, he was writing what amounted to a multivolume sequel to that book.

DAVID M. FAHEY is professor of history at Miami University in Ohio. He is the author of *Temperance and Racism: John Bull, Johnny Reb, and the Good Templars.*